Experimental Criticism

Experimental Criticism: Franco Moretti and Literature

Edited by
Francesco de Cristofaro
and Stefano Ercolino

Translated by
Richard Braude

London • New York

This English-language edition first published by Verso 2026
First published as *Critica sperimentale. Franco Moretti e la letteratura*

The publisher and editors extend their gratitude to the publications where the following essays appeared first: 1, 'Unrestrained Individuation: The Young Franco Moretti', *Historical Materialism* 29: 2 (2021); 11, 'The Roads to Rome: Literary Studies, Hermeneutics, Quantification', *New Left Review* 124, July–August 2020; 14, 'Between History and Theory: The Novel Form in the Work of Franco Moretti', *New Left Review* 148, July–August 2024; 15, 'Lukács's Theory of the Novel', *New Left Review* 91, January–February 2015

The manufacturer's authorized representative in the EU for product safety (GPSR) is LOGOS EUROPE, 9 rue Nicolas Poussin, 17000, La Rochelle, France
contact@logoseurope.eu

1 3 5 7 9 10 8 6 4 2

Verso
UK: 6 Meard Street, London W1F 0EG
US: 207 East 32nd Street, New York, NY 10016
versobooks.com

Verso is the imprint of New Left Books

ISBN-13: 978-1-80429-507-6
ISBN-13: 978-1-80429-509-0 (US EBK)
ISBN-13: 978-1-80429-508-3 (UK EBK)

British Library Cataloguing in Publication Data
A catalogue record for this book is available from the British Library

Library of Congress Cataloging-in-Publication Data
A catalog record for this book is available from the Library of Congress
Library of Congress Control Number: 2025946528

Typeset in Minion by Biblichor Ltd, Scotland
Printed and bound by CPI Group (UK) Ltd, Croydon, CR0 4YY

Contents

Criticism as Experiment

Francesco de Cristofaro and Stefano Ercolino

1.

> Now, it's time for some answers. But those are for others to provide. Like the Turkish child who has planted herself at the little table where I am writing these lines, and every time I get an idea pushes me away from the laptop and taps out her name with her index finger (Gizem), somewhere there is a girl, or a boy, who is reading these pages – attentively, yes, but deep down convinced that they can do better. And so it will be. To them, good luck.[1]

These heartfelt words, written at the Pierre Loti café overlooking the Golden Horn in Istanbul, represent Franco Moretti's farewell in the final volume of *Il romanzo* (*The Novel*), the impressive, 'restless' work he conceived and edited for Einaudi at the turn of the century.[2] Through the enchanted and expectant gaze of little Gizem, they speak to us – not only of the serenity that should always accompany any natural passing of the torch between generations, but also of a very sincere hope for further intellectual encounters, to be conducted with the right amount of courage, humility and, of course, restlessness. And this perhaps

1 Franco Moretti, *Il romanzo* (Turin: Einaudi, 2001–03), vol. V, p. xiv. In English: *The Novel*, 2 vols (Princeton, NJ: Princeton University Press, 2006). This introductory essay was written, in its first part, by Francesco de Cristofaro (sections 1 and 2); and in its second part by Stefano Ercolino (section 3).

2 Moretti, *Il romanzo*, p. xiv.

encapsulates the spirit of intellectual exchange that animates this collection.

When we first discussed the idea for this book, we immediately agreed about one aspect in particular. We did not really want to produce a book about Franco Moretti; it seemed more fitting and useful to place his work at the centre of our reflections, as a springboard for a polyphonic discussion about the fundamentals of literary theory in the here and now. We put together a list of themes and considered which colleagues we could involve. The project took off without too much difficulty. After a few months, as the responses began to come in, it became clear that, despite their different theoretical starting points, the scholars we had invited converged in recognising in Moretti's criticism not only a distinct originality of mind, but also a strongly *experimental* character. Whether in works that deal with a particular genre (such as *The Way of the World*) or a with problem in cultural history (such as *The Bourgeois* or the 'five easy pieces' of *Far Country*); whether the method leans more towards close or distant reading; whether the interpretative dimension prevails or instead the mapping of complex patterns, perhaps with the aid of digital tools, the drive, the motivation behind Moretti's work, always remains that of pushing criticism beyond the pillars of Hercules, generating innovative hypotheses that are – ideally at least – also falsifiable ones. Such a venture, which recovers the heuristic and 'operationalisable' character of scientific research, is perhaps the only way to endow criticism with a degree of *positivity*:

> I think that in everything that involves the meeting of different objects and fields, the most important thing is a sense of limits and of precision. This is something that the failures – *especially* the failures – of quantitative studies have taught me: how much you understand, how much you don't. Because it is never all or nothing; there is always something. But how much is something? Something where? Something how? 'It is always something' would be a good title.[3]

3 Francesco de Cristofaro and Giuseppe Episcopo, 'È sempre qualcosa. Intervista a Franco Moretti', *L'Indice dei libri del mese* 36: 3 (March 2019), an interview to mark the Italian translation of *The Bourgeois*.

In a paper titled 'Simulations, Forms, History', delivered to the 2019 Compalit convention in Siena, Moretti's first move is to make this gambit, as it were, more tangible. Addressing an audience of humanists who are discussing literature over the *longue durée*, he recounts his experience of creating in his laboratory 'the digital equivalent of a die with 100 sides' to measure the percentage of lines in a play spoken by a given character. Simulations, he explains, 'allow us to imagine alternatives, and almost to conduct experiments with reality'. More specifically, the unrealised goal was to develop a 'periodic table of dramatic networks'. In relation to the team's intentions, the die would be rolled a hundred times. However, while it is true that 'a throw of the die will never abolish chance' (Mallarmé), a loaded die ends up doing just that, because a virtual polyhedral conceived in this manner – reflecting, that is, the *actual* distribution of characters' statements – does not correspond to a pure, formal model generated through procedures based on the calculation of probabilities. This prevents measurement of the deviation of a given text (or class of texts) from that abstract model, 'in order to better understand its logic'.[4]

As Moretti notes, the working group soon realised that it needed to draw on more sophisticated methods. Crucially, it is only at this point, after acknowledging a procedural error, that Moretti can go on to illustrate the simulation – without skimping on any of the arithmetical details that can be difficult, even vexing, for the typical literary scholar. He then reviews the corpus of texts, from Sophocles to Racine, Shakespeare to Ibsen; the methodological paradigm, namely network theory; the basis of the algorithm, which is the dialogue between characters; and finally the various operational parameters which are gradually identified in the course of the experiment.

Trying to summarise here the intricate development of that paper would do it an injustice: from the effectiveness of the model when applied to a classic text of Racine, *Alexandre Le Grand*, through to its apparent impasse when applied to *The Master Builder*, with those enigmatic, nameless figures that appear in the final scene, and which end up disrupting the

---

4 Franco Moretti, 'Simulating Dramatic Networks: Morphology, History, Literary Study', *Journal of World Literature* 6: 1, pp. 2–3, 20.

abstract design and very physiology of Ibsen's dramaturgy. It seems more appropriate to highlight a positive takeaway, namely the idea that the configuration of an abstract model primarily serves to measure, and then interpret, the distance of individual literary objects from it; and, conversely, the acknowledgment of a sort of limitation intrinsic to the method used, relating to the fundamental question posed of that particular conference occasion:

> Beginning by constructing the model, and introducing historical works in order to 'test' it, were choices that had gone almost without saying; in fact, they had established *a complete subordination of history to morphology.* Morphology was the model, the hypothesis, the idea; it was *our work*; history, a test . . . Morphological imagination was everything; historical reality, very little.[5]

Yet it is precisely this 'mishap', as he calls it, that has allowed us to learn something: not by taking the conventional route, but through a process of estrangement. As is typical of experimental criticism, in fact.

2.

Now for an older picture: let's call it *Sangue Romagnolo* (Romagnolo Blood), partly as a tribute to the location, partly for the daring quality it signifies. On a Friday afternoon in 1994, at one of the first *Colloqui malatestiani* in Santarcangelo, dedicated that year to spatial configurations in the European novel, Moretti – casual trousers, shirt, a loosely knotted tie – summarised, through some initial case studies and suggested readings, his project for a 'historical atlas of literature'. The words of this professor, so unconventional, both unsettled and captivated his audience: an audience that included many deans and masters who are no longer with us, among them Francesco Orlando, Remo Ceserani, Alessandro Serpieri and Luciano Zagari. Not quite forty-four years old, Moretti had by then completed his move across the Atlantic, and was known as the author of a small classic

5 Ibid., p. 20.

work dedicated to the *Bildungsroman*; not to mention that he was about to publish another important essay, a bold theoretical study of those elusive textual objects which today we call 'world literature'. In other words he was a comparatist who, over the years, had done battle with canonical authors including Shakespeare, Balzac, Stendhal, Dickens, Eliot, Joyce . . .

But on that spring evening he did something very different. He began to project onto a screen, one after another, a series of maps – maps no one had ever seen before. They were diagrammatic representations he had developed using artisanal methods and rigorous processes of abstraction, even if it was an abstraction rich with history: the two Englands of Jane Austen – the deep homeland versus the transactions of the national marriage market along the south coast; the Latin Quarter of the *Comédie humaine*, orientated according to the characters' desires; and much more that would later form the backbone of *Atlas of the European Novel*. That presentation, with its adamantine clarity, posed an uncompromising challenge to existing methodologies. It was already clear that one had either to take it or leave it.

It was also clear, furthermore, that there were at least two Morettis – both undoubtedly theorists, but practitioners of different genres of theory. One was hermeneutic, sometimes even philosophical, inclined towards close readings of texts; the other was engaged instead in a daring form of distant reading, a sort of telescoping of the phenomenology of forms in a quantitative and sociological history of literature. And in this notion of literature, truly all literature came within range – even the 'normal' literature ordinarily destined for oblivion, even the vast, yet measurable, unread that does not enter the canon, and perhaps cannot enter it. Indeed, anyone who hears Moretti speak today, whether in public or private, about his *livre à venir* on tragedy – observing how he still stubbornly and faithfully draws on a critical lineage that stretches from Lukács to Szondi – or instead about quantitative experiments and the digital humanities, cannot help but feel that those two souls still cohabit the same body, even if they are perhaps not quite so different as they might seem (the current volume includes some demonstrations of this, starting with the first essay). Take *The Bourgeois*: a book apparently much closer in tone to *The Way of the World*, but in which new readings of works dominated by bourgeois characters – from *Robinson Crusoe* to Ibsen's plays – are corroborated and defended through the use of empirical data derived from linguistic analysis of corpora and databases. Of course, this is only a light skirmish compared to the unalloyed experimentalism of *Distant Reading* or *Canon/Archive*, an anthology of pamphlets from the Stanford Literary Lab, where, in support of what we have tried to argue here, one can find the following informal but epistemologically crucial statement: 'By frustrating our expectations, failed experiments "estrange" our natural habits of thought, offering us a chance to transform them.'[6] Above all, it is here that the reader finds the most surprising things: new and more sophisticated maps; graphs supported by complex computational processes; diagrammatic trees that allow one to visualise the morphology of genres and techniques (from the detective novel to the interior monologue). All matters which, for any normal literary critic, cannot but provoke a mix of excitement and disorientation, scepticism and exultation. Moretti's working method is so radical at first contact that it can cause confusion, even shock.

It really is like that: take it or leave it. Or, to steal a musical metaphor from a beautiful song of a few years ago, take it *and* leave it: analytical rigour and theoretical imagination; picking a side and dialectical self-criticism. In the end, this is what is always necessary if one wants to attempt to combine research with inspiration.

3.

Graphs, Maps, Trees opens emblematically with a celebrated passage from Robert Musil's *The Man Without Qualities*, chosen as the epigraph: 'A man who wants the truth becomes a scientist; a man who wants to give free play to his subjectivity may become a writer; but what should a man do who wants something in between?'[7] Ulrich – the protagonist of Musil's masterpiece – replies that this man will perhaps become an essayist. This is an answer that probably wouldn't displease Moretti.

---

6 Franco Moretti, 'Literature, Measured', *Pamphlet 12* (2016) of the Stanford Literary Lab, p. 4 – at litlab.stanford.edu.

7 Robert Musil, *The Man Without Qualities*, transl. Sophie Wilkins (London: Picador, 1997), p. 274.

The essay, Musil writes, is 'the strictest form attainable in an area where one cannot work precisely'. It is the tool used by both Ulrich and Musil to explore the vast, fragmented territory of the 'nonratioid' – that domain of the consciousness from which rational certainties are banned, but which nevertheless demands examination. In this sense, the essay is an 'attempt' (*Versuch*), 'the unique and unalterable form assumed by a man's inner life in a decisive thought'; 'nothing is more foreign to it than the irresponsible and half-baked quality of thought known as subjectivism'; 'the irresponsibility and mediocrity of ideas'.[8]

Versuch: yes, in German it means *attempt, essay* (as in the subtitle to Lukacs' *Theory of the Novel*, a numinous presence throughout much of Moretti's work), but also *scientific experiment*. Perhaps no other single expression so immediately grasps one of the more characteristic features of Moretti's criticism: that it is not only rigorous and experimental, but also subjective and free-spirited, as we have attempted to communicate in this book. Because if Musil is right, and the essay is the form which 'the interior life of a person' assumes in a 'decisive' moment, it will inevitably start from a core experience, from a particular and subjective encounter with the world, and then expand outwards into the abstraction of theoretical speculation. And if we add, still agreeing with Musil, that nothing is further from the essay than 'the irresponsibility and mediocrity of ideas', we might arrive at a fairly accurate description of the kind of criticism that Moretti has practised since his earliest writings: stubbornly iconoclastic, provocative, incendiary in methods, content and tone, yet also deeply self-aware. And even amid his tireless pursuit of new ways to reinvigorate literary studies, it is a mode to which he has remained, in essence, remarkably committed.

Awareness. In Chapter 30 of Thomas Mann's *Doctor Faustus*, following the outbreak of the First World War, Serenus Zeitblom is in Munich to complete his preparations before leaving for the front. He takes the opportunity to visit his old friend Adrian Leverkühn in Pfeiffering,

---

8 Robert Musil, '[On the Essay]', in *Precision and Soul: Essays and Addresses*, ed. and transl. Burton Pike and David S. Luft (Chicago: University of Chicago Press, 1990), p. 48; Musil, 'Sketch of What the Writer Knows', in ibid., pp. 61–5; Musil, *Man Without Qualities*, p. 273.

with whom he enters into a long conversation. Re-enacting the novel's typical short-circuit between political discourse and avant-garde musical theory, at a certain point Adrian claims: 'There is at bottom only one problem in the world, and this is its name. How does one break through [*Wie bricht man durch*]? How does one get into the open? How does one burst the cocoon and become a butterfly?'[9] Reflecting on Kleist's famous essay on puppet theatre and the work in which he was engaged during that time, the *Gesta Romanorum*, Adrian sharply poses the problem of the search for the *new* in art – a problem that, as we know too well, was central to modernist aesthetics and much of postmodernism, especially in the Anglophone world, until at least the mid-1990s.

Bidding adieu to the dark and captivating *Doctor Faustus*, and returning to the realm of literary criticism, we believe that very few critics have interrogated with Moretti's lucidity and awareness the problem that obsesses Adrian in his musical research: How to 'break through'? How to advance; towards what, and why? The numerous retrospective parentheses scattered throughout Moretti's mature work (such as *Distant Reading*) testify to this. They are precious documents about what it should really mean to be sustained in one's intellectual passions by an uncommon and uncompromising research ethic. Indeed, it is not emphasised enough how different each of Moretti's works are from each other, whether a monograph, a short essay, a collection of writings, or an edited volume; how scrupulously he avoids repeating or citing himself, and how little he leaves to chance in his writing. Given Moretti's intense productivity, we are surely looking here at something exemplary in its method – something that many of us would strongly wish for.

In this sense, one might say that Moretti's criticism is imbued with that differential logic which, according to Niklas Luhmann, underpins the symbolic apparatus of modernity's apparatus – a logic that is intimately Cartesian, and quite distinct from the poststructuralist temperament and the strand of irrationalism characteristic of certain

9 Thomas Mann, *Doktor Faustus* (Frankfurt am Main: Fischer, 2008), p. 412; *Doctor Faustus*, transl. H. T. Lowe-Porter (Oxford: Oxford University Press, 1949), pp. 307–8.

positions within French theory.[10] The latter, which emerged in France in the late 1960s and was then successfully transplanted to the United States in the 1970s, had already begun to gain traction before Moretti's work had garnered broad critical acclaim – beginning in the mid-1980s, both in English-speaking countries and in Italy. Indeed, Moretti has always remained bound to a certain idea of criticism that has its roots in the austere and anti-dialectical Italian Marxism of the 1960s and '70s, and in the eclectic Marxism of the Frankfurt School – traditions that Moretti has creatively revisited in a scientistic and Popperian key since at least the late 1980s, and right up to the radical computational turn of the early 2010s.

In its structure and content, this volume aims to reflect the themes outlined thus far. Part I, 'Towards an Intellectual History', reconstructs Moretti's intellectual journey from his student years at the Sapienza University of Rome to the present day. The essays by the two editors, along with that by Giuseppe Episcopo, focus on different moments in this journey and their significance: the years between 1976 and 1986 (the Italian years, during which Moretti grappled with his Marxist training and Trotskyist activism; this was also the period in which his distinctive style and idiosyncratic authorial voice took shape); the years from 1990 to 2005 (the American years, in which Moretti seems to work without pause, more or less under the radar, on a long and extremely complex 'discourse on method'); and, finally, the years from around 2011 to today (those of the computational turn and the Stanford Literary Lab pamphlets, but also *The Bourgeois* and *Far Country*).

Part II is titled 'Experimental Criticism'. Like the volume whose title it shares, it brings together contributions that illuminate the fundamental features of Moretti's protean experimentalism, engaging with themes and questions central to his reflections on literature, or which shed light on important aspects of his work: essayism (Mazzoni), literary morphology and evolutionary theory (Miconi), Marxism and literary history

---

10 Niklas Luhmann, *Beobacthungen der Moderne* (Opladen: Westdeutscher Verlag, 1992); See François Cusset, *French Theory* (Paris: La Découverte, 2003); Galin Tihanov, 'Romanticism's *Longue Durée*: 1968 and the Projects of Theory', *Interventions* 23: 3 (2021), pp. 463–80.

(McManus), the sociology of literature (Sapiro), literary theory (Bertoni), world literature and distant reading (Thomsen) and the Digital Humanities (David).

Part III, 'On the Novel', is devoted to the literary form most closely associated with Moretti's name. We felt it important to include essays that engage with his complex conception of the novel from various perspectives: the relationship between the serious and the tragic (Fiorentino), the study of the nineteenth-century novel (Lavocat) and the tension between the novel and the tragic form (Villari).

Finally, the book is enriched by three texts by Moretti himself: the methodological essay 'The Road to Rome: Literary Studies, Hermeneutics, Quantification', which appeared in *New Left Review* in 2020; the short and elegant essay 'Lukács's *Theory of the Novel*', also first published in *NLR*; and 'Time Passes', a provisional epilogue to the journey charted in this volume, in which Moretti reflects on many of the questions raised by the authors of the essays collected herein.

We would like to thank Franco Moretti sincerely for the intelligence, enthusiasm and generosity with which he has participated in this project. We would also like to give sincere thanks to all those who contributed their essays to the volume: Federico Bertoni, Jérôme David, Giuseppe Episcopo, Francesco Fiorentino, Françoise Lavocat, Guido Mazzoni, Patricia McManus, Andrea Miconi, Gisèle Sapiro, Mads Rosendahl Thomsen and Enrica Villari. Our gratitude also goes to the colleagues and friends with whom we discussed the idea of the book: Elisabetta Abignente, Mimmo Cangiano, Elvira Di Bona, Fredric Jameson, Gianni Maffei, D. A. Miller, Raffaello Palumbo Mosca, Matteo Palumbo, Gabriele Pedullà, Valentina Sturli and Galin Tihanov.

I

TOWARDS AN INTELLECTUAL BIOGRAPHY

1

Unrestrained Individuation: The Young Franco Moretti

Stefano Ercolino

1. Franco Moretti, 1976–86

In 1976, the first monograph published by Franco Moretti, *Letteratura e ideologie negli anni Trenta inglesi* (Literature and Ideologies in England in the 1930s), begins with a lengthy quotation from Trotsky's *Whither England?*[1] The second quotation we encounter in the book is taken instead from Lenin's *Imperialism, the Highest Stage of Capitalism*, which appears in a note.[2] Earlier, as an epigraph, we find a passage from Paul

1 'The crowding out of England from its position of world ruler thus begins to appear clearly as early as the last quarter of the nineteenth century, giving rise, at the beginning of the present century, to a condition of internal uncertainty and ferment in the upper classes and profound molecular processes, basically of a revolutionary character, in the working class. Mighty conflicts of labour and capital played the chief part in these processes. Not only was the aristocratic position of English industry in the world shaken, but also the privileged position of the labour aristocracy in England . . . The war of 1914–18 interrupted this revolutionary process and stopped the growth of the strike wave. Ending in the destruction of Germany, it seemed to restore to England the role of world hegemony. But it soon became apparent that, instead of retarding the decline of England, the war had actually accelerated its decline': Moretti, *Letteratura e ideologie negli anni Trenta inglesi* (Bari: Adriatica Editrice, 1976), p. 7 (translations are original unless otherwise stated); Trotsky, *Whither England?* (New York: International Publishers, 1925), pp. 16–17.

2 'It must be observed that in Great Britain the tendency of imperialism to divide the workers in this way, to encourage opportunism among them, and cause

Nizan's novel *The Conspiracy*.[3] Ten years later, in 1986, the first three quotes from *The Way of the World: The* Bildungsroman *in European Culture*, in order of appearance, are taken from Mannheim's 'The Problem of Generations', Panofsky's *Perspective as Symbolic Form*, and Marx. Unlike the ones that open *Letteratura e ideologie*, these are shorter. The first two are interspersed with Moretti's own words.[4] The third quotation refers instead to Marx's concept of 'permanent revolution', but appears without bibliographical indications and, in the original Italian version of *The Way of the World*, without quotation marks.[5]

Letteratura e ideologie coincides roughly with Moretti's graduation thesis. It is a book devoted exclusively to English literature from the

---

temporary decay in the working-class movement, revealed itself much earlier than the end of the nineteenth and the beginning of the twentieth centuries . . . Marx and Engels systematically traced this connection between opportunism in the labour movement and the imperialistic features of British capitalism for several decades': Moretti, *Letteratura e ideologie*, p. 8 n. 2; Lenin, 'Imperialism, the Highest Stage of Capitalism', in *Essential Works of Lenin: 'What Is to Be Done?' and Other Essays*, ed. Henry M. Christman (New York: Dover, 1987 [1917]), p. 252.

3 'They were stirred more by disorder, absurdity and outrages to logic than by cruelty or oppression, and really saw the bourgeoisie, whose sons they were, less as criminal and murderous than as idiotic. But they wished to fight not for the workers – who, fortunately, had by no means waited for them – but for themselves: they viewed the workers merely as their natural allies. There is a great deal of difference between wanting to sink a ship and refusing to sink with it': Moretti, *Letteratura e ideologie*, p. 6; Paul Nizan, *The Conspiracy*, transl. Quintin Hoare (London: Verso, 2011 [1938]), p. 39.

4 'In "stable communities", that is in status or "traditional" societies, writes Karl Mannheim, "Being Young" is a question of biological differentiation"'; 'The *Bildungsroman* as the "symbolic form" of modernity: for Cassirer, and Panofsky, through such a form "a particular spiritual content [here, a specific image of modernity] is connected to a specific material sign [here, youth] and intimately identified with it"': Moretti, *The Way of the World: The* Bildungsroman *in European Culture*, transl. Albert Sbragia (London: Verso, 2000 [1986]), pp. 4, 5.

5 'Marx's words' become Moretti's 'Modernity as – in Marx's words – a permanent revolution that perceives the experience piled up in tradition as a useless deadweight, and therefore can no longer feel represented by maturity, and still less by old age': *Way of the World*, p. 5. Here and elsewhere, translations have been modified slightly for greater adherence to the original text or for stylistic reasons.

1930s, mostly poetry. It is political, militant, austere and subtly workerist.[6] From today's perspective, it is somewhat moralistic:

> There was certainly an embarrassing vertical collapse of the leading organs of the trade unions, which abandoned millions of workers in the decisive moment of the clash . . .[7]

> The deepest roots in the defeat of the general strike, in conclusion, reside perhaps more in the disaggregation of the English proletariat and society as a whole than in the 'betrayal' of the summits and the sudden end to the struggle . . .[8]

> Here we see Auden and Orwell, attempting in different ways to recreate in poetry and in literature that first-hand information, so precise and cutting, which official sources had covered over with hypocritical silences . . .[9]

Letteratura e ideologie is a book that can be squared with the context of late 1960s and early 1970s left-wing Italian academic culture, and one that is consistent with Moretti's Marxist formation and his Trotskyist political militancy in those years. Already completed as a manuscript in

---

6 The courses in Italian literature held by Alberto Asor Rosa at the Sapienza in 1969–70 and 1970–1, both of which Moretti attended – one on the division of intellectual labour, the other on the historical avant-gardes – might have played a role in lending a perhaps unwittingly workerist hue to Moretti's first book. It has to be noted, however, that Asor Rosa's main influence on the young Moretti was not through his most famous work from 1965, *Scrittori e popolo* (The Writer and the People – published in English in Seagull Books' Italian List, edited by Alberto Toscano), but rather through his 1971 book on Thomas Mann, *Thomas Mann o dell'ambiguità borghese* (Thomas Mann, or, On Bourgeois Ambiguity), which had previously appeared in serial form in the journal *Contropiano*. Asor Rosa's general lack of interest in theoretical and methodological questions related to the practice of literary criticism, as well as his predominant expertise in Italian literature, prevented Moretti from viewing him as an essential source of inspiration.

7 Moretti, *Letteratura e ideologie*, p. 10.

8 Ibid., p. 14.

9 Ibid., pp. 31–2.

1974,[10] it was published two years later in the series *Biblioteca di Studi inglesi* (Library of English Studies) overseen by Agostino Lombardo for Adriatica Editrice in Bari. Mostly ignored by critics, and rarely mentioned by the author himself, it has never been reprinted, nor has it been even partially translated in English (or, to my knowledge, any other language).

The Way of the World is an entirely different matter: a classic of literary criticism and theory of the twentieth century that is immensely admired, endlessly cited, and which has been translated into several languages. Published in Italian by Garzanti a few years after the first edition of *Signs Taken for Wonders* (1983) and preceded by the 1983 and 1985 essays 'Waterloo Story' and 'The Comfort of Civilisation', appeared in the journals *Quaderni piacentini* and *Representations*, *The Way of the World* was the book that made Moretti's name, in Italy as well as abroad. The stylistic shift from *Letteratura e ideologie* is noticeable from the start. From the beginning of the book, the writing is direct, anxious:

> Achilles, Hector, Ulysses: the hero of the classical epic is a mature man, an adult. Aeneas, carrying away a father by now too old, and a son still too young, is the perfect embodiment of the symbolic relevance of the 'middle' stage of life. This paradigm will last a long time ('*Nel mezzo del cammin di nostra vita* . . .'), but with the first enigmatic hero of modern times, it falls apart. According to the text, Hamlet is thirty years old: far from young by Renaissance standards. But *our* culture, in choosing Hamlet as its first symbolic hero, has 'forgotten' his age, or rather has had to alter it, and pictures the Prince of Denmark as a young man.[11]

The syntax is broken, more muscular and agonistic, even colloquial – a stylistic trait that, from *Signs Taken for Wonders* and *The Way of the World* on, will characterise Moretti's writing:[12]

---

10 Moretti informs us of this in an asterisked note: ibid., p. 33.

11 Moretti, *Way of the World*, p. 3.

12 In the 'Acknowledgements' section of *Signs Taken for Wonders*, Moretti laments the fact that the 'general tone' of the English translation of the essays collected in the volume is 'slightly more "highbrow"' than his use of Italian in the original pieces, which he describes as 'very idiomatic and colloquial': *Signs Taken*

> Mobility and interiority. Modern youth, to be sure, is many other things as well: the growing influence of education, the strengthening of bonds within generations, a new relationship with nature, youth's 'spiritualisation' – these features are just as important in its 'real' development. Yet the *Bildungsroman* discards them as irrelevant, abstracting from 'real' youth a 'symbolic' one, epitomized, we have said, in mobility and interiority. Why this choice?[13]

The change in authorial posture, which becomes bold and idiosyncratic, is pronounced:

> This novel marks simultaneously the birth of the *Bildungsroman* (the form which will dominate or, more precisely, make possible the Golden Century of Western narrative), and of a new hero: Wilhelm Meister, followed by Elizabeth Bennet and Julien Sorel, Rastignac and Frédéric Moreau and Bel-Ami, Waverley and David Copperfield, Renzo Tramaglino, Eugene Onegin, Bazarov, Dorothea Brooke . . .[14]

In *The Way of the World*, the argument concentrates on the novel and on a specific genre. From English literature of the 1930s – the topic of Moretti's first book – the field of enquiry stretches back chronologically and broadens geographically to include German, English, Russian and French literature of the 1700s and 1800s, ranging more or less from 1795–96 and Goethe's *Wilhelm Meister's Apprenticeship* to 1876 and George Eliot's *Daniel Deronda*. The writers discussed in *Letteratura e ideologie* – primarily Orwell, Upward, Day Lewis, Auden and Spender – disappear from *The Way of the World* (as they do from the essays in *Signs Taken for Wonders*), in which only Orwell is cited, and then only as an interpreter of Dickens.[15] There seems to be no trace of the political, militant tension of his 1976 debut. The ideological and cultural frame of the first book, so

---

for Wonders: Essays in the Sociology of Literary Forms, transl. Susan Fisher, David Forgacs and David Miller (London: Verso, 1983), p. vi.

13 Moretti, *Way of the World*, pp. 4–5.

14 Ibid., p. 3.

15 Ibid., p. 192.

characteristic of Italian Marxism in the 1960s and 1970s, and the references to Italian intellectuals such as Della Volpe, Colletti and Asor Rosa, which once meaningfully featured in *Letteratura e ideologie*, are (except for the latter, still present in *Signs Taken for Wonders*) nowhere to be found.[16]

Finally, in *Letteratura e ideologie*, the methodological horizon is already that of the Marxist sociology of literature. The insistence on the social and political dimension of literary form – a constant hum in the background of Moretti's work, from his debut to his computational turn – is repeated: '[H]ere one can understand the importance of the methodological assumption from which we began, according to which a stylistic procedure always has deeply social and political motivations and aims'.[17] Nonetheless, one notes the absence of theoretical elements that, in the next ten years, would confer a different depth on Moretti's sociological imagination: the Russian formalists, early Lukács, Wilhelmine sociology, the *Annales* school in historiography; these are all subjects that will be taken up in *Signs Taken for Wonders* and, with even greater density, in *The Way of the World*, where, depending on the given instance, they will have more or less of an impact on the argument.[18] The case of Hegel is especially striking. Quite present in *Signs Taken for Wonders*, and especially in *The Way of the World*, the German philosopher is mentioned only once in *Letteratura e ideologie* – and this in a note, in the context of a quotation from Della Volpe's *Il verisimile filmico e altri saggi* (Cinematographic Verisimilitude and Other Essays), in relation to aestheticism understood as a phenomenon that is innate, rather than antagonistic, to capitalism.[19] If, on the one hand, Hegel's absence from Moretti's first book can be explained by way of his

16 Trotsky himself has one brief mention: Moretti, *Way of the World*, p. 109.

17 Moretti, *Letteratura e ideologie*, p. 29; cf. pp. 20–33.

18 Shklovsky, who is so central in Moretti's 'mature' reflection on literary forms, is mentioned only once, in a note and within a parenthetical aside (*Letteratura e ideologie*, p. 288 n. 7). Jakobson is the only other thinker related to Russian formalism whose name appears in the book. There is just a single mention of *Theory of the Novel* (*Letteratura e ideologie*, p. 235), one of the texts that had been most influential in establishing Moretti's work on forms. The Lukács that interests Moretti in *Letteratura e ideologie* is specifically the Lukács of the 1930s.

19 Moretti, *Letteratura e ideologie*, p. 216 n. 42.

affinity, in the early 1970s, with the rigidly uncompromising anti-Hegelian Marxism of Della Volpe and Colletti, on the other hand, the marked expansion of space devoted to Hegel in Moretti's later production will, among other things, be an even stronger signal of intellectual emancipation on his part.

Beyond the obvious differences in content between the books produced from 1976 to 1986, that is, *Letteratura e ideologie* (1976), *Signs Taken for Wonders* (1983) and *The Way of the World* (1986), the shift in theoretical and ideological horizons, style, research interests and critical acuity in Moretti's work is so profound that it cannot be explained in terms of a normal process of maturation or the intellectual curiosity of a young scholar. What happened? How did Moretti go, within the arc of ten years, from a book that is well documented, militant, Trotskyist and measured in its thematic and temporal arc in comparison to his later works, to a masterpiece of literary criticism and theory that is highly personal, spellbinding and written in the language of the Nietzschean grand style? What are the experiences that were decisive in determining this transition?

2. *Reductio ad Unum*

To answer this question, one could begin in 1972. Apart from being the year in which he defended his thesis, 1972 is also the year when Moretti met two individuals who would go on to have different, but important and long-lasting effects on his professional and intellectual life: Perry Anderson in London, while Moretti was conducting research towards what would become *Letteratura e ideologie*; and D. A. Miller at Gabriele d'Annunzio University of Pescara, where Moretti was a research fellow (from 1972 to 1975), and where Miller was a lecturer.[20]

The year 1972 is also when Colletti took up a permanent post at the Sapienza University of Rome. The influence of his relationship with

20 For these and other details not directly mentioned in Moretti's published works or that cannot be inferred from those, I have availed myself of private conversations with Moretti himself.

Colletti on the development of Moretti's thought was considerable. In 1974 and 1975, Moretti audited Colletti's lectures on Marx's *Capital* in the packed main hall of the Faculty of Literature and Philosophy at the Sapienza. Colletti is cited in both *Letteratura e ideologie* and *Signs Taken for Wonders* – specifically in the essays 'The Long Goodbye' and 'Clues'.[21] In 1974, Moretti was present when Anderson interviewed Colletti for the *New Left Review*, a meeting that became the basis of what would be published as 'A Political and Philosophical Interview', translated by Moretti himself into Italian and published by Laterza the following year.[22] On the theoretical level, Colletti instilled in Moretti an antidialectical prejudice, one that he would never abandon and that had already come to him through reading Della Volpe's *Critique of Taste*, a text assigned in Emilio Garroni's aesthetics courses, which Moretti attended at the Sapienza. As for Colletti, his most palpable influence on Moretti was at the level of style and authorial voice, especially with respect to the search for an expository clarity and a rather apodictic form of enunciation. One thinks of certain passages from Colletti's works, such as the lightning strike that begins the first chapter of the second section of *Marxism and Hegel*, an anti-Hegelian critique of Marxist humanism and dialectical materialism carried out through the reconstruction of the differences between the Marxist interpretation of Hegel's philosophy and that of thinkers belonging to, or at least close to, dialectical materialism: 'The central theme of Hegel's thought is his thesis of the identity of idealism and

---

21 The first citation, taken from Lucio Colletti, *From Rousseau to Lenin: Studies in Ideology and Society*, transl. John Merrington and Judith White (New York: Monthly Review, 1972 [1969]), confronts the question of the relationship between structure and superstructure and the problem of the mirror structure of ideology (*Letteratura e ideologie*, p. 241 n. 82); the second, from the same essay collection, refers to the manifest and hidden aspects of capitalism, and to the causal bond that ties the former to the latter (*Signs Taken for Wonders*, pp. 151, 258 n. 31); the third, from Colletti and Napoleoni, eds, *Il futuro del capitalismo: crollo o sviluppo?* (Bari: Laterza, 1970), addresses the crises of production in the capitalist system (*Signs Taken for Wonders*, pp. 184, 262 n. 5).

22 Lucio Colletti, 'A Political and Philosophical Interview', *New Left Review* I/86 (July–August 1974), pp. 3–28.

philosophy.'[23] Or consider the beginning of the 1959 essay 'Marxism as Sociology', later collected in *From Rousseau to Lenin*, comprising essays critical of modern bourgeois society:

> We may start by turning to the preface written for the first edition of *Capital*. Two important circumstances stand out immediately, the first of which is as follows. Unlike all the economists who had discussed society 'in general' before him, Marx is concerned with *one* society only, modern *capitalist* society. He claims to have examined the laws of development of *this* society and none other . . . Which means that the analysis concerns not an *idea* (an ideal object) but a *materially determined* or real object. This is the first point of departure.[24]

Or, again, note the beginning of the 1968 essay 'From Hegel to Marcuse' – also included in *From Rousseau to Lenin* – on Marcuse's romantic and regressive Marxism, in which Colletti, commenting on the *Science of Logic*, defines the central points of Hegel's philosophy:

> Hegel's philosophy is based on three propositions. The first is that philosophy is always idealism: . . . The second is that the problem of philosophy is *to realise* the principle of idealism: . . . The third is that the realisation of the principle of idealism implies the *destruction of the finite and the annihilation of the world . . .*[25]

What is striking here is the certainty and clarity of the exposition, the insistent use of italics for emphasis, the analytic decomposition of problems, the orderly disposition of ideas, the illustrative enumerations. What is striking in Colletti's writing, here as elsewhere, is its Cartesian spirit and its cheekiness: two traits that, though hardly present in *Letteratura e ideologie*, would, starting with *Signs Taken for Wonders* come to

---

23 Lucio Colletti, *Marxism and Hegel*, transl. Lawrence Garner (London: Verso, 1979 [1969]), p. 7.

24 Colletti, *From Rousseau to Lenin*, p. 3.

25 Ibid., p. 111.

permanently characterise Moretti's prose.[26] See, for example, the beginning of 'Homo palpitans' in *Signs Taken for Wonders*:

> This essay will endeavour to demonstrate three hypotheses. First, that the metropolis (in our case, Paris in the middle of the nineteenth century) calls for a change in the perception not so much of space as of the *flow of time*. To come to terms with the urban experience, literature must excogitate a new rhetoric of temporality . . . Second, I will maintain that this peculiar rhetorical arrangement moves from literature into the daily life of urban dwellers . . . The third hypothesis . . . is that the connection Benjamin established between the urban experience and literary production in his essays on Baudelaire . . . is probably far less convincing and exemplary than one would tend to believe, and therefore must be re-examined.[27]

Or take a look at a famous passage from 'The Soul and the Harpy', the first methodological piece authored by Moretti, and also the essay that opens *Signs Taken for Wonders*:

> On the other hand, in the rather frenetic world of literary criticism, theoretical speculation enjoys the same symbolic status as cocaine: one

---

26 In this regard, one need only briefly reread the four 'precepts', which, in his *Discourse on Method*, Descartes posits as the basis of modern epistemology: 'The first was never to accept anything as true that I did not plainly [*évidemment*] know to be such; that is to say, carefully to avoid hasty judgement and prejudice; and to include nothing more in my judgements than what presented itself to my mind so clearly and distinctly [*si clairement et si distinctement*] that I had no occasion to call it into doubt. The second, to divide [*diviser*] each of the difficulties I would examine into as many parts [*parcelles*] as possible and as was required in order better to resolve them. The third, to conduct my thoughts in an orderly fashion [*par ordre*], by commencing with those objects that are simplest and easiest to know, in order to ascend little by little, as by degrees [*par degrés*], to the knowledge of the most composite things, and by supposing an order even among those things that do not naturally precede one another. And the last, everywhere to make enumerations [*dénombrements*] so complete and reviews [*revues*] so general that I was assured of having omitted nothing': René Descartes, *Discourse on Method and Meditations on First Philosophy*, 4th edn, transl. Donald A. Cress (Indianapolis, IN: Hackett, 1998), p. 11.

27 Moretti, *Signs Taken for Wonders*, p. 109.

> *has to* try it. Readers will judge for themselves whether in my case it has been worthwhile or whether they have simply had dust thrown in their eyes.[28]

The time of the 'embarrassing vertical collapse of the leading organs of the *Trade Unions*' and the 'hypocritical silence' of the 'official sources' against which Auden and Orwell fought seems quite distant. And yet, only a few years had passed since 1976 and *Letteratura e ideologie.* We persist, then, in asking: What happened? Or, rather, what was happening at the time? Starting from 1972, the encounters with Anderson, Miller, and especially Colletti were all influential, as I have noted. But what else took place?

It would be difficult to answer this question without giving due emphasis to Moretti's experience in the group that founded and edited the journal *Calibano.* Born from the desire to give new life to a Marxist critical orientation to Anglophone and American studies in Italy and internationally, *Calibano: rivista semestrale di ricerche sulla letteratura inglese e americana* (Caliban: Biannual Journal of Research in English and American Literature) was founded in Rome in 1976, began publishing in 1977, and continued to be active until 1983. The team comprised a group of relatively young scholars, many of whom were originally from Rome and had been educated at the Sapienza, among whom we may recall Moretti, Benedetta Bini, Guido Carboni, Paola Colaiacomo, Mario Corona, Nadia Fusini, Barbara Lanati, Alessandro Portelli and Carole Beebee Tarantelli, later joined by Beniamino Placido and Niccolò Zapponi. Beyond serving as an occasion for intense and prolonged intellectual discussion, for Moretti *calibano* was a writing lab that allowed him to explore an essayistic style more freely – something that contributed significantly to his change in authorial posture with respect to *Letteratura e ideologie.* It is no accident that Moretti published in *calibano* half of the essays that,

28 Ibid., p. 2. The piece originally appeared in Italian in 1982 in the fifth issue of the new series of *Quaderni piacentini*. 'L'anima e l'arpia. Riflessioni sugli scopi e i metodi della storiografia letteraria', would reappear in English translation in *Signs Taken for Wonders* with a few introductory pages added, from which the citation is drawn – pages omitted from the reissue of the essay from the first Italian edition of the collection – Moretti, *Segni e stili del moderno* (Turin: Einaudi, 1987).

translated into English, would make up the first edition of *Signs Taken for Wonders*: 'Dialectic of Fear' (1978), 'The Great Eclipse: Tragic Form as the Deconsecration of Sovereignty' (1979), 'From *The Waste Land* to the Artificial Paradise' (1980) and 'Kindergarten' (1981).

Alongside his work with *calibano*, another crucial experience with respect to the definition of Moretti's writerly voice was his collaboration on the new series of *Quaderni piacentini*, through which he published two important essays that would ultimately appear in *Signs Taken for Wonders*: 'Homo Palpitans' (1981) and 'The Soul and the Harpy' (1982). From this point of view, it is interesting to note that, in the first Italian edition of *Signs Taken for Wonders*, titled *Segni e stili del moderno*, published by Einaudi in 1987, the only essays of the collection published by Verso in 1983 that he excluded were those which were conceived of separately from his experience with *calibano* and *Quaderni piacentini*: 'The Long Goodbye: *Ulysses* and the End of Liberal Capitalism', which appeared in the 1976–77 issue of *Studi inglesi* (English Studies), and 'Indizi [Clues]', an introduction to the volume *Polizieschi classici* (Classic Detective Stories), edited by Moretti in 1978 for the publisher Savelli.

Surveying the essays in *Signs Taken for Wonders*, one can see how, in their pages, in comparison to *Letteratura e ideologie*, Moretti's intellectual world had widened considerably. The presence of Adorno, Benjamin, Freud, Hegel and early Lukács becomes more intense. Anderson, the *Annales* school, Auerbach, Barthes, Bakhtin, Cassirer, Eco, Foucault, Frege, and even Baudrillard make their appearance. We also find Kant, Marcuse, Nietzsche, Orlando, Panofsky, Propp, Schmitt, Simmel, Wallerstein, Watt and Weber. Trotsky vanishes. Apart from Russian formalism, which is still not particularly present (its weight will start to grow, though not in a particularly perceptible way, starting with *The Way of the World*), in *Signs Taken for Wonders* we find most of the cultural references taking shape that would become constant in Moretti's work thereafter. From a methodological and ideological point of view, Moretti moves with conviction towards the Grand Hotel 'abyss [*Abgrund*]' of eclectic Marxism that is generally sceptical towards the possibility of revolutionary developments in advanced capitalist societies – a form of Marxism more or less explicitly advocated by the Frankfurt School, which was a scintillating place, rich with ferment, in which Moretti seems to feel at ease; a place that is in many ways incompatible with the cloistered, anti-Hegelian and anti-dialectical Marxism of Colletti and (though less so) of Della Volpe.[29]

If we wanted, then, to fix the principal coordinates of the evolution of Moretti's work in the decade between 1976 and 1986, we could do so along three axes: those of (1) style, (2) theory and ideology, and (3) political militancy. Regarding style, we saw how, after *Letteratura e ideologie*, the influence of Colletti, the experience with *calibano*, and the collaboration on *Quaderni piacentini* – along with a no less crucial drive to keep his writing conversational and approachable, in a voice that often seems reminiscent of the lecture form – allowed Moretti to rapidly develop a highly personal, essayistic style of writing, characterised by expository clarity and speculative audacity. With respect to theory and ideology, the opening towards an eclectic, freer Marxism along the lines of the Frankfurt School seems to relegate to the background the more rigid Italian Marxism of the 1960s and 1970s. With respect to political militancy, to which I will return soon, there seems to be in Moretti's work a general detachment, which one can especially see in his abandonment of more engaged tones and the eclipse of Trotsky's influence, which had shone so brightly in *Letteratura e ideologie*.

One could envision the common denominator of these three changes in the form of a double movement: a collapse into a point that is followed by an immediate, impetuous release. The collapse was that of most of the cultural and ideological world of the years of his university education and political militancy, a world that would continue to have a precise significance for Moretti until at least 1976 or 1977. This collapse had the effect of releasing him from a particular type of context within which he had long lived and worked, and it also involved a kind of *reductio ad unum* of the epistemological foundations of his way of doing criticism. From then on, his *subjectivity* became a starting point, ever more central to an impetuous intellectual inquiry. But what did this mean? What provoked the collapse?

---

29 On the *Grand Hotel Abgrund*, see Georg Lukács, *The Destruction of Reason*, transl. Peter Palmer (Atlantic Highlands, NJ: Humanities, 1981), p. 243.

3. 'History is what hurts'

In Italy in May 1976 – while *Letteratura e ideologie* was in press, the first of the essays that would go on to appear in *Signs Taken for Wonders* was published, and the *calibano* period was starting – the first trial against the Brigate Rosse (Red Brigades) was taking place in Turin.[30]

In the June elections, the Partito Comunista Italiano (Italian Communist Party) enjoyed great electoral success, in contrast to left-wing groups inimical to it. For the first time since 1947, the PCI did not vote against the formation of a Christian Democratic government: from then on, the rupture with left-wing extra-parliamentary groups would prove irreparable. A few months later, at the Congress of Rimini, the group Lotta Continua (Continuous Struggle) would dissolve. Some of those who left Lotta Continua and Potere Operaio (Workers' Power), which dissolved in 1973, founded the group Prima Linea (Front Line). In October, the Italian dimension of the Lockheed scandal came to light. In a climate of exacerbated political and social conflict in February 1977, in a student-occupied Sapienza, right-wing extremists seriously wounded the student Guido Bellachioma. Two weeks later, at the Sapienza again, Luciano Lama, the leader of the Confederazione Generale Italiana del Lavoro (General Italian Confederation of Labour), was bitterly confronted by the autonomists.

In March, the Movement of 1977 was at the centre of violent clashes with the police in Bologna and later in Rome, following the killing of the Lotta Continua member Pier Francesco Lorusso. On 5 July, Sartre, Foucault, Deleuze, Guattari, Barthes, Sollers and others signed in the pages of *Lotta Continua* an appeal against the repression of those in Italy who fought against the so-called 'historical compromise'. In Bologna, in September, the conference on repression took place – the last assembly of the Movement of 1977 – during which the divergences between various factions of the movement once again proved insurmountable, and in the face of which it did not survive.[31]

---

30 Fredric Jameson, *The Political Unconscious: Narrative as a Socially Symbolic Act* (London: Routledge, 2002 [1981]), p. 102.

31 See Luca Falciola, *Il movimento del 1977 in Italia* (Rome: Carocci, 2015); Davide Steccanella, *Gli anni della lotta armata. Cronologia di una rivoluzione*

After his time at the Gabriele d'Annunzio University of Chieti, Moretti spent the years between 1975 and 1979 at the Sapienza as a researcher, where he witnessed the frantic events described above. Moretti had never signed up with the PCI, belonging since his years of study to groups connected to the extra-parliamentary left, such as the Nuclei Comunisti Rivoluzionari (Revolutionary Communist Nuclei, 1969–71) and the group around *il manifesto* (1974–76).[32] Moretti was not connected to the Movement of 1977, both for ideological reasons and because a personal political crisis had slowly emerged in the preceding years. This was a result of the endemic isolation experienced by young Trotskyist students at the Sapienza (an isolation recounted by Colletti in his interview with Anderson), of the too-often violent bent assumed by socially antagonistic forces, and of events such as the dramatic end of the Allende government in Chile and the missed radicalisation of the Carnation Revolution in Portugal, which for many young people in Italy and throughout the world had represented the hope for a relatively peaceful path towards revolution.[33] If, as Weber wrote, one of the key experiences of the modern era is that of disenchantment, for Moretti, on the political front, this experience matured from 1972 to 1977, during a period in which everything in Italy continued to aim, if not for long, in the opposite direction: towards increasing extremism in political struggle.[34]

---

mancata (Milan: Bietti, 2018), pp. 149–94; Alberto Pantaloni, *La dissoluzione di Lotta continua e il movimento del '77* (Rome: DeriveApprodi, 2019).

32 The Nuclei Comunisti Rivoluzionari was a small Trotskyist formation of the extra-parliamentary left created after 1968 by those who had left the Gruppi Comunisti Rivoluzionari (Revolutionary Communist Groups), the Italian section of the Fourth International. Until their dissolution in 1971, the leaders of the group were Paolo Flores d'Arcais and Franco Russo. From 1971 to 1972, the schismatic fringe guided by Flores published the magazine *Soviet*, in the pages of which appeared Moretti's very first piece, in 1972, namely 'Ombre rosse, ombre cinesi, ('Red Shadows, Chinese Shadows').

33 In 'A Political and Philosophical Interview', Colletti analyses the crisis of Marxist thought and the consequences it had for the Italian and European workers' movement, in what is, in its profundity and acumen, a veritable intellectual history of post-war Italy (and beyond). Among other things, Colletti observes how, in that moment, Trotskyism was a minority position among the youth at the Sapienza, who were closer to Maoist or neo-Stalinist positions.

34 'The fate of our times is characterised by rationalisation and intellectualisation and, above all, by the disenchantment of the world [*vor allem: Entzauberung der Welt*]. Precisely the ultimate and most sublime values have retreated from

In the moment in which it came to light in 1976 and presented its author as a young and serious Trotskyist critic, for Moretti himself *Letteratura e ideologie negli anni trenta inglesi* had already been superseded from an ideological and cultural point of view: his debut was, in this sense, already an ending. In this regard, the closing passage strikes a prophetic note. Commenting on the ending of Orwell's *Nineteen Eighty-Four*, Moretti writes:

> With this double exaltation of individual freedom and integrity . . . both Orwell's life and his work come to an end; and it is significant that, at the end, we (re)discover the problem that was first at the origin: that of the role the individual (Orwell) can and ought to play in society. Except that here the landing point marks a regression: no longer to do with individuating social forces, oppressed or revolutionary, in allegiance to which one can reconstruct one's identity – but with assuming one's own single, private, possessive, isolated dimension as a unique, albeit precarious, point of departure [*ma di assumere la propria dimensione singola, privata, possessiva, isolata come unica, se pur precaria, base di partenza*]. Orwell takes up one of the values most dear to the bourgeois ideology and projects it out of time, with a decisiveness and violence unknown to the intellectuals of the 1930s, though he shares with them (and there is nothing to be done about this) the laboured decline.[35]

'[A]ssuming one's own single, private, possessive, isolated dimension as a unique, albeit precarious, starting point': this could be a summary of what Moretti would go on to do soon after in the essays of *Signs Taken for Wonders* and in *The Way of the World*, where the new critical and theoretical 'landing point' was born precisely out of a political 'regression' and a process of folding-in on one's own individuality. To adopt an expression from Adorno, what Moretti arrived at in *Signs Taken for Wonders* and *The*

---

public life either into the transcendental realm of mystic life or into the brotherliness of direct and personal human relations': Max Weber, 'Science as Vocation', in *From Max Weber: Essays in Sociology*, ed. and transl. H. H. Gerth and C. Wright Mills (Abingdon: Routledge, 1991 [1917/1919]), p. 155.

35 Moretti, *Letteratura e ideologie*, p. 344.

Way of the World, following the political crisis of 1976–77, was an 'unrestrained individuation [*rückhaltlos(e) Individuation*]'.[36]

In 'On Lyric Poetry and Society', Adorno contends that 'the lyric work hopes to attain universality through unrestrained individuation'.[37] By 'unrestrained individuation' Adorno means a process of radical reduction of life to the meaning that its varied manifestations have for a single individual – a process that has a fundamentally social character, as a sign of a 'protest against a social situation that every individual experiences as hostile, alien, cold, oppressive'.[38] That of the lyric poet configures itself, then, as a subjective, idiosyncratic, utopian and anti-capitalist form of 'social antagonism [*gesellschaftliche Antagonismus*]':

> In its protest the poem expresses the dream of a world in which things could be different. The lyric spirit's idiosyncratic opposition to the superior power of material things is a form of reaction to the reification of the world, to the domination of human beings by commodities that has developed since the beginning of the modern era, since the industrial revolution became the dominant force in life.[39]

For Adorno, modern lyric poetry bears within itself a 'rupture [*Bruch*]' between the 'I' and the world, making itself an expression of the subjectivity of an individual that 'defines and expresses itself as something opposed to the collective, to objectivity', and that tries paradoxically to re-establish a harmony with things, and to reach the universal in history precisely by 'immersion in the "I" itself [*in Selbstversenkung*]'.[40] Moretti's way of working between 1976 and 1986 bears a striking resemblance to that of the modern lyric poet as described by Adorno. In 1976 and 1977, Moretti's reflection on literature always begins with himself, from a radical, free, antagonistic extroversion of his personality and his taste. The political crisis experienced

36 Theodor Adorno, 'Lyric Poetry and Society', in *Notes to Literature*, ed. Rolf Tiedemann, transl. Shierry Weber Nicholson (New York: Columbia University Press, 1991 [1957]), p. 60.

37 Ibid.

38 Ibid., p. 61.

39 Ibid., pp. 66, 40.

40 Ibid., p. 41.

around the middle of the 1970s *encodes* the overt political militancy and social antagonism of *Letteratura e ideologie* into a new way of expressing oneself, in a strongly subjective style and a theoretical eclecticism that voiced at the same time unease, protest and defiance towards a historico-political reality that was perceived as 'hostile, alien, cold, oppressive'. For if the eclecticism, personalised style, and disengagement towards which Moretti moved from 1976 to 1986 were, on the one hand, a response to experiencing a political crisis, on the other, they did not signify an ideological abjuration. Moretti – neither at the height of the mid-1980s nor after this – never rescinded his connection to the context from which he came, that of historical materialism. On the contrary, he remained profoundly tied to it and, in his own way, he reinterpreted it, constantly keeping himself distant from irrationalist theoretical positions (such as those expressed by the deconstructionist critics of the Yale school, those fostered by the Lacanianism pervasive in certain Italian left-wing intellectual circles in the 1970s, or the positions advanced in Gilles Deleuze and Félix Guattari's *Anti-Oedipus*, a work that was important for the Movement of 1977 – a movement with which, as I have mentioned, Moretti was not involved).

It thus happened that Moretti came progressively closer to the methods of science, in an increasingly sturdy desire to achieve exactness and in the utopian attempt – one that had already been theorised in 'The Soul and the Harpy' – to formulate falsifiable hypotheses (the computational turn of the early 2010s representing the apex of this tendency).[41] Moretti remained tied to his origins, moreover, also through a certain type of seriousness and a work ethic that hearkened back to European bourgeois culture – which he had known and appreciated from the time of his courses with Asor Rosa at the Sapienza – and to Italian Marxism of the 1960s and 1970s, which he never fully forgot: a seriousness and a work ethic that have always been mobilised, in Moretti's work, towards

41 Carolyn Lesjak traces the roots of Moretti's aspiration towards the formulation of falsifiable research hypotheses to Colletti's Popperian criticism of Marxism as a pseudoscience. See Lesjak, 'All or Nothing: Reading Franco Moretti Reading: A Review of *Distant Reading* and *The Bourgeois: Between History and Literature* by Franco Moretti', *Historical Materialism* 24: 3 (2016), pp. 192–3 n. 28, and Moretti's reply, 'History, Materialism, Historical Materialism: A Response to Carolyn Lesjak and Stefano Ercolino', *Historical Materialism* 29: 4 (2021), pp. 263–71.

the construction of vast and profound discourses of truth, in keeping with the most prestigious Marxist critical and theoretical tradition of the twentieth century (and other traditions as well).

Beyond the intrinsic merit of the works, one might be tempted to think that one of the reasons Moretti's writings have garnered such great and continued appreciation among the public, and especially among younger scholars, resides in the fact that Moretti seemed to accelerate, in 1976–77, a tendency of the world in which we currently live – and likewise, of present-day criticism; a tendency that made itself explicit only at the end of the 1980s and the early 1990s, with the articulation and the rise of the neoliberal subject: that of a radical self-reference of our experience of the world. In this essay, I have suggested that, for Moretti, arriving at an Adornian 'unrestrained individuation' with respect to critical activity was a form of coming-to-terms with a political and cultural crisis that arose in those years 1976–77; the coming-to-terms with his Marxist–Trotskyist training, with his years of militancy, with the political culture and climate of Italy in the early 1970s. But in the 1980s, a reader encountering *Signs Taken for Wonders* or *The Way of the World* without wondering about the genesis of these works or knowing much of the starting point of Moretti's intellectual trajectory could not imagine such a thing, and would likely have had the immediate impression of finding him- or herself confronting an original critical language – a language endowed with great force, free and creative in its stylistic choices as well as in its objects of study. Towards the end of the 1980s and the start of the 1990s, when the historical and cultural foundations that in modernity had legitimised the principle of intellectual authority were already in ruin, and the dominion of *doxa* had come to define itself in the sphere of public discourse, Moretti's critical work seemed capable of speaking the same subjective, broken language of the late-capitalist, neoliberal world, of making itself an interpreter of its euphoric promise of freedom.[42] I say 'seemed' because, as we have seen, Moretti never broke his bond with the cultural hinterland from which he had emerged, or with an antagonistic and utopian vision of critical activity, understood as the intimately

42 See Guido Mazzoni, *I destini generali* (Rome and Bari: Laterza, 2015); 'Democrazia e critica letteraria', *Le parole e le cose*, 8 October 2018.

contradictory but necessary construction of cross-sections of meaning capable of going beyond the details of a given work to extend themselves towards the general and the collective of history.[43]

Retrospectively speaking, one could say that the caesura of 1976–77 in Moretti's work was a perhaps unwitting way of *smuggling in and allowing to survive*, under a seductive vestige of idiosyncratic individualism, an antagonistic critical discourse in a world that, if it was not already hostile towards it, would soon become so. It was, at the time, a visionary act, one that today, in the tribal and particularistic anarchy of methods and aims of contemporary criticism and theory – often indifferent towards the need for an authentically antagonistic reflection on literature, or prone to conformist international, pseudo-progressive research agendas – seems more relevant and desirable than ever.[44]

---

43 See Stefano Ercolino, 'GN-z11, Homesickness for Ice, and Literary Theory', transl. Dylan J. Montanari, *b2o: an online journal*, 24 July 2019; 'Una lama. Critica, forma, totalità', *L'ospite ingrato* 10 (2021), pp. 19–27.

44 See Federico Bertoni, *Letteratura. Teoria, metodi, strumenti* (Rome: Carocci, 2018); 'La resistenza alla teoria', *Ermeneutica letteraria* xiv (2018), pp. 29–36; 'La teoria alla prova', *Comparatismi* 3 (2018), pp. 39–49.

2

Discourse on Method

Francesco de Cristofaro

A taste for the 'concrete' is usually something conservatives have. Beniamino tried to introduce it among people who were anything but. I am thinking of that way he has of discussing matters in a low voice, looking down and around him every now and again, as if the truth were to be found just an inch above the earth, and if you were to look up at the sky you might just miss it; a speech that would begin with a little clearing of the throat, as if to say, 'Certainly matters are just as you say. Yet I recall that . . .'. Or his legendary exam question on Huckleberry Finn, *when in the middle of long discussions – the right ones, but long – on childhood, racism, America and freedom, he would ask: 'Listen, but why do they go down the river on a raft? I mean, why a raft exactly? And not a canoe, or a little boat?'*[1]

1. 1990: Comparative Literature

In 1990 Franco Moretti began his American 'second life', one that would span a quarter of a century between New York and Stanford. The author of *The Way of the World*, then a professor at Verona, was invited to take up the chair in English and Comparative Literature at Columbia University. Meanwhile, on the European side of the Atlantic, comparative literature was facing resistance from many specialists – philologists

1 Franco Moretti, 'Perché proprio una zattera?' ('Why Exactly a Raft?'), in Alberto Abruzzese et al., *Caro Beniamino: Scritti per una festa di compleanno* (Rome: Edizioni della Cometa, 2006), p. 110.

and others – who promoted a kind of text-centred scholarship not without its neo-positivist shades, and a historicism that had somehow emerged unscathed from the collapse of ideologies. But what seems still stranger today, at a generation's distance, is the widespread revival in both research and teaching curricula of a scientific paradigm marked by a kind of intellectual autarky, set in stark opposition to the forces of late-capitalist globalisation that were reshaping the economy, anthropological models, and artistic forms; as if it were the task of criticism – more or less consciously perceived as such – to safeguard the 'genius' of peoples from the Babel of languages, cultures and trends. In a decade that opened with the Gulf War, what Francesco Orlando in a dense lecture at the Sapegno Foundation called 'the other within us' was not universally regarded as a positive value.[2] Far more interesting and urgent was the homeland: a *patria* whose boundaries, to be clear, were variable – sometimes coinciding with a single nation-state, at others with a continental zone (the 'Europe' of Maastricht was born in 1992), or even with the West in its entirety.

The story is well known. In most cases, there was a value-laden confrontation – centred on the United States – between the last defenders of the canon and the apologists for Cultural Studies, a confrontation that was always political. Harold Bloom had published *The Western Canon* in 1994 to international acclaim. By the flick of an editorial wand, a series of hermeneutical rhapsodies was transformed into something like a Macedonian phalanx of classics, a Viconian 'School of the Ages'. Meanwhile, an axiological conflict that had claimed many victims was being reduced to intellectual bickering. What played out, particularly across European screens, was a scholarly drama in which the 'villains' were inevitably academics from the Global South, ethnic and other minorities, postcolonial cultures, and multiple, hybrid identities. The Yale professor branded them the 'School of Resentment'. The little old world of literary criticism had never felt so small, or so old.

Let us narrow the focus a bit, to get an idea of the Italian scene in those closing years of the twentieth century. In Italy, two leading figures, both

2 Francesco Orlando, *L'altro che è in noi. Arte e nazionalità* (Turin: Bollati Boringhieri, 1996).

professors of literary theory, were presenting the results of their extraordinary intellectual undertakings. These were, in fact, theoretical works of international range and significance: Mario Lavagetto's *La cicatrice di Montaigne* ('The Scar of Montaigne') and Francesco Orlando's *Obsolete Objects in the Literary Imagination* – the latter built around a central thesis that could, at first glance, appear almost as a *petitio principii*. A few years earlier, two other elegant, dense studies had also stood out: Giancarlo Mazzacurati's *Pirandello nel romanzo europeo* (Pirandello in the European Novel) and Carlo Ossola's *Figurato e rimosso* (The Figurative and the Repressed). Both had rejected narrow particularism, drawing from the rich Italian tradition they were deeply rooted in – a paradoxical source of curiosity and freedom for their authors.

Meanwhile, on the other side, in the *soi-disant* comparative camp, Piero Boitani's eulogy to 'impure theory' in the well-received *The Shadow of Ulysses* and Remo Ceserani's pre-emptive retreat from abstract models in *Treni di carta* (*Paper Trains*) could be seen as symptoms of a certain unease, a reflection of that difficult search for a halfway house between objects and ideas which Jean Starobinski had already pointed to back in the 1960s.

It was an enigmatic season: a great intellectual fervour, an unprecedented plurality of methods, but also the feeling (or perhaps the obsession) that something had been lost. Some even spoke of a crisis: diagnosed early on by Cesare Segre in *Notizie dalla crisi* (News from the Crisis) and later confirmed by Mario Lavagetto in *Eutanasia della critica* (The Euthanasia of Criticism). As for the discipline at the centre of it all, no one really understood what a comparatist was, or what they were actually supposed to do. Claudio Guillén's now famous *Entre lo uno y lo diverso* (*The Challenge of Comparative Literature* [1985]), translated into Italian in 1992, offered some tentative definitions laced with witty barbs: the comparatist is someone who gets in the way, someone who knows a bit of everything, someone who's just plain impertinent. It is no surprise, then, that this body of knowledge was met with condescension in university faculties, where strong methodological identities and territorial affiliations were being reaffirmed and channelled into large-scale projects: monumental editions, comprehensive reference works, or materials designed for teaching. In the meantime, the literary canon was reasserting itself with vigour, and the long shadow of the author once again loomed over literary studies. Few had the appetite to talk about genre, let alone to think about form. With the fervour of structuralism spent, and the euphoria over interdisciplinary 'theodicies' having fizzled out, the field was reorientating itself. To speak plainly: it was a return to order.

Thus, when *Opere mondo* (*Modern Epic*) came out in 1994, it seemed to some like a disconcerting object, despite not representing that much of a break from Moretti's previous work. A book seemingly devoid of scientific criteria, historical linearity or systematic organisation ('nothing is as rare as a plan', Moretti would later write, quoting Napoleon).[3] A book that was supposed to be something else, namely an essay on modernism. A book whose opening poses a candid, almost self-evident question ('Take *Faust*, what is it?') that arises more from the realm of *doxa* than from that of *episteme*. A book that not only brings together works distant in time and space, but also seeks principles of classification. A book that often glosses over secondary literature, but at the same time invokes to support its theses the conceptual elaborations of Freud, Darwin, Koselleck, and many others who did not think about literature – or at least, not professionally. Furthermore, it is a lopsided, synecdochic book that examines two hundred years through as many monumental and incommensurable case studies; it traverses a masterpiece like *Das Rheingold* and a crucial technique like stream of consciousness; it concludes with a brilliant epilogue on a recent classic of world literature. It is a book, finally, that grows out of flashes of insight, intuitions and serendipity; and that, as we will see, views writers as *bricoleurs*, but at the same time performs a kind of bricolage criticism. So, what kind of book is this?

2. 'The sky will not satisfy your hunger for words'

At the centre of the dust jacket of *Opere mondo* is a collage by Jiří Kolář, *The Sky Will Not Satisfy Your Hunger for Words*. In the foreground, the face of Ingres's *Mademoiselle Caroline Rivière* is crossed by a translucent

3 Franco Moretti, 'Literature, Measured', *Pamphlet 12* (2016) of the Stanford Literary Lab, p. 4 – at litlab.stanford.edu.

band, possibly plastic, fastened with a clip; behind her, the sky is visible, but it too sinks into a sea of printed words (apparently taken from an essay on Gertrude Stein) that the artist has first shredded and then mixed; beneath that typographic chaos, finally, there flows another sea: a map showing a stretch of the Norwegian coast, with its characteristic sequence of fjords. The image is an intelligent choice, symbolising the 'games of truth' that play out across different planes of representation: from the expressive-mimetic level of the portrait to the cartographic-conventional one of the map, all the way to the most prominent and expansive one: that of language – the 'words' that might perhaps satisfy the woman's 'hunger'. In her gaze, art critics have often discerned a sensual desire, not negated but rather intensified by the purity of her flesh; the reader of *Opere mondo* will instead perceive a nostalgia for a lost, harmonious origin – and the painful awareness of being suspended between that fullness and a modernity shaped by self-consciousness, loss of aura and the endless deferral of meaning.

The postmodern semiotic storm unleashed by Kolář reveals the fundamental terms of the complex interplay that Moretti stages in his essay, a threefold encounter between literature, history and geography. The central argumentative thrust – explicitly indebted to Ernst Bloch's concept of the 'contemporaneity of the non-contemporaneous' – proposes that the oxymoronic phrase 'modern epic' becomes intelligible once one understands that geography can function as a metaphor for history, and history for geography.

The secularised epic draws sustenance from a spatial dimension that enfolds all epochs and locales, supplanting the ancient drive towards the construction of a national identity with a broader aspiration (as exemplified in *Faust*); in other words, it derives its energy from a temporal dimension that catalyses and condenses an entire life, or indeed the life of the world itself (with *Ulysses* standing as its paradigmatic text). In this way, the singular voice of a subject – even the most fragile and elusive, such as Leopold Bloom or Mademoiselle Rivière – might paradoxically achieve a polyphonic, and irreparably fractured, form of totality: this, precisely, is the modern epic.

It is no accident that the title of the English translation of *Opere mondo*, published in 1996 by Verso, is simply *Modern Epic*. The *opere* ('works') disappear and the *mondo* ('world') too seems to fade – although it re-emerges in the new subtitle, *The World System from Goethe to García Márquez*, which, by openly acknowledging the influence of the economic historian Immanuel Wallerstein, replaces the more austere *Saggio sulla forma epica dal 'Faust' a 'Cent'anni di solitudine'* (*Essay on the Epic Form from 'Faust' to 'One Hundred Years of Solitude'*) and the tagline on the back cover, *La genealogia e destino dell'epica moderna* ('The genealogy and destiny of the modern epic'). Regardless of whether these adjustments were the author's own refinements or merely publishing strategies, they are revealing.

Perhaps Moretti had gradually become convinced that the wager was paying off – that a loose and approximate genealogy could indeed give rise to a reliable genology, and that his 'world works' were not merely a categorical abstraction (a 'nebula', to borrow an image later dear to the proponents of the New Italian Epic), but rather an ontologically grounded class: a transversal genre, or *metagenre*. We should not overlook the predicate in the original subtitle: 'epic form', not 'epic mode' (as we are more inclined to say today, following Northrop Frye).[4] In literature, while epic often manifests as a mode, it can also exist as a form: the two perspectives neither exclude nor invalidate one another, but refer instead to different orders and aspects of the same theoretical problem. A work can have elements, functions and features proper to epic – but it may also *be* an epic in its own right, even unintentionally. And it is precisely this second possibility that most fascinates Moretti.

How could this somewhat old-fashioned passion for morphology be communicated – and perhaps even made contagious? Moretti made the choice, all the bolder in a book so radically formalist, not to remain confined to the realm of pure form, but rather to open his inquiry to other domains of knowledge. From this perspective, the method deployed in *Modern Epic* may even appear heretical: a glance at the thick undergrowth of notes makes it clear that among the thinkers discussed and engaged with we find Hegel, but also Nietzsche; Bakhtin, but also

---

4 [Translator's note: 'New Italian Epic': a term coined by Wu Ming in 2008. See Maurizio Vito, 'A Narrative Discourse of the Twenty-First Century: The New Italian Epic', *Italianist* 30: 3 (2010), pp. 395–412.]

Blanchot; Marx, but also Schmitt; Lukács, but also Spitzer; Curtius, but also Barthes. And the list could go on, though such an exercise would quickly become tedious.

Yet within this phantasmagoria of authors and concepts, one cognitive paradigm stands out with particular clarity: the evolutionary model, which acts as the true *relais* of this phase of Moretti's intellectual history – for it not only motivates and sustains his critical reasoning, but, as we shall see, even illuminates its very mode of operation.

We must return to 1987, the year when Moretti took part in the Convergence in Crisis conference organised by Fredric Jameson at Duke University. On that occasion, he put the Darwinian model to the test of literary history (the paper would later be published, prominently, as a coda to the second edition of *Signs Taken for Wonders*). The contribution not only enjoys one of the rare and carefully rationed self-citations in *Modern Epic*, but also constitutes a strategic point in its introduction. More discreet, though no less incisive, is the reflection that Moretti develops from the specific idea of a scientist who would come to play a key role in his theoretical vision: Stephen Jay Gould. As often happened in the essays of those years, this reflection is tucked away in a footnote, which is worth reproducing in full:

> Polemic against anyone who extols the 'perfection' of natural evolution is one of the arguments dearest to Stephen Jay Gould, who has counterposed the 'Panda principle' of the inevitable imperfection of every product of evolution: '[Perfection] is a lousy argument for evolution, for it mimics the postulated action of an omnipotent creator. Odd arrangements and funny solutions are the proof of evolution – paths that a sensible God would never tread, but that a natural process, constrained by history, follows perforce.' . . . As for literary criticism, it is divided equitably between creationist faith (the text is a complete and perfect world, and the author is the watchmaker who foresees everything) and deconstructionist gnosis (at the slightest contradiction, the text collapses into total chaos). Once again, Russian formalism – and especially Shklovsky – had sketched the solution: to accept the 'imperfect bond' between the various parts of the text as an absolutely normal fact, to be neither hidden nor exaggerated. Identical to the stance of Erwin

> Panofsky, who presents the evolution of artistic technique as a very concrete process of cut and thrust: made up of chance opportunities and 'perplexities', structural problems and 'acrobatic solutions' – or even ones that are 'courageous, though not quite honest'. I take these expressions from *Perspective as Symbolic Form* . . . and, especially, *Gothic Architecture and Scholasticism* . . . with its marvellous discussion of the 'problem of the rose window in the West facade' and the difficulties this created for French Gothic.[5]

These lines allow us to see how Moretti positioned himself within the debate on method; but they also reveal something more general about his characteristic style and what we might call his mode of thought. The former speaks for itself: clear, idiosyncratic, uncompromising – yet never cold; on the contrary, it operates on a temperature scale that tends towards higher values, and which in the final sentence rises higher still (how much enchantment there is in the use of the adjective 'marvellous' to describe an essay by Panofsky!). Above all, however, this style serves a free-thinking mind, which in the cited example moves nimbly from biology to hermeneutics, and from hermeneutics to iconology.

Now, by 1994 it had already become common knowledge – even within the compulsory education system – that fields of knowledge were no longer isolated silos; but the transdisciplinary dialogue at work in *Modern Epic* is not simply a discussion of isolated themes or aspects, but rather a much deeper exchange between entire paradigms. Evolutionism – the true theoretical motor behind a history of forms made up of false starts, lost paths, impossible attempts, bricolage – offered Moretti a golden opportunity to achieve a meaningful degree of abstraction, not through the algebras devised by structuralism, nor through philosophies of art, but rather through a cognitive model that was both scientific and historical – where the latter adjective points to a very long duration, to a deep history. Moreover, this model was not imposed from above or applied mechanically; rather, it served as an initial hypothesis, the epistemological basis for a critical reasoning that was itself built, in turn,

5 Franco Moretti, *Modern Epic: The World System from Goethe to García Márquez* (London: Verso, 1996), p. 22.

through a process akin to bricolage: a patient labour of approximations, attempts, hesitations, bifurcations, conjectures.

Conjectures: consider, for example, the 'twisted motion' described in the opening of the second chapter. After a quotation from Goethe, Moretti invokes a passage from Hans Blumenberg's *The Legitimacy of the Modern Age* (1966), on the gravitational pull that the past exerts over the present, imposing 'inherited problematics' upon it. He then asks: 'Was there really any *need* for this symbolic form, between the eighteenth and nineteenth centuries?'[6] He responds, via Blumenberg, that it was simply 'an inherited form'. Then he breaks off, leaves a blank line, and starts again: if that thesis is valid, 'then the question that I have just formulated . . . must be changed completely. Because of pressure from the past, a modern epic could not help but emerge; the proper question is *whether it could ever succeed*.' One notes here a kind of mimetic effect, not so much of spoken language as of thought itself: as if the flow, the very evolution of the reasoning were being captured in its unfolding; and even – through typographical devices, punctuation, the decelerating effect of italics, the inferential leaps of reasoning – the suprasegmental traits of an inner voice. Thus, a virtuous circle is created, along with a double empathy: between literature and the critic, and between the critic and the reader.

3. 1999: World Literature

Conjectures: of course. 'Conjectures on World Literature' (2000) is the title of the essay marking Moretti's second major turn, which took place at the end of that decade and was once again tied to a conference occasion. In this case (as explained in one of the valuable introductory notes in *Distant Reading*), what was at stake was the reorganisation – or perhaps the splitting up – of the Department of English and Comparative Literature at Columbia University.[7] During a symposium at Columbia's Italian Academy, Moretti raised the stakes, inviting participants to look

6 Ibid., p. 36.

7 Franco Moretti, *Distant Reading* (London: Verso, 2013), p. 43.

beyond the skirmishes between defenders of the Western canon and culturalists mentioned at the outset, and to consider *Weltliteratur.* The paper was published in *New Left Review* at a moment that could hardly have been more epochal: January 2000. This also means that 'Conjectures' was conceived, delivered and published in a nation which, as Moretti would later write in an epilegomenon, had been experiencing 'an unprecedented symbolic hegemony', as well as a political one, for two decades – a hegemony that would soon begin to falter after the attack on the United States on 11 September 2001.[8] When the essay appeared, the feared heavenly apocalypse had not occurred, but an earthly apocalypse was just around the corner.

Despite the modesty of the title, 'Conjectures' was a true manifesto-essay. Its style was even more crystalline than Moretti's usual register, and its propositions were anything but casual. First of all, the 'theological' practice of close reading was now to be replaced by its opposite, provocatively named 'distant reading' (replacing the milder 'serial reading' initially selected). This was followed by an apologia for the division of intellectual labour; a call for the return of sociology and politics to literary studies; a preference for experimental procedures as a pathway to greater abstraction; the rejection of canons and the simultaneous expansion of the field of research, from the Western core to the entire globe; and, finally, a productive use of cognitive models developed by history and the 'hard sciences'. The cornerstone of Moretti's argument was Max Weber's idea that 'It is not the "actual" interconnection of "things", but the *conceptual* interconnection of *problems* which define [*sic*] the scope of the various sciences', because 'A new "science" emerges where a new problem is pursued by a new method.'[9] From this, it followed that world literature does not simply constitute the same object on a larger scale, but rather a new order of problems – an original 'chain' of epistemic inquiry. The global literary-historical system to be pursued would, like Wallerstein's

8 Franco Moretti, 'Conjectures on World Literature', *New Left Review* II/1 (January–February 2000), p. 119.

9 Max Weber, 'Objectivity in Social Sciences and Social Policy', in *The Methodology of the Social Sciences* (Glencoe, Ill.: The Free Press, 1949 [1904]), p. 68 – cited in Moretti, *Distant Reading*, p. 46.

'world-economy', have a centre, periphery and semi-periphery; and the influences operating within it would be neither symmetrical nor bidirectional, given that central codifications often ignore those on the peripheries, over which they exercise influence while themselves remaining immune. Finally, to observe such relations, a synoptic perspective would be necessary – one capable of dialectically combining the heterogeneous findings of specialists into a broader synthesis.

The essay declared a 'formalism without close reading' in which details are not erased but illuminated by schemas and patterns; where the criteria for comparison become more rational; where the value of the artwork can be measured and thus removed from the arbitrariness of aesthetic judgement and taste; where literary relations are read as 'power relations'; and where a political, even militant, impulse re-emerges – however restrained: 'the way we imagine comparative literature is a mirror of how we see the world'.[10] It is easy to see how, within such a framework, the mandate of the literary historian and critic, especially that of the comparatist, would also be transformed: no longer – or no longer merely – someone who, from within their own national tradition, gazes outward at the Other and reflects on what their culture has ultimately absorbed, but rather a stateless collector (or, borrowing a metaphor from thermodynamics, a convector) tasked with revealing, even when working 'second-hand', the irreducible constants, general logics and underlying structures that govern a kind of universal economy of forms.

What appeared most difficult to accept at that time – when methodological debate was increasingly threatened by academic fashions – was the conviction that 'world literature' could be understood only by adopting a perspective located elsewhere, on the 'second moon' of theory: distance, Moretti insisted, was indispensable:

> *A condition of knowledge*: it allows you to focus on units that are much smaller or much larger than the text: devices, themes, tropes – or genres

---

10 Moretti, *Distant Reading*, p. 65. He added: '"Conjectures" tried to do so against the background of the unprecedented possibility that the entire world may be subject to a single centre of power – and a centre which has long exerted an equally unprecedented symbolic hegemony'. Moretti, *Distant Reading*, p. 119.

> and systems. And if, between the very small and the very large, the text itself disappears, well, it is one of those cases when one can justifiably say, Less is more. If we want to understand the system in its entirety, we must accept losing something.[11]

Here, Moretti's prose became more militant than ever, even bordering on the apodictic (and the sloganistic). In the closing passage, after presenting a vision of comparative literatures as permanently antagonistic, the author borrows a wonderful line from *The Red and the Black*: '"Don't delude yourself", writes Stendhal of his favourite character: "for you, there is no middle road." The same is true for us.'[12] On the battlefield of *Weltliteratur*, one had either to advance together or abandon the cause completely.

No one could have considered Moretti's path in those years as middle-of-the-road or conciliatory. The vast project on the novel, published by Einaudi, which he conceived and directed, was a site of intense activity.[13] From the release of the first volume in 2001, it became immediately clear to everyone that a substantial shift had occurred – not only in the scope of the work, but also in the very protocols of comparative literature. I attempted to illustrate the novelty of the project in a lengthy review published a few months after the fifth volume appeared.[14] Here, I will simply reiterate that *The Novel* was, in a way, an *impure* product of comparative literature: a comparatism understood as collective labour, built upon a foundation that was at once shared, deliberately constructed, and subject to negotiation. Whether one agrees with the results or not, it is impossible not to acknowledge the titanic effort of imagination and coordination that its editor undertook – during tumultuous years – without holding back or succumbing to the routines of academic compilation; the responsibility he assumed for identifying the cognitive foundations of the project, even seeking them in fields whose terminologies were already

11 Ibid., pp. 48–9.

12 Ibid., pp. 62.

13 Franco Moretti, ed., *Il romanzo*, 5 vols (Turin: Einaudi, 2001–2003).

14 Francesco de Cristofaro, 'Mondo, storia, vita: Considerazioni in margine a *Il romanzo* (con alcune considerazioni sulla letteratura comparata)', *Intersezioni* 24: 3 (2004), pp. 359–80.

firmly established; the way he designed the work as an assault on the material from multiple positions (five fields for the five volumes: cultural-anthropological, morphological, historical-geographical, thematic, and finally hermeneutic); and, most importantly, how he dismantled, particularly in his own contribution, the centrality of the realist model and the idea that its success was due to any intrinsic structural virtues. He also rejected the canonising and typological method that tends to select only the peaks of the genre, while neglecting the vast expanse of 'normal literature' (as he had already called it, following Roland Barthes, in a seminal essay published in 1982).[15]

After all, the tree of stories has infinite branches, and *The Novel* bears the marks of this theoretical approach on every page. I will cite just one example. In a contribution on Japanese fiction, Jonathan Zwicker stressed how the vocabulary and conceptual framework of the natural sciences prove productive at the level of knowledge, insofar as they transcend a purely historical logic:

> the sciences focus on the structural potential of concepts while virtually ignoring the moments of their illocution. By taking a step outside of history and looking for purely formal patterns where traditional history has seen only discontinuity and division we can begin to conceive of a different type of history that is historical in its own right but belongs to a different register than the history of texts and events. This is what Koselleck means when he writes that *formal categories are the conditions of possible histories*, that is, conditions for histories that do not yet exist but remain to be written.[16]

We are dealing here with an exemplary procedure, one worth retracing in order to grasp the method by which the Einaudi volumes were conceived. Confronted with the nebulousness and even terminological

15 Franco Moretti, *Signs Taken for Wonders: Essays in the Sociology of Literary Forms*, transl. Susan Fisher, David Forgacs and David Miller (London: Verso, 1997 [1983], 2nd edn 1988), p. 15.

16 Jonathan E. Zwicker, 'The Long Nineteenth Century of the Japanese Novel', in Franco Moretti, ed., *The Novel*, vol. 1 (Princeton, NJ: Princeton University Press, 2006), p. 578.

instability of his topic, Zwicker chose to draw upon the resources of 'historical semantology' and to embrace the 'notion of structure', adopting a macro-categorical 'machine' that allowed him to group texts into a 'class.' This kind of 'compositional rule' appears to have guided the design of the entire project: only by heuristically fixing 'the novel' as a gnosiological hypostasis could one begin to discern the outline of a shape: an entity that, although multiple and complex ('a great thicket of related forms'), could then be analysed for its constants and variations. In other words, the task was to write a 'possible history' – which is ultimately nothing other than a 'falsifiable criticism' translated from the level of the individual element to that of the system.[17] It is striking to realise that both *Modern Epic* and *The Novel* – despite all their obvious differences (beginning with the distinction between a single-authored monograph and a collective work) – do not concentrate on something already given, but rather construct a new problem, progressively defining its field. There is, in the methodology Moretti developed over this decade, a restlessness that does not mar criticism but instead constitutes its foundation – its very precondition. Today, bureaucrats of academic evaluation would call this 'originality' or, worse still, 'innovation'. Perhaps the right word is 'courage'.

4. Angelus Novus

'General, you make use of maps during a campaign, I believe. But why should you do so, when the country they represent is right there?'[18] Moretti includes this strange quotation, taken from a story recounted in Charles Sanders Pierce's 'Prolegomena to an Apology for Pragmaticism' (1906), in the opening pages of *Atlas of the European Novel*. The remark seems like an objection, but it is actually a counter-objection, formulated in hindsight – like a classic *esprit de l'escalier* – by the great American semiotician and founder of pragmatism. Moretti employs it in a passage

17 Franco Moretti, 'Mille domande intorno a un romanzo', *La Repubblica*, 19 January 2002, p. 42.

18 Franco Moretti, *Atlas of the European Novel* (London: Verso, 1998), p. 4.

that, in retrospect, reads as a kind of initiation ritual into the methodological approach – built upon abstraction, quantification, and the interpretation of patterns – that he would later define as 'distant reading'. From this moment on, alongside his ongoing effort to redefine the vast morphological plain stretching between epic and novel, another theoretical demon begins to take hold of him.

The dialogue between *Atlas of the European Novel* and *Distant Reading*, whose chapters first appeared in English in the *New Left Review*, resembles something like a game of dominoes: if the final pages of *Modern Epic* had opened the way for *Letteratura europea*, and the latter for *The Novel*, now the epilogue of the *Atlas* – while also pointing ahead to the broader design of *The Novel* – revisits and refines two of the 'Abstract Models for a Literary History' (the English subtitle of the 2005 triptych) – namely, maps and graphs. Surveying Moretti's work across the turn of century, one might say that the admired cognitive paradigm of 'punctuated equilibria' operates beneath the surface of his thinking as well; nor could one fail to notice that the critical turning points tend to occur in the conclusions, as if there a stronger surge of conceptual energy were released, capable even of projecting a bridge towards the next book to come.[19]

The 'geographical campaign' had already begun in 1991, spurred by a passage from one of the masterpieces of the *Annales* school's 'historiographical revolution', Fernand Braudel's *The Mediterranean*, which lamented the absence of 'artistic atlases'.[20] The utopia – which would remain such – of an 'historical atlas of literature' was at the centre of Moretti's thoughts over those years. In 1992, he launched a seminar series at Columbia, together with a handful of doctoral students; and in 1993, during the first of the *Colloqui malatestiani* dedicated to spatial configurations in novels, he set off along a path distinct from those taken by the other speakers (beginning with Orlando, who, in his recently published *Obsolete Objects*, had argued for particular attention to space rather than time). Moretti, by contrast, chose not to focus on the

19 The reference is to Stephen Jay Gould, *Punctuated Equilibrium* (Cambridge, MA: Belknap, 2007).

20 Moretti, *Atlas of the European Novel*, p. 6.

description of landscapes and settings within novels, but on the intuition of a space that does not merely host literary history but *shapes* it; a geography understood as an actor rather than as mere background.[21]

The *Atlas* is perhaps Moretti's most elegantly written work, but it is also the least fruitful – like a startup that fails to yield the expected results. It really consists of two books: an amphibious essay, divided – almost like *Angelus Novus* – between the critic's past and future. The first two chapters look back to his work of the 1980s, to the plots of Balzac and Dickens, to figures that had already appeared in *The Way of the World*. In contrast, the third chapter seems to anticipate the quantitative, computational turn of the 2000s, with its *histoire modèle* shaped by novel cognitive categories – divergent traits, morphospaces, niches, latencies, ramifications, divergences and cultural anastomoses, formal catastrophes, allopatric speciations . . . Thus, when the reader, already two-thirds of the way through the book, turns the page and realises that the geography *in* literature investigated up to that point has abruptly transformed into a geography *of* literature, in the form of a bibliographic inquiry, they may well be left somewhat disorientated.

There is nothing truly organic or seamless in the transition from the seductive topographical maps of the Latin Quarter – interpreted as a magnetic field in which the characters' desires shape the narrative trajectories – to the cold diagrams derived from the catalogues of nineteenth-century English circulating libraries. And yet, this ends up being a hidden strength of the book: through that very conspicuous 'structural imperfection', the *Atlas* reveals its own nature as a work-in-progress, a collective and evolving experiment – without doubt the most significant contribution of this period in Moretti's work.

As for the second aspect of the volume, the lesson of the *Annales* school once again proved decisive. Moretti had grasped how the vertiginous 'quantitative challenge' posed by the French historians offered an excellent opportunity for literary studies – partly because it helped overcome the thorny impasse between *intentio operis* and *intentio*

---

21 Franco Moretti, 'Verso un atlante storico della letteratura', in Loretta Innocenti, ed., *Scene, itinerari, dimore. Lo spazio nella narrativa del '700* (Rome: Bulzoni, 1995), p. 185.

lectoris, finally bringing together comparative literature, the history of the book, and reception studies. Only a few years later, a critic beyond suspicion of sociologism would observe that, in order to conceive of a literary history capable of integrating both materialistic and formalistic dimensions, it is not enough merely to postulate a 'horizon of expectation' or a 'repertoire' to be transgressed, text by text, by individual works.[22] This 'cadastral' territory must be known in a concrete – and, why not, statistical – way. We must know what readers actually consumed, how they consumed it, and how much: not only the educated readers who left behind written records (the ones primarily employed by reception aesthetics, thus perpetuating the same old hermeneutic routine contemplating 'great writers'), but the ordinary readers as well. Compagnon's vision was strikingly close to the one Moretti – at the same historical juncture, though on the other side of the world – was already putting into practice.

5. 2005: Abstract Models

This, it seems to me, was in fact the principal challenge of *Graphs, Maps, Trees*, especially in the chapters on 'Graphs' and 'Trees'. A challenge whose origins lay much farther back – namely, in the already mentioned foundational essay of 1982, where Moretti had judged it urgent to graft historiography onto rhetoric, arguing that the Lukácsian dichotomy 'between the warmth of life and the purity of form' was mistaken, and had called for a literary history that would be 'slower' and 'more discontinuous', not consecrated solely by those few works saved for the canon.[23] It is surely no accident that 'The Soul and the Harpy' opens – under the splendid Hobbesian epigraph 'Form is power' – both the Italian and the English editions of his essays from the 1980s. Nor is it by chance, perhaps, that the Italian edition of *Signs Taken for Wonders* omitted an even earlier essay, 'Clues', which had originally served as an introduction to an

22 See Antoine Compagnon, *Le Démon de la theorié* (Paris: Seuil, 1998).
23 Moretti, *Signs Taken for Wonders*, p. 12.

anthology of detective stories.[24] 'Clues' analysed the genre according to interpretative protocols (and fetishes) diametrically opposed to those Moretti would later employ in 'The Slaughterhouse of Literature', the pilot study on which 'Trees' was based. It may be useful to take a retrospective and comparative look at this shift, in dialogue with the contribution by Stefano Ercolino that opens the present volume.

We do not know – nor, perhaps, does it matter – whether Moretti truly renounced 'Clues'. In any case, it is never mentioned in his later works, by now entirely liberated from the spectre of Marx. What is certain is that this introduction, written by a young researcher still in his twenties, and published by a countercultural publishing house in Rome (Savelli, which also published the journal *calibano*), in a series significantly titled 'Political Culture', began from a methodological premise imbued with the atmosphere and theoretical jargon of its time: the dilemma between syntagm and paradigm paved the way for an adventurous and stylistically severe argument aimed at demonstrating nothing less than that 'the detective story dispels from the consciousness of the masses the individualistic ethic of "classic" bourgeois culture', giving rise to 'an aesthetic model that implies the *impossibility of verifying* cultural forms, and thus overturns the experimental assumption that shaped early bourgeois "public opinion".' And furthermore: 'the victim has *asked for it*', in part because he is 'still attached to his small capital'; 'money is always the motive of crime in detective fiction, yet the genre is wholly silent about *production*'; 'detective fiction is a hymn to culture's coercive abilities'; and so on.[25] These fragments, extrapolated and torn out of context in a way that does not do justice to the complexity and internal coherence of the argument, are nonetheless sufficient to highlight *ex negativo* the shift initiated by the Moretti of 'Trees', who had shed his ideological arsenal and developed a passion for critical distance. Like a skilled domino player, he returns to the same material but asks new questions of it.

---

24 Franco Moretti, 'Introduzione', in *Polizieschi classici*, ed. Franco Moretti (Rome: Savelli, 1978) – published in English as the chapter 'Clues' in *Signs Taken for Wonders*, pp. 130–56.

25 Moretti, *Signs Taken for Wonders*, pp. 134, 136, 139, 143.

'Clues' takes two leading figures of the detective story, Arthur Conan Doyle and Agatha Christie, and attempts to test on them one of the most famous controversies of the structuralist period: the debate between Propp and Lévi-Strauss concerning the supposed absence of 'the content of tales' from the morphology of narrative.[26] With regard to Poirot's mysteries, Moretti sided with Propp, since he observed an actual predominance of the syntagm ('only the determining function of the formal mechanism of syntax remains'); but when it came to the Sherlock Holmes stories, he saw things differently. Here, the paradigm asserted itself forcefully – a paradigm encompassing science, the individual, and the bourgeoisie. It was, in fact, the real cypher in the construction of the tale. In this case, then, Lévi-Strauss was right.

Twenty years later, with an experimental and ground-breaking theoretical proposal, Moretti finally decides to sketch a diagram of the genre: a historical, not logical, 'tree', unfolding from left to right along an evolutionary timeline. The question he seeks to answer is: How is one of the most significant specimens of 'genre literature', namely detective fiction, constituted, and what selective criterion is first applied by readers and then by literary history? The competition between syntagm and paradigm is reopened: even on Baker Street, the syntax of functions can prevail over the contents of 'structure', but only on the condition that a different kind of paradigm – this time a strictly formal one – is acknowledged. The procedure adopted is now far more systematic.

Preferring the archive over the canon in the selection of the corpus, Moretti discovers that in the very same years when Sherlock Holmes was becoming an emblem of the Victorian era, the darling of an enthusiastic and stratified readership (such that the judgement of value becomes a judgement of surplus value), the works of authors who ignored the artisanal device of the clue – a fundamental element in both the epistemology and the narrative technique of the time – withered away as dead branches, falling from the 'tree' of the genre. Nor are the 'rivals' of Conan Doyle spared when they misuse the device, failing to uphold the tripartite standard (necessity, visibility, decodability) that silently governs its function – or falling into absurd errors, as in *Race with the Sun*, an

26 Ibid., p. 141.

obscure 1897 detective novel, where the character drinks from the very cup of coffee in which he had discovered a sleeping potion. 'This is truly "perplexing & unintelligible"', Moretti wryly comments, 'and the only possible explanation is that these writers realized that clues were popular, and tried to smuggle them into their stories – but hadn't really understood *how* clues worked, and so didn't use them very well.'[27] This is a far cry from the claim that 'detective fiction is a hymn to culture's coercive abilities'. Instead, we are invited to a celebration of intelligence and style (and enjoyment, for both author and reader), framed within that vast, singular discourse on method that Moretti had been writing continuously from 1990 to 2005.

'The method is all', we read in one of the most sincere and candid pages of the *Atlas*: a method that always brings 'a taste for the concrete' to theoretical development, applied as much to things as to the words that designate them.[28] (The exam question, 'Why *a raft* exactly?', cited in homage to his friend Beniamino Placido and included here as an epigraph, would not sound out of place coming from Moretti himself.) Thus, for example, in the test case of the tree of detective stories, the purely stylistic elements – the localised narrative techniques, the skilful delineation of characters and their relationships, the registers and codes employed – in short, all those elements that contribute to the celebrated literary quality of Conan Doyle's novels – are deliberately glazed over, because only the feature deemed crucial from a morphological and historical-cultural point of view needs to be made pertinent. The clue thus becomes the *passepartout* granting access to a class of texts otherwise unknown: something already familiar (and therefore old) is lost, but something new is gained. Distant reading, applied empirically on a large scale, opens up a far more articulated and profound understanding of the literary system. And the more the scholar works on unknown productions – works culled by the slaughterhouse of literature, which is as ruthless as the slaughterhouse of history imagined by Hegel – the more the tree branches out, and the sharper the analysis becomes: 'the more one looked in the archive, in other words, the more complex and

27 Franco Moretti, *Graphs, Maps, Trees* (London: Verso, 2005), p. 72.

28 Moretti, *Atlas of the European Novel*, p. 5.

"Darwinian" became the genre's morpho-space.'[29] Here, finally, lies the secret: theory not only does not die from an excess of books, but in fact grows stronger because of them; for that sea of words may succeed in satisfying us in a way that the sky of ideas never can.

29 Moretti, *Graphs, Maps, Trees*, p. 74.

3

The New Anatomy Table

Giuseppe Episcopo

> *The point isn't the word, but its meaning, and you think of the meaning as a thing of the same kind as the word, though also different from the word. Here the word, there the meaning. The money, and the cow that you can buy with it. (But contrast: money, and its use.)*
>
> Ludwig Wittgenstein, *Philosophical Investigations*

1. Bricolage and Revolution

May 1765, a Saturday afternoon. The technical breakthrough that delivers the decisive push to the Industrial Revolution is conceived during a walk by a mechanical engineer from the University of Glasgow. He had been tasked with repairing one of the models of the Newcomen steam engine and, as he would recall years later: 'It was in the Green of Glasgow. I had gone to take a walk.'[1] Boilers, pistons and cylinders had already existed for over fifty years, but their power was limited by the low efficiency with which steam was used:

> I was thinking upon the engine at the time . . . the idea came into my mind, that as steam was an elastic body it would rush into a vacuum, and as a communication was made between the cylinder and the exhausted vessel, it would rush into it, and might be there condensed

1 Henry Winram Dickinson ed., *James Watt: Craftsman and Engineer* (Cambridge: Cambridge University Press, 1936), p. 36.

> without cooling the cylinder . . . Two ways of doing this occurred to me . . . I had not walked [very far] when the whole thing was arranged in my mind.[2]

The mind in which the idea took shape belonged to James Watt, and the 'whole thing' was the design of the separate condenser – an improvement from which followed a series of modifications so extensive that listing them individually would amount to describing the steam engine in its entirety – which, indeed, would come to bear Watt's name.

There are many ways to invent something, but (turning on its head an expression familiar to Moretti's readers) there are few ways to improve it. Almost all of them involve bricolage. James Watt himself recounted this when he addressed the Glasgow Archaeological Society, recalling the adventurous story that began with the repair of a defective model. Moretti reminds us of it as well, in the notes accompanying *Distant Reading* (2013), where he reflects on the occasions of writing, the process of composing his texts, the questions that gave rise to them, and the reactions his arguments provoked. These ten reflections – written at different intervals after the original articles – lay out the master's tools on the dissection table, among them Ernst Mayr's concept of 'allopatric speciation':

> I took forms as the literary analogues of species, and charted the morphological transformations triggered by European geography: the differentiation of tragedy in the seventeenth century, the novel's take-off in the eighteenth, the centralization and then fragmentation of the literary field in the nineteenth and twentieth. The notion of 'European literature', singular, was replaced by that of an archipelago of distinct yet close national cultures, where styles and stories moved quickly and frequently, undergoing all sorts of metamorphoses. Creativity had found an explanation that made it seem easy, and almost inevitable.[3]

---

2 Ibid.; Robert Hart, 'Reminiscences of James Watt', *Transactions of the Glasgow Archaeological Society* 1 (1868), p. 4.

3 Franco Moretti, *Distant Reading* (London: Verso, 2013), p. 1.

Also among them was Immanuel Wallerstein's conceptual model of the world-system:

> Wallerstein's tripartition of core, periphery, and semi-periphery appeared to me because it explained a number of empirical findings I had slowly gathered in the course of the 1990s: France's continental centrality, so often mentioned in the essay on European literature; the peculiar productivity of the semi-periphery, analyzed in *Modern Epic*; the unevenness of narrative markets of the *Atlas of the European Novel* – all these, and more, strongly corroborated Wallerstein's model.[4]

Now, anyone seeking to outline the seriotemporal structure of evolutionary science and economic development theory within Moretti's critical work must also acknowledge the role they play as a counterbalance – offsetting the double torsion, both necessary and necessitating, that emerges in his turn towards *quantity*. In this section, the relationship to the object of study itself shifts, and the object, like water undergoing a phase transition, expands in volume and alters both its scale and properties.

The use of data and network theory, the methodologies for collecting that data and for visualising networks, and the strategies of interpretation – anyone seeking to sketch a profile of these must keep in mind that they are not disconnected from narrative practices. Indeed, all these elements allow Moretti, on the one hand, to put into practice the falsifiable criticism whose outlines he had already traced in 1983 in 'The Soul and the Harpy', and, on the other, to renew – in a new territory – Roman Jakobson's famous challenge to literary criticism as mere *causerie*, and to its language, which follows all the rules of informal conversation, beginning with the imprecise, generalised and indefinite use of expressions (that is, essentially lamenting, according to a well-established position of Russian formalism, the absence of a truly scientific terminology).[5] Whichever way you approach them, at the heart of these debates we

---

4 Ibid., pp. 43–4.

5 Roman Jakobson, 'On Realism in Art', in Krystyna Pomorska and Stephen Rudy, eds, *Language in Literature* (London/Cambridge, MA: Belknap, 1987 [1921]), pp. 19–27.

constantly find 'realism': for Jakobson the most unfortunate term of all, because the uncritical use to which it has been subjected has led to 'fatal consequences'; for Moretti, at the close of his *Novel* project, realism is the bottleneck through which theories and the history of the novel have been funnelled, thereby narrowing the range of possible approaches to a narrative prose tradition that is millennia old, global in scope, and protean in its morphology.[6] 'There are many ways of talking about the theory of the novel, and mine will consist in posing three questions: Why are novels in prose? Why are they so often adventure stories? And, why was there a European, but not a Chinese rise of the novel over the course of the eighteenth century?'[7]

The opportunity to voice these questions aloud was an excellent one: the conference on contemporary theories of prose, held in February 2007 at Brown University to mark the anniversary of the journal *Novel: A Forum on Fiction*. In the first of the three volumes collecting the proceedings of the conference, Nancy Armstrong – who acknowledges the broad consensus among scholars regarding Moretti's 'social-historical assumption', according to which the novel spreads into new niches by following the paths of capitalism and print culture, incorporating local material along the way – introduces, in her opening editorial, the authors of the two plenary addresses:

> Along with a good two-thirds of the original conference papers, these issues include the texts of plenary talks by Franco Moretti and Roberto Schwarz – two very different but equally controversial demonstrations of how to read novels for the secret of their global reach and the transformations enabling their persistence through time and across cultural boundaries. The author of several highly influential studies of the novel that have moved steadily away from the canon as their primary object of knowledge, Moretti here makes the startling claim that we should take 'the style of the dime novels as the basic object of study and [explain] James's [*Ambassadors*] as an unlikely by-product' – because, as he puts

6 Franco Moretti, ed., *Il romanzo*, 5 vols (Turin: Einaudi, 2001–3), pp. vii–xvii.

7 Moretti, *Distant Reading*, pp. 160–1.

> it, 'that's how history has proceeded.' To follow this injunction, one has to overturn the traditional priority of 'the formal' over 'the quantitative' counter not only to reader practices (to read James we will have already read any number of dime novels like *Dashing Diamond Dick*) but also to the operations of the book market. The novel goes where the book market takes it, and the demands of the market consequently reshape the novel (witness the triple-decker). Unless I'm terribly mistaken in my reading of Moretti's full-tilt-forward, headier-than-usual argument, novels not only follow the book market, they also make sense of the willy-nilly growth of the market itself. The novel holds onto the adventure story, Moretti suggests, because this premodern chronotope provides a model as well as the motor for the opportunistic expansion of capitalism.[8]

This paragraph shows how, in one way or another, and in one context or another, it is most often the question of genre that gains the most attention and captures the headlines. At the same time, however, Armstrong's argument proves to be a suitable place to bring into view precisely what might seem to lie outside its frame: namely, morphology – the 'tool' with which Moretti addresses one of the most complex problems of literature, that of 'influence'.[9] 'Influence' is a more neutral term than others – such as impact, tradition, canon, each of which carries a heavier theoretical legacy inherited from specific critical contexts. Here instead we mean the influence of a technique within a genre, or of a genre over a cultural system; the way in which a given technique or a genre comes to prevail over others, determining both its own destiny and that of others. Far from representing an extramural incursion, reference to the problem of influence by means of the formula coined by Jonathan Arac – 'formalism without close reading' – makes it possible to place another element on the anatomist's table, one that – whether intentionally or not in Arac's expression – bends the inquiry towards the 'Serapion Brothers': that

8 Nancy Armstrong, 'Editor's Introduction: The Way We Read Now', in *Novel: A Forum on Fiction* 42: 2 (2009), p. 168.

9 [Translator's note: Episcopo uses the term *influsso* ('influence'), distinguishing it from *influenza* ('impact') in the following phrase.]

critical school which, with Jurij Tynjanov in 1927, closely linked formal problems of the artistic process with the study of literary evolution. It is important here to recall at least the outlines of Tynjanov's work, since his primary objective was, significantly, to transform (as Chomsky would later say in relation to language) mysteries into problems:

> The relationship between form and function is not accidental. The comparable combination of a particular lexicon with particular meter . . . is not accidental. The variability of the functions of a given formal element, the rise of some function of a formal element, and the attaching of a formal element to a function are all important problems of literary evolution . . . I would like to say only that the whole problem of literature as a system depends on further investigation of this argument.[10]

In the illuminating pages preceding my own, Stefano Ercolino asks:

> Retrospectively speaking, one could say that the caesura of 1976–77 in Moretti's work was a perhaps unwitting way of *smuggling in and allowing to survive*, under a seductive vestige of idiosyncratic individualism, an antagonistic critical discourse in a world that, if it was not already hostile towards it, would soon become so.[11]

Might we see, in later years, a similar break? Could we say that the period from 2005 to the first productions of the Stanford Literary Lab was an incubation phase, one that served to 'smuggle in and allow to survive' – how best to put it here – Leon Trotsky and a science-oriented methodology in a world that was beginning to observe the digital humanities with interest, but where that interest had not yet fully taken off?

---

10 Jurij Tynjanov, 'On Literary Evolution', in Ladislav Matejka and Krystyna Pomorska, eds, *Readings in Russian Poetics: Formalist and Structuralist Views* (London/Cambridge, MA: MIT, 1971), pp. 66–78, translation modified.

11 See Chapter 1, above.

2. Celibate Machines

> The first graduate seminar that Matthew Jockers and I offered in 2004, called 'Electronic Data and Literary Theory', had one student. But we insisted and insisted and insisted. And then one day in 2010 I told Matt, 'Look, let's take a piece of paper, write "Stanford Literary Lab" on it, put it on a door and let's see if this changes things.' I went to the Chair of the English department and said, 'can we have the room that's always empty?' We were given the room, I printed out the paper and we put it up there with Scotch tape. One thing that happened was that we found a way for graduate students to count their work at the Lab for some credits. Then the Lab received some money from the university for its first two years. It was exactly 20,000 dollars for two years. Since we had to buy computers, screens and everything, it was nothing really. But beside that we didn't need a lot of money. What we needed, and this is something we got, was some free time. That's something we need much more than money. Some free time to think, to read, to study, to talk.[12]

These words are from an interview Moretti gave in Prague to František A. Podhajský in February 2020, as a guest of the Academy for Fine Arts and the Czech Academy of Sciences. Strange as it may seem, this is one of those rare cases where the pioneering beginnings appear almost less compelling than the adventurous trajectory that unfolded after the conclusion of Moretti's years as director of the Stanford Literary Lab. It is from that moment that the Lab's international life begins, outside the walls of Stanford, with the collection and translation of its pamphlets.

Let us be clear: all the original articles produced by the Literary Lab are free and available in English; they can be read, downloaded and printed without any restrictions – i.e. as many times as one wishes – and without any geographical limitations – i.e. anywhere in the world. But is this alone enough to ensure the circulation of ideas? The editorial

---

12 František A. Podhajský, 'Free Time is What Scientists Need More than Money, Says Stanford Professor Emeritus', in *Universitas: Magazine for Universities*, at universitas.cz/en, translation modified.

adventure of the pamphlets, despite their being written in the dominant language of global scientific discourse, provides further evidence that, in order to enter and circulate within other cultural contexts, ideas must come into contact with other languages and undergo the transformations this contact entails.[13] This is something Moretti himself taught us to observe, and as his readers we have already seen it happen many times with literary forms. It is also something that, to provide some external corroboration, can be explained by what Francesco de Cristofaro writes in the conclusion to his chapter 'Discourse on Method': 'Here, finally, lies the secret: theory not only does not die from an excess of books, but in fact grows stronger because of them.'[14] De Cristofaro, it should be said, has played an important role in the European history of the pamphlets, creating the conditions that made the Italian edition of *Literature in the Laboratory* (*La Letteratura in laboratorio*) possible.[15]

However, we must not forget to return to the discussion on method, which we left off in 2005 with a single question split into two: How can different conceptual models be made to work together? And what is to be done with the different levels of explanation in terms of literary history?[16] This question of Moretti's arose in a specific moment in the development of the digital humanities in the United States. We can describe this context using the words of Stephen Ramsay during his talk 'High Performance Computing for English Majors' at the 2006 Modern Language Association convention:

> Over the last twenty years, we have spent millions digitizing texts and putting them online. The resulting digital full-text archives are among the greatest achievements in digital humanities. Yet for all their wonder, they remain committed to a vision of digital textuality firmly ensconced within the metaphor of the physical library. You can browse the text, read the text, search the text, and even download the text, but you can't

---

13 Franco Moretti and Giuseppe Episcopo, eds, *La letteratura in laboratorio* (Naples: Federico II University Press, 2019).

14 See chapter 2, above.

15 Available online at the website of the Federico II University Press in three formats, pdf, epub, mobi: fedoabooks.unina.it.

16 Franco Moretti, *Graphs, Maps, Trees* (London: Verso, 2005), p. 92.

> really do much beyond that. It is time to start thinking of ways to exploit this data with analytical tools and visualizations. Ideally, such tools should be an integral part of the experience of working with Web-based text collections.[17]

To describe the landscape at the end of the period of rupture marking Moretti's second American decade – which we hypothesised earlier – we can cite Ramsay again. In 2011, within the same context, during another session of the MLA convention, he noted:

> Personally, I think Digital Humanities is about building things. I'm willing to entertain highly expansive definitions of what it means to build something. I also think the discipline includes and should include people who theorize about building, people who design so that others might build, and those who supervise building (the coding question is, for me, a canard, insofar as many people build without knowing how to program). I'd even include people who are working to re-build systems like our present, irretrievably broken system of scholarly publishing. But if you are not making anything, you are not – in my less-than-three-minute opinion – a digital humanist. You might be something else that is good and worthy – maybe you're a scholar of new media, or maybe a game theorist, or maybe a classicist with a blog (the latter being a very good thing indeed) – but if you aren't building, you are not engaged in the 'methodologisation' of the humanities, which, to me, is the hallmark of the discipline that was already decades old when I came to it.[18]

We have held together a few different threads: Moretti's question about the tools needed to further advance the study of culture's deep structures, and the call for methodological rigour within the American academic context (specifically that of the digital humanities).

---

17 Stephen Ramsay, 'High Performance Computing for English Majors', paper given at the Modern Language Association Annual Convention, Philadelphia, 2006.

18 Ibid.

It would not have made sense to separate these two moments at the beginning of this discussion, and not only because they coincided. If they do not fully collapse into one another, it is only due to a subtle yet distinct difference in where knowledge is situated, and to what it can ultimately be attributed. In modern literary theory, Franco Moretti adds the function of 'measurement' to the series of formalisations that constitute the intersection between the morphological approach to literature and the development of algorithmic procedures, along the lines of a 'process that is absolutely central to a new field, that of critical computation – or, to give it the preferred name, the digital humanities'.[19]

At its most basic level – that is, in a strictly technical context – Moretti adopts the definition proposed by the American physicist Percy Williams Bridgman, who understands a concept in terms of actual operations, considering it synonymous with the procedures that determine it and thus make it definable through them. 'Operationalisation', then, corresponds to the construction of a link that leads from the concepts of literary theory to literary texts through some form of quantification – where quantification, precisely, is the transformation of a concept into a series of operations that can be applied to texts, rather than to one text in particular.

There are two crucial points here. First, the legitimation of scientific knowledge within the humanities. The history and tradition of this relationship (even if we limit ourselves to the twentieth century) run so deep that there is no point in attempting to explore them fully here; it will be enough to gather the gold dust that clings to one's fingers from merely scratching the surface. Within the Stanford Digital Humanities (at least during the years when Moretti was at the helm), legitimation did not consist in merely borrowing terminology from the domains of statistics; rather, its defining feature lay in establishing the necessary falsification processes to determine which statements could be deemed prescriptive and which could not.

In a fine book that, through Lyotard, investigates what it means and what it entails to computerise narrative knowledge, Bruno Moroncini

19 Franco Moretti, 'Operationalizing', *New Left Review* II/84 (November–December 2013); *Pamphlets of the Stanford Literary Lab* 6 (2013), p. 1.

writes that, as a preliminary to any (scientific) logic of discovery, it is necessary 'to identify the order of discourse or reconstruct the "genealogy" . . . of what, at any given time, is taken as true'.[20] In other words, where are we to find the rules for producing the tools capable of synthesising literary facts? Now, let us move to point two: the concepts that Moretti operationalises.

In the pamphlet on the role of measurement in modern literary theory, Moretti engages with the space of words and the system of characters, transforming two concepts into tools for quantitative analysis. The first is character-space, as proposed by Alex Woloch in *The One vs. the Many*; the second comes from Graham Alexander Sack's analysis of the frequency of characters' names in *Simulating Plot: Towards a Generative Model of Narrative Structure*.[21] The character-space is a textual space – that is, the space of words – while the frequency of names represents the protagonist's connection to the system of characters. Moretti does the following: he outlines an analytical methodology that allows for a literary-historical formula in which theoretical questions are transformed into objects that can be measured and calculated. Style, narrative functions and structures (whether those previously highlighted by the Russian formalists or those emerging from large textual corpora), cultural emotions, and the performativity of institutional discourse – all these become measurable.

Choosing a research framework based on problems, however, is not a lesson learned from machines; it is the lesson of Fernand Braudel, Marc Bloch and Lucien Febvre. The guiding ideas behind the *Annales* school, as Peter Burke observed, lie above all in the replacement of a history 'focusing on events' with 'a history that is analytically oriented towards problems'.[22]

---

20 Bruno Moroncini, *Il discorso e la cenere. Dieci variazioni sulla responsabilità filosofica* (Naples: Guida, 1988), p. 44.

21 Alex Woloch, *The One vs. the Many: Minor Characters and the Space of the Protagonist in the Novel* (Princeton, NJ: Princeton University Press, 2003); Graham Alexander Sack, 'Simulating Plot: Towards a Generative Model of Narrative Structure', in *Complex Adaptive Systems: Energy, Information and Intelligence. Papers from the AAAI Fall Symposium*, eds Mirsad Hadzikadic and Ted Carmichael (Palo Alto, CA: AAAI Press, 2011), pp. 127–36.

22 Peter Burke, *The French Historical Revolution: The Annales School 1929–1989* (Stanford, CA: Stanford University Press, 1990).

3. They Say Those Skies Were Made for Horses, and the Streets Are Stage Dust

The Bourgeois was published in America on the exact same day in 2013 as *Distant Reading*, almost as if to suggest, in that perfect temporal synchronicity, a stereoscopic vision of the literary phenomenon. In Italy, editorial circumstances produced other, retrospectively significant coincidences: *Il borghese* was published in 2017; accompanied by 'The Bourgeois Makes the World' (*Il borghese fa il mondo*), edited by Francesco de Cristofaro and Marco Viscardi – a volume that concluded the 'bourgeois trilogy' begun at the Opificio di Letteratura Reale of the Federico II University of Naples, directly inspired by the American edition of Moretti's book.[23] In terms of publication date, *Il borghese* is closer to *Un paese lontano* (2019, also in its English edition) than to *Distant Reading*, a book that would be encountered again in its Italian translation under the title *A una certa distanza* (2020). Thus, perhaps significantly, *The Bourgeois* is in many ways a homecoming. The Prague interview from 2020, which I referred to above, bears witness to this:

> Back in the 1970s, in my twenties, I was a militant in the New Left – the Trotskyist, anti-Stalinist New Left – and a literary student, a young scholar. None of my friends studied literature, they were all philosophers, economists, journalists, historians, and when I was thinking about myself, I knew that I needed to earn some bread, and so I would need to be a professor. At the same time, I was thinking that the nice thing to be would be to be an intellectual. That is, someone whose intellectual life is not only spent inside the university, but whose work can have meaning also outside of their discipline, and maybe in political terms, in a loose sense. In the 1970s and 1980s I could still have this

23 For the bibliography, see Francesco de Cristofaro and Giovanni Maffei, eds, *Borghesia. Sette Approssimazioni*, vol 1: *Abbecedario* (Pomigliano D'Arco: Diogene, 2015); Francesco de Cristofaro and Marco Viscardi, eds, *Il borghese fa il mondo. Quinidici accoppiamenti giudiziosi* (Rome: Donzelli, 2017); Maria Greco, Marilisa Moccia and Pasquale Palmieri, eds, *Borghesia. Approssimazioni* (Campobasso: Diogene, 2017).

> belief or delusion about myself that I really was an intellectual. When I went to the United States, I clearly became a professor. I was a very good professor – as you pointed out I founded two institutions that have been incredibly successful. But I was just a professor. That my last act there was founding a lab was even more professor-like, because it was a small, very specialized place within the university. Now, it's too late to change my life, but it's nice to return to a situation where, if I cannot actually do it, at least I can feel it, I can smell the intellectual figures around me.[24]

As does the 2017 interview with *Il Venerdì*, the weekly supplement to *la Repubblica*:

> [The bourgeois] is a figure that has fascinated me ever since my university days, at the end of the 1960s. At that time, it was a keyword – much used and also much abused. Over the decades, I was often tempted to write about it, but the question always seemed enormous. In the end, I told myself: this is a piece of cultural history that has been lost. Perhaps I am not the person best suited to bring it back into play, but I am the person who wants to do it.[25]

It is a keyword of an era in which, as McKenzie Wark recalls in her 2013 review of *The Bourgeois* for the *Los Angeles Review of Books*, 'It used to be a terrific insult to call someone or something "bourgeois".'[26] Today, however, this is no longer the case, as the review continues, partly because no one really knows or remembers what the word even means: 'While pretty much everyone, from left to right, agrees that our world is a capitalist one, the notion that the culture of those who rule it is "bourgeois" seems no longer to hold.' What happened? Because, as Franco Moretti suggested in his 2017 interview, 'capitalism is stronger than ever, even as

---

24 Podhajský, 'Free Time is What Scientists Need More than Money', translation adjusted.

25 Simonetta Fiori, 'La borghesia è ormai un fantasma: ma chi l'ha uccisa?', *il Venerdì – di Repubblica*, 1 March 2018.

26 McKenzie Wark, 'The Engine Room of Literature: On Franco Moretti', *Los Angeles Review of Books*, 5 June 2013.

embodiment seems to have vanished into thin air'.[27] Wark, however, might not be entirely convinced of this, if we take literally the title of one of her more recent books published by Verso, *Capital Is Dead*. In it, she offers a kind of media-age update of the Lacanian formula, suggesting that the death of capital leads to something even worse (*pire*) than the father (*père*): an immaterial capitalism where information becomes the new capital, and the bourgeoisie its ultimate commodity.

Returning once again to *The Bourgeois*, Wark offers a politically engaged reading of Moretti's analysis of narrative dispositions: there is the movement of verb tenses, a grammar of growth that makes room for things, and then an astonishing number of fillers. These fillers occupy a large part of *Robinson Crusoe*, described by Moretti in the interview as that 'strange novel . . . split in half between an adventure story and a story of the relentless labour on the island'.[28]

But it is precisely at this point that Wark, without mediation – almost as a pure ideological gesture – welds together the world described by Marx in the opening lines of *Capital* ('The wealth of those societies in which the capitalist mode of production prevails, presents itself as "an immense accumulation of commodities", its unit being a single commodity') with the fillers, which, according to Moretti, '*rationalize the novelistic universe*, turning it into a world of few surprises, fewer adventures, and no miracles at all'.[29] Perhaps I have lingered too long on this point: we all know about fillers, and we have already encountered them while reading the chapter on the 'serious century' in *The Novel*. However, Moretti's writing – and this must be emphasised clearly – creates unexpected constellations and astonishing encounters like the one we have just seen with McKenzie Wark, and like the one we are about to see.

Still on the topic of fillers in literature: anyone who has read Amitav Ghosh's latest nonfiction work, *The Great Derangement* (2016), will find a precise analysis of fillers that the Indian writer develops from

27 Horea Poenar, interview with Franco Moretti, 'Gusta Transilvania', *TVRCLuj*, 28 January 2017, at youtube.com.

28 Fiori, 'La borghesia è ormai un fantasma'.

29 Franco Moretti, *The Bourgeois: Between History and Literature* (London: Verso, 2013), p. 82.

reflections on a catastrophic event he personally experienced: the first tornado ever to strike the city of Delhi. Ghosh, whose novels often feature floods and extreme weather conditions, has never incorporated the tornado into any of his stories, because he has never believed it could be successfully translated into narrative terms: 'Surely, only a writer whose imaginative resources were utterly depleted would fall back on a situation of such extreme improbability?'[30]

The decisive point hinges on the word 'improbable'. It is not simply the opposite of 'probable', but rather something outside probability itself. As Ghosh notes by citing Ian Hacking, probability is 'a "manner of conceiving the world constituted without our being aware of it."' He continues:

> Probability and the modern novel are in fact twins, born at about the same time, among the same people, under a shared star that destined them to work as vessels for the containment of the same kind of experience. Before the birth of the modern novel, wherever stories were told, fiction delighted in the unheard-of and the unlikely. Narratives like those of *The Arabian Nights*, *The Journey to the West* and *The Decameron* proceed by leaping blithely from one exceptional event to another. This, after all, is how storytelling must necessarily proceed, inasmuch as it is a recounting of 'what happened' – for such an inquiry can arise only in relation to something out of the ordinary, which is but another way of saying 'exceptional' or 'unlikely'. In essence, narrative proceeds by linking together moments and scenes that are in some way distinctive or different: these are, of course, nothing other than instances of exception.
>
> Novels too proceed in this fashion, but what is distinctive about the form is precisely the concealment of those exceptional moments that serve as the motor of narrative. This is achieved through the insertion of what Franco Moretti, the literary theorist, calls 'fillers' . . . Thus was the novel midwifed into existence around the world, through the banishing of the improbable and the insertion of the everyday. The process can be

30 Amitav Ghosh, *The Great Derangement: Climate Change and the Unthinkable* (Chicago, IL: University of Chicago Press, 2016).

> observed with exceptional clarity in the work of Bankim Chandra Chatterjee, a nineteenth-century Bengali writer and critic who self-consciously adopted the project of carving out a space in which realist European-style fiction could be written in the vernacular languages of India.[31]

Everyday details, then, function as the 'opposite of narrative', yet allow for the evocation of 'entire universes'. Here, Ghosh makes another significant move, linking the emergence of the rhetoric of the everyday with the rise of a statistical system shaped by ideas of probability and improbability, which during those same years was beginning to refashion society.

How does this happen? It happens because the geological theories of gradualism pushed catastrophism into the background; and so, as nature became more predictable, the novel could also relegate every anomaly to the margins. Ghosh's argument builds on Franco Moretti's insights into the arts, combining them with Stephen Jay Gould's *Time's Arrow, Time's Cycle* (1987), which – after adopting a long-term historical perspective that leads him to some interesting conclusions – Ghosh ultimately describes as 'an essay about narrative'.

At this point, it is almost irresistible to follow the branching paths that Moretti's thought has taken in the work of others, or to trace his voice serendipitously through a collection of interviews, threading together its key moments and grouping them into clusters. But I must resist these temptations. Not for fear of being shipwrecked – like Crusoe – but rather because of the danger of straying from the intended course: which, in these last two stops, consists of materials I was not sure I would be able to find. Given the occasion, I would like to treat them as small gifts, and, in keeping with my initial promise, I will wrap them in the simplest sugar paper.

The first is the hero of 'pragmatism' and 'methodical coordination', as read by Galvano della Volpe in one of the five fragments on ethics appended to *Rousseau and Marx*. These are the pages dedicated to 'The Good Robinson':

---

31 Ibid., p. 16.

A recent American edition of *Robinson Crusoe* brings us back to this hero of our childhood, reconsidering his true meaning and philosophy, partly through the merit of its new introduction by the acute critic Louis Kronenberger.

Robinson, as K. writes, is full of a general sufficiency and, just like his author, a profound hypocrisy; but if it is true that he represents all that which is dry and brutal in the British character (Dickens rightfully pointed out that *Crusoe* is the only great novel that provokes neither smiles nor tears), it is also true that he excellently represents that for which this same character is admired: Robinson is tenacious, faithful to himself, practical and unshakeable; to the extent that he manages to single-handedly transform a raw Eden into a 'well-ordered little England' and manages – with the presence of his 'slave', Friday, to create a 'little India'; after which 'he is allowed to sail back'.

Furthermore, one does not believe that our hero and school-boy model does not lack a certain class consciousness, proclaiming at the opening of the tale how much he follows in the name of his fatherly teaching: 'Mine was the middle state . . . which he had found, by long experience, was the best state in the world, the most suited to human happiness, not exposed to the miseries and hardships, the labour and sufferings of the mechanic part of mankind', etc.

How this typical image of seventeenth-century English bourgeois resourcefulness was erected as a model for human resourcefulness in general, and celebrated in an absolute sense when it was none other than solitary, private, individualistic – in a word, bourgeois – human initiative; how this happened is not a mystery for the Marxist who knows the economic, social, historical roots of *Robinsonism*, as with every other ideology, and therefore knows which (cultural) tools of the class struggle are 'absolute' models and ideals. While the others, the non-Marxists, find themselves in the same condition of blessed faith shared by school-boys – and not only in relation to Robinsonism. They do not suspect, furthermore, that it is merely the *infancy* of our present society (in crisis) which the good Robinson represents and yearns for.[32]

---

32 Galvano della Volpe, *Rousseau e Marx e altri saggi di critica materialistica* (Rome: Editori Riuniti, 1964), p. 211.

The second material comes in the form of a facsimile reproduction. On the one hand, in a kind of circular movement, the text returns to the years dealt with by Stefano Ercolino and closes on 1983; on the other, it throws open a window onto the future, points to the work on the horizon, and lets light in on its foundations. 'Literature as Values' appeared on Sunday, 4 September 1983 in the *New York Times Book Review*. Next to it one finds a review by Walter Kendrick of Terry Eagleton's *Literary Criticism*. 'Literature as Values' is Edward W. Said's review of *Signs Taken for Wonders*. The opening is striking: in the natural sciences, research takes place within accepted and shared norms and conventions. Discoveries that shift paradigms are exceedingly rare, and they create problems of stability because a new common framework must be organised. Paradigm-shifting discoveries are exceedingly rare – and when they occur, they create instability, because they require the reorganisation of a common ground and a new framework of understanding. Literary studies and criticism, by contrast, have imposed novelty as a duty: and in this system, works – novels, poems – are used as instruments of struggle, and of governance. Having established this framing, Said introduces Moretti's book into the vast and terrifying world with an extraordinarily measured gesture:

> Literary studies, he says, ought to make the conventions of such genres as the novel an object of serious investigation, especially since genres furnish the stability of what we call literature, which in turn is part of the apparatus producing consent in the major Western industrial states. By consent, Mr Moretti means what his great compatriot Antonio Gramsci, the Marxist philosopher, meant when he spoke of the maintenance of hegemony (as opposed to direct domination) in the field of ideas through rational consent. This is a critical discrimination between coercion in a police state and the powerful influence of ruling ideas in liberal societies.[33]

It is clear that Said is not merely presenting a book to a cultured and wide-ranging readership; nor, in fact, is he simply welcoming a young

33 Edward Said, 'Literature as Values', *New York Times Book Review*, 4 September 1983, pp. 9–18.

overseas colleague onto the academic stage. Rather, he is recognising a 'valuable critic', affirming that we are in the presence of an important scholar, and that it is good to have him 'on the intellectual scene'.

In conclusion, let us turn to the foundations: *Signs Taken for Wonders* is a collection of essays – as is *Far Country* (2019). But *Far Country* is also a return, an implicit act through which Moretti resumes a critical engagement with the problems of cultural life.[34] He does so with the same anti-dogmatic spirit he brings to literary texts (the canonical masterworks, to put it plainly), and with the same systematic rigour with which he transforms the problem an algorithm must address into a set of homogeneous questions (this time working not with books, but with corpora made up of hundreds of millions of words). 'Stanford, Salerno' – the opening chapter of the 'five easy pieces' that make up the book ('Five Easy Pieces' was meant to be the title, but copyright issues left no room for negotiation) – starts from an era, in the later 1970s, when anti-intellectualism was the primary risk to the university. With a gaze that grows close and familiar, it arrives at our own time, in which the new enemy of a university increasingly shaped not by politics but by the forces of the world itself is its dystopian–utopian relationship with the future. In light of all this, then, is the true foundation of Moretti's critical practice – his anatomist's table – which strips works of their aura of wonder and removes the cult of personality from the aesthetic experience, not, above all, an intellectual mission?

---

34 A decisive confirmation of this reading from Moretti himself can be found in 'C'era una volta', the introduction to the new edition of *Segni e stili del moderno* (Rome: Del Vecchio, 2020).

II

EXPERIMENTAL CRITICISM

4

Essayism: Franco Moretti

Guido Mazzoni

1. Styles

In a passage from *Far Country*, Moretti alludes to a well-known methodological discussion. In November 1938, Adorno wrote to Benjamin. The former was in exile in New York, the latter in Paris. Benjamin had provided the Institute for Social Research with a sample from his book on the Arcades, the essay 'The Paris of the Second Empire in Baudelaire', and awaited an opinion.[1] Adorno's response carried practical significance, since the Institute might have been able to secure financial support for Benjamin through a patron.[2]

Adorno is sceptical. He begins by praising Benjamin's intelligence and the project's value, as one does in such cases; but then he arrives at the part that does not convince him. It seems to Adorno that Benjamin connects the actual content of Baudelaire directly to contemporary social history – linking superstructure to structure – while skipping over the necessary mediations. Benjamin replies a month later with a rather curt letter, in which he defends his essay without wavering or making concessions.

It is a disagreement over method (Adorno envisions a more classically Hegelian–Marxist way of connecting the particular to the universal

1 Franco Moretti, *Far Country: Scenes from American Culture* (London/New York: Verso, 2019), pp. 8–9.

2 Bernd Witte, *Walter Benjamin* (Reinbek bei Hamburg: Rowohlt, 1985), p. 128.

through a progressive broadening of perspective; Benjamin, by contrast, is developing his idea of the monad and the dialectical image) and, at the same time, a disagreement over form. The approach to linking parts not through mediation but through montage, that leap from empirical history to concept – so characteristic of Benjamin, and the first thing a reader notices about him – does not convince Adorno, who sees it instead as a strange hybrid of positivism and magic.[3]

We could discuss at length the philosophy implicit in this exchange, but it is just as interesting to reflect on its *a priori*.[4] The *a priori* – to use a concept of Hegelian origin that Adorno develops in *Philosophy of Modern Music* and *Aesthetic Theory* – is the idea that form is always semantic, that style carries a latent content prior to any manifest content. Some years later, speaking of music, of art more generally, and then of the family of texts that since the second half of the eighteenth century has come to be called literature, Adorno names this latent content 'sedimented content'.[5] But this idea applies to every text, not just to works of art or literature. It applies especially to those texts that use the medium of the concept, and which a scientistic view of knowledge or an inflated, illusory view of philosophy would like to see removed from such concerns. Twenty years after his letter to Benjamin, Adorno completed his *Essay on Form* (1954–58); twenty-eight years earlier, Lukács wrote a letter to Leo Popper that opens his *Soul and Form* (1910), giving rise to a Central European debate on the essay as a literary form.

2. The Essay as Form

For those who first encountered Franco Moretti's work in the second half of the 1980s (the two books that made him known were *Signs Taken for Wonders*, written between the late 1970s and early 1980s and published

3 Walter Benjamin, *Charles Baudelaire: A Lyric Poet in the Era of High Capitalism* (London: Verso, 1997).

4 Giorgio Agamben, *Infancy and History: Essays on the Destruction of Experience*, transl. Liz Heron (London: Verso, 1993 [1978]), pp. 107–23.

5 Theodor W. Adorno, *Aesthetic Theory*, transl. Robert Hullot-Kentor (Minneapolis: University of Minnesota Press, 1997 [1970]), p. 5.

in English in 1983, and *The Way of the World*, published in Italian in 1986), the form of his essays mattered almost as much as their content. Moretti wrote in a style entirely foreign to the dominant modes of Italian academic criticism at the time. By contrast, his first book, *Letteratura e ideologie negli anni Trenta inglesi* (English Literature and Ideologies in the 1930s), published in 1976 by Adriatica Editrice in the Library of English Studies series edited by Agostino Lombardo, was fully aligned with one of those prevailing styles. The first section laid out the historical framework of English society, economy and politics in the era of the crisis of imperialism; the second discussed the social function of literature in Britain – and so on, progressing from context to texts, from structure to superstructure, with the layered motion typical of the expressivist model of causality embraced by a certain strain of Marxist historicism.[6] And the writing followed the same pattern, proceeding slowly and methodically:

> The brief historical analysis just outlined provides the foundation, without which it becomes impossible to understand the work of the authors discussed in the following essays or to grasp its specificity in relation to other literary phenomena – whether earlier, later, or contemporary. If, in fact, the literature of the 1930s aimed to define itself as a literature of 'opposition' to the bourgeois and 'decadent' tradition, any judgment of it must depend on assessing the extent to which it was able to articulate, on the literary level, the antagonism that had emerged in the struggles waged between the two wars by the British and international workers' movements.[7]

There were also idealistic, and above all positivistic, versions of this procedure, which updated the paradigms of the late-nineteenth-century historical school for the twentieth and twenty-first centuries. Even today, most Italian literary criticism follows a similar model: it seeks to study an individual

---

6 Louis Althusser and Étienne Balibar, *Reading Capital*, transl. Ben Brewster (London: Verso, 2007 [1968]); Fredric Jameson, *The Political Unconscious: Narrative as Socially Symbolic Act* (London: Methuen, 1981).

7 Franco Moretti, *Letteratura e ideologie negli anni Trenta inglesi* (Bari: Adriatica, 1976), pp. 20–1.

work or a series of works philologically, and to situate texts within their historical context according to a mechanical and punctual idea of causality – the influence of one writer on another, of a milieu on an artistic movement, of patronage or the market on a literary genre. Ten years later, *The Way of the World* was written in a completely different style: montage, argumentative suspense, fragmented periods, sudden associations:

> 'Nineteenth-century bourgeoisie' – the worst sort, for Balzac: usurers, convicts, 'wolves', 'blood-thirsty hunters' (Adorno). Together with their 'spiritual mobility', and their perspicacity in 'a knowledge of the weaknesses and defects of one's surroundings', that characterises for Sombart the Faustian figure of the 'entrepreneur', these characters display, as is inevitable, some of the most repugnant features of capitalist society: cynicism, cruelty, heedless indifference to the fate of others, or a predatory promptness to take advantage of it. Balzac, as is well known, not only does not tone down these aspects, he stresses them. Because of Lukács's celebrated 'incorruptible artistic integrity' which is responsible for the equally famous 'triumph of realism'? I doubt it.[8]

There is a certain family resemblance to the method of certain Italian essayists born between the late 1930s and 1940s (Ginzburg, Jesi, Agamben), all of whom were influenced, in their style of writing, by the first translations of Benjamin published by Einaudi during the 1960s and 1970s, and all of whom were equally distant from the traditional modes of Italian essay writing. Moreover, Moretti was – and would remain – equally distant from the dominant modes of argumentation in the Anglo-American world. The rhetoric of making a point and of advancing an argument through linear procedures, following the *ordo naturalis* and a certain model of rationality, never pertained to him. Two stylistic features were typical of his approach. First, the sudden insertion of quotations from works of history, the social sciences, philosophy or literary criticism in order to explain a literary text by referencing a historical process or an anthropological constant:

---

8 Franco Moretti, *The Way of the World: The* Bildungsroman *in European Culture*, transl. Albert Sbragia (London: Verso, 2000 [1986]), pp. 138–9.

> It appears to me instead the uncanny challenge of one who realizes that certain ideas and deeds, not in spite of their loathsomeness, but *due to it*, have given this new class a power, and with it a *power of vision*, previously unknown. After five hundred years, this contradictory development has once again made possible a *universal narration*: a 'comedy' that dares the analogy with its divine precedent. This new comedy is the vision of a heartless usurer, and we must not forget it; but it is the *Comédie Humaine*, and this too must not be forgotten . . .
>
> A generation goes by, and the demon that had spoken through Balzac reappears. This time, under the name of Jacob Burkhardt: 'The mind must transmute into a possession the remembrance of its passage through the ages of the world. What was once joy and sorrow must now become knowledge, as it must in the life of the individual. Therewith the saying *Historia vitae magistra* takes on a higher yet humbler sense. We wish experience to make us, not shrewder (for next time), but wiser (for ever). How far does this result in scepticism? True scepticism has its indisputable place in a world where beginning and end are all unknown, and the middle in constant flux . . . Of the true kind [of scepticism] there can never be enough.'[9]

And, second, a syntax that imitates the rhythms of spoken language (especially the lecture form), at times verging on interior monologue, like a kind of Stephen Dedalus reflecting on Aristotle on the beach at Sandymount:

> Take *Faust*, what is it? A 'tragedy', as its author states? A great philosophical tale? A collection of lyrical insights? Who can say. How about *Moby Dick*? Encyclopaedia, novel or romance? Or even a 'singular medley', as one anonymous 1851 review put it? How about *The Nibelung's Ring*, with its millenarian notion of being a 'total art-work': drama, opera or myth? Ezra Pound described *Bouvard and Pécuchet* in 1922 as 'no longer a novel'; 'it is no longer a novel' T.S. Eliot repeated of *Ulysses* a few months later. But if not novels, then what are they? And *The Cantos*, or *The Waste Land*? Is *The Last Days of Mankind* a theatrical work? How

---

9 Ibid., p. 139.

> about *The Man Without Qualities*: novel or essay? And those splendid stories arriving from Latin America and India? 'Magical realism'? As if we did not know that contradictions in terms are quite meaningless.[10]

In Moretti's work, we can distinguish two different phases, as I will discuss, but his style and intellectual stance never change. If we open any essay from the second phase at random – 'The Slaughterhouse of Literature', for example – we find the following:

> But why is Conan Doyle selected in the first place? Why him, and not others? Here the economic model has a blind spot: the event that starts the 'information cascade' is unknowable. It's there, it *has* to be there, or the market wouldn't behave as it does, but it can't be explained. Moviegoers 'discover what they like', but we never discover *why* they like it. They're the blind canon makers, as it were. Now, this is understandable for economic theory, which is not supposed to analyze aesthetic taste. But literary history is, and my thesis here is that what makes readers 'like' this or that book is – form. Walter Benjamin, *Central Park*: 'Baudelaire's conduct in the literary market: Baudelaire was, through his deep experience of the nature of the commodity, enabled, or perhaps forced, to acknowledge the market as an objective . . . He devalued certain poetic freedoms of the romantics by means of his classical use of the Alexandrine, and classical poetics by means of those *caesurae* and blanks within the classical verse itself. In short, his poems contain certain specific precautions for the eradication of their competitors.'[11]

In early-twentieth-century reflections on the essay as a genre, the opposition between the treatise-form and the essay-form frequently recurs. The former is the genre of science and philosophy conceived as formal logic or deductive metaphysics; the latter is a hybrid between philosophy and literature, between science and art. The treatise seeks – or claims – to

---

10 Franco Moretti, *Modern Epic: The World System from Goethe to García Márquez* (London: Verso, 1996), p. 1.

11 Franco Moretti, *Distant Reading* (London: Verso, 2013), p. 70. The quote is from Walter Benjamin, 'Central Park' (1937–38), *New German Critique* 34 (1985), p. 37.

abolish the subjectivity of the person writing it, while the essay exalts it. Now, even in the second phase of his work – the one marked by explicit scientific, quantitative and impersonal ambitions – Moretti proceeds through intuitive associations that begin from texts or data. In other words, he remains fundamentally an essayist: more than presenting content, he presents a process of thought. The epigraph from *The Man Without Qualities* that opens *Graphs, Maps, Trees* serves almost as a self-portrait: 'A man who wants the truth becomes a scientist; a man who wants to give free play to his subjectivity may become a writer; but what should a man do who wants something in between?'[12] Moretti is an essayist in the sense that both the young Lukács and Musil gave to the term. In *The Bourgeois*, he discusses the difference between Walter Scott's historical novel and the model that Scott himself admired, Maria Edgeworth's *Castle Rackrent*. In Scott, the narrator recedes into the background as an objective voice; in Edgeworth, the narrator is a character within the story – an individuated, tangible narrative presence.[13] Moretti behaves not like Scott, but like Edgeworth – as do the majority of contemporary historical novelists, who have returned to the intradiegetic narrator, abandoning Scott's model. This is one reason his books convey a sense of openness rather than closure, as if posing problems were more important than arriving at rigid conclusions. And they communicate the movement of an 'I' – an 'I' for whom discussion seems more important than assertion, and interrogation more important than definition.

3. Two Seasons

The introductions to the essays republished in *Distant Reading* are particularly interesting because they allow the author to reflect on the journey he has taken. In the opening essay, originally published in 1991

12 Robert Musil, *The Man Without Qualities*, transl. Burton Pike and Sophie Wilkins, vol. 1 (New York: Knopf, 1995 [1930–42]), p. 274; Franco Moretti, *Graphs, Maps, Trees* (London: Verso, 2005), p. 1.

13 Franco Moretti, *The Bourgeois: Between History and Literature* (London: Verso, 2013), pp. 90–1.

in Einaudi's *Storia d'Europa*, Moretti makes a distinction between the first and second phases of his work. The essay he discusses belongs to the first phase, which Moretti looks back on with mixed feelings:

> Somehow, I found the right tone; possibly, because of my total reliance on the canon of European masterpieces (as a colleague pointed out, the word 'great' seemed ubiquitous in the essay; and it was, I used it fifty-one times!). The canon allowed for comparative analysis to take place: Shakespeare and Racine, the *conte philosophique* and the *Bildungsroman*, the Austrians and the *avant-gardes* . . . As the years went by, I would move increasingly away from this idea of literature as a collection of masterpieces; and in truth, I feel no nostalgia for what it meant. But the conceptual cogency that a small set of texts allows for – that, I do miss.[14]

A similar distinction reappears in the introduction to the debate with Christopher Prendergast:

> The second point concerns the role of the 'market' in my explanations; specifically, the fact that this notion ends up playing a greater role in 'Darwinian' pieces like 'Slaughterhouse', 'Trees', or 'Style, Inc.', than in explicitly 'Marxist' ones like 'Conjectures' or 'Planet Hollywood'. The reason for this seeming paradox is probably this: once literary history is conceived as an evolutionary process, it splits into two distinct (though interacting) series: on one side, the often random variations arising from formal experiments; on the other, the broad social processes that underlie cultural selection. Ideally, the analysis of these two series should form a unity; in practice, their two causal chains are so completely different that I have always ended up concentrating on one of the two, and evoking the other only in a simplified form. And this is what happened in the chapter criticized by Prendergast, where 'the market' is brought in largely as a place-holder for an analysis that is still to come.
>
> The next essay in this collection presents the opposite type of one-sidedness: I spend several pages analyzing the features of novelistic markets in early modern China and Europe – and rely on a simplified

14 Moretti, *Distant Reading*, p. 2.

summary of the morphological issues at stake. Maybe, one day, I will learn to do the two things together.[15]

Moretti's work thus contains two seasons and two ways of understanding criticism. The first season derives from Marxism and, even earlier, from German Idealism – often filtered through certain twentieth-century interpretations: the young Lukács, Panofsky, Auerbach, Szondi. In his earliest essay on method, 'The Soul and the Harpy' (1982), Moretti attacks the use of the zeitgeist and the philosophy of the history of art we find in Hegel's *Aesthetics*.[16] Yet many of Moretti's essays would be inconceivable without a philosophy of history derived from the Hegelian–Marxist tradition: it is enough to read the opening chapter of *Modern Epic* to see this. Moreover, the concept of symbolic form developed by Cassirer and Panofsky, to which Moretti often turns in his interpretations of literary genres, is itself a reworking of the Hegelian idea that 'the sensuous aspect of art is spiritualized, since the spirit appears in art as made sensuous'.[17] Or, as Adorno puts it, that artistic forms are sedimented contents. This way of thinking about criticism assumes a precise canon: 'Shakespeare and Racine, the *conte philosophique* and the *Bildungsroman*, the Austrians and the *avant-gardes*' – and, more broadly, within the tradition of the novel, Goethe and Austen, Scott and Balzac, Stendhal, Flaubert, George Eliot and Henry James, Tolstoy and Dostoevsky, Stevenson and Conrad, Mann, Musil and Kafka, Joyce and Woolf, and so on; in short, the great bourgeois canon, more or less the same canon on which Lukács and Auerbach worked.

The other season of Moretti's work is Darwinian and scientific in its dominant orientation. It emerges forcefully with 'Conjectures on World Literature' and continues through *Distant Reading*, the Stanford Literary Lab, and *La letteratura in laboratorio*. But this was not a sudden shift.

Moretti's interest in science as a discourse of truth and an antidote to the vagueness of Idealist-Romantic aesthetics and the hybridisations of

15 Ibid., p. 138.

16 Franco Moretti, *Signs Taken for Wonders: Essays in the Sociology of Literary Forms*, transl. Susan Fisher, David Forgacs and D. A. Miller (London: Verso 1997 [1983], 2nd edn 1988), pp. 25–41.

17 Hegel, *Aesthetics*, vol. 1, trans. T. M. Knox (Oxford: Clarendon, 1975), p. 39.

Idealism and Marxism, was already present in his early essays. The third section of 'The Soul and the Harpy', for example, is titled 'Towards a "Falsifiable" Criticism'. It was there in intellectual formation, especially in the influence of Della Volpe, Colletti, and their scientific, non-Hegelian readings of Marx.[18]

The two seasons follow one another, but they also overlap. The first begins with the essays collected in *Segni e stili del moderno*, continuing through *Il romanzo di formazione* and *Opere mondo* (*Modern Epic*). The second opens with *Atlante del romanzo europeo* (*Atlas of the European Novel*), followed by *Graphs, Maps, Trees* and many of the essays in *Distant Reading*. That said, 'La letteratura europea', 'Serious Century', *The Bourgeois* and *Far Country* still belong to the first phase – and in any case, the hybridisms are continuous.[19]

Between the two phases lies a shift in the intellectual landscape that was deeply felt by the generations born in the second half of the twentieth century, a shift that led many to question the assumptions underpinning the earlier period. Moretti experienced this transformation intensely: he moved from Italy to the United States, from the Italian university system to the American one, and then from Columbia to Stanford – from the most European of American cities to the heart of the digital revolution. He lived, in particularly acute form, the three major transformations that reshaped the contemporary cultural landscape:

1. *The radical critique of the inherited image of the past, and of the canons we have taken for granted.* The expansion of geographical horizons, the rise of new collective subjects who were once silent or marginalised, and the spread of relativism as the dominant ideology of the humanities have all called into question the visible, surviving portion of literature preserved in official histories – the very body of work that the early Moretti engaged with, and that also underpinned the writings of Lukács, Bakhtin, Auerbach and Szondi.

---

18 Moretti, *Graphs, Maps, Trees*, p. 2; Moretti, *Distant Reading*, pp. 139, 155.

19 Franco Moretti, 'La letteratura europea', in Carlo Ginzburg et al., *Storia d'Europa, vol 1: L'Europa oggi* (Turin: Einaudi, 1993). 'Serious Century' was published as an essay in Moretti, *Il romanzo*, vol. 1 (Turin: Einaudi, 2001), pp. 689–725.

2. *The change in scale in the demographics of research.* Since the 1960s, the number of people involved in the production of history and culture has grown enormously; since the 1980s, computing has made it possible to access texts, bibliographies and data with a degree of ease unimaginable fifty years earlier. The result has been an expansion without precedent of specialised knowledge. The great philosophies of literary history developed between the early nineteenth and early twentieth centuries were made possible by the scarcity of information: knowing a few exemplary things still allowed one to mitigate the damage that history does to life. For Nietzsche, 'life' included the capacity to form a synthetic idea of the past: 'How learned we would be if we knew only five or six books well', Gustave Flaubert wrote to Louise Colet on 17 February 1853.[20] The nineteenth century saw the spread of atomised knowledge and its dialectic without synthesis – its tragedy. The first major reflections on this phenomenon, from Nietzsche to Simmel, emerged between the late nineteenth and early twentieth centuries. But this is nothing compared to what is happening now, just as the nineteenth- and early-twentieth-century literature on urban experience was written in the shadow of cities one-tenth or one-twentieth the size of today's megacities. Moretti's distant reading is an attempt to use big data to respond to the damage big data does to life: to the narcissistic wound it inflicts when it reveals how infinitesimal our first-hand knowledge really is, and how partial and elitist an image of the past is conveyed by our canons.

3. *The political crisis of traditional humanism.* One of the most significant developments of the twentieth century is the rise of pop culture. While a culture for the modern masses has existed for two centuries, what happened in the second half of the twentieth century was unprecedented in both scale and impact. Generations born from the 1940s onward are culturally bilingual. They grew up between two paradigms: the first, traditional humanistic culture, was mostly encountered in school; the second, pop culture, was absorbed from the discursive aether of their time. The former retained direct political influence as long as

---

20 Gustave Flaubert, *Correspondance*, vol. 2 (Paris: Gallimard, 1980 [1851–58]), p. 247.

society preserved hierarchies rooted in the authority of intermediary bodies – that is, in structures of aristocratic or pastoral power. But the more society transitions from one governed by elite hegemony into a true mass society, the more the political weight of traditional culture wanes, while that of pop culture grows.

In Moretti's words:

> In the span of a single generation, everything changed. And the next generation, wouldn't you know it, wants to change things again: studying film, television, advertising, comics. The Norwegian critic who wrote the excellent essay on contemporary fiction for *Il romanzo* left his literature professorship a few months ago to work at a research centre focused on video games. And I think he made the right choice.[21]

When this happens, literature can truly be viewed from afar.

4. Zeitgeist and numbers

The research programme and 'reflections on the goals and methods of literary historiography' that Moretti laid out in 'The Soul and the Harpy' closely align to what he would go on to pursue in the years that followed – so much so that his most recent methodological essay, the introduction to *Far Country*, reprises many of the ideas first articulated in 1982. An era produces symbolic forms, signs that are saturated with social meaning, and the most significant and recognisable symbolic forms in literature are its genres.

If, according to Moretti's reading, Hegelian historicism holds that 'every historical epoch has in essence *one* ideal content to "express", and it gives "sensible manifestation" to it through one artistic form', for Moretti the symbolic forms an era produces are plural and locked in struggle.[22] The guiding notion he adopts to conceptualise this kind of

21 Franco Moretti, *La letteratura vista da lontano* (Turin: Einaudi, 2005), p. 4.
22 Moretti, *Signs Taken for Wonders*, p. 25.

conflictual plurality is rhetoric. Rhetoric is the discourse of partisanship par excellence; the symbolic forms of literature – its genres and subgenres – are rhetorical formations vying for hegemony. A crucial point, one Moretti reiterates over time, is that literature is formed through compromises, 'problem-solving devices'.[23] It is an attempt to mediate psychic, social and political forces by forging temporary equilibria and defusing tensions. This idea (which draws on various sources, including Francesco Orlando and his Freudian theory of literature) is elaborated in various ways.[24] What Moretti emphasises is that literature tends towards consensus; it reveals a connection between form and power that utopian or critical-negative aesthetics typically underestimate.[25] What changes between the first and second phase of his work is, above all, the way in which that consensus is interpreted.

In 'The Soul and the Harpy', while rejecting the unified, monistic conception of historical epochs that he sees as implicit in Hegel's *Aesthetics*, Moretti also deprecates what he calls 'the zeitgeist fallacy':

> One succumbs to the allure of the sweeping generalization and falls into what we could call the '*Zeitgeist* fallacy'. Does the rhetoric of detective fiction imply a certain attitude towards science? Right then: 'the society of Conan Doyle's time', 'England in the eighteen nineties', 'the imperialist phase of capitalism' – whatever else one cares to invoke – all '*share that attitude*'.[26]

In truth, up until the phase of his quantitative research, Moretti often relies on explanations grounded in the zeitgeist: a form triumphs or fades, gains prominence or is forgotten, because it corresponds to the

---

23 Moretti, *Distant Reading*, p. 141.

24 In 'The End of the Beginning: A Reply to Christopher Prendergast' (Moretti, *Distant Reading*, pp. 137–58), Moretti cites Freud, Lévi-Strauss, Althusser, Orlando, Jameson and Eagleton. In 'The Soul and the Harpy' (Moretti, *Signs Taken for Wonders*, pp. 1–41), Moretti cites Orlando's *Towards a Freudian Theory of Literature* (Baltimore, MD: John Hopkins University Press, 1978) and *Lettura freudiana della 'Phèdre'* (Turin: Einaudi, 1971).

25 Moretti, *Signs Taken for Wonders*, pp. 27ff; Moretti, *Far Country*, pp. 10–11.

26 Moretti, *Signs Taken for Wonders*, p. 25.

becoming of social being – or, to put it more bluntly and without excessive scruples over vocabulary, because it corresponds to a particular epoch. While Moretti is fully aware of the plural, conflictual and competitive nature of forms – as opposed to a certain scholastic interpretation of idealist historicism – the ontological engine driving the process remains essentially the same.

Take, for example, Chapter 6 of *Modern Epic*. The subject is *Ulysses*. Moretti asks why stream of consciousness took hold so quickly and enjoyed such success that it had already become a topic of conversation by the late 1940s. He begins by citing Simmel's *The Metropolis and Mental Life* (1903) (fragmentation and the shocks of urban experience); he continues with Zola's *The Ladies' Paradise* (1883) (the fetish of the commodity, the nervous stimuli of advertising, the organised chaos of department stores); and then references *Les Voleuses des Grands Magasins* (1902) by Paul Dubuisson, head of the Sainte-Anne asylum in Paris and expert witness in the city's courts – one of the first to speak in clinical terms about the new psychology allegedly produced by urban, market-driven modernity.

Bourgeois inventions (the modern city, department stores, advertising) pervert bourgeois psychology because they destroy the supposed integrity of the bourgeois self. At this point, Moretti introduces *Ulysses*. Joyce is not merely a product of his time: he is one of literature's responses to a state of affairs, to a condition of the world.[27] But if that response succeeds – if it outcompetes other ways of interpreting its time – it is because *Ulysses* gives form to aspects of what, despite the disavowal we read in 'The Soul and the Harpy', two centuries ago was called the zeitgeist. And there is nothing wrong with that – quite the contrary. If up close it seems that Benjamin is right in criticising Hegel and Ranke, and Bourdieu is right in criticising Proust (history written by the victors erases the symbolic struggles that once divided an era; the historian's task is to read against the grain, to bring those contradictions back into view, to recover the standpoint of the defeated), then seen from afar, Hegel and Proust take the upper hand . Everyone who lived in a given time ends up resembling each other; the verdicts that emerge from the battles that once divided

27 Moretti, *Modern Epic*, pp. 123–66.

them become absolute in the eyes of later generations, who have different struggles and different thoughts; thousands of refined symbolic worlds lie forgotten, along with the passions that animated them and the conflicts that once set them ablaze; and if once it was impossible to confuse the Guermantes and the Verdurins, for a new generation the Verdurins *are* the new Guermantes. The short-sightedness of this way of doing cultural history has a solid ontological justification.

Moretti had both the merit and the strength to revisit and revise those premises. At the root of this intellectual shift lie the transformations previously discussed: scepticism towards traditional humanistic culture, but above all the geographical and social expansion of the literary field. In *Atlas of the European Novel*, and later in the multi-volume *Il romanzo*, Moretti grapples with the problem of the representativeness of the canon and with literary globalisation. His response consists of multiple strategic moves. It includes developing a model for understanding world literature (*Atlas*, *Distant Reading*); collaborative research (*Il romanzo*, *La letteratura in laboratorio*); quantitative data analysis; and a geopolitical model of global literary exchange in which numbers and flows tend to replace canons, and Darwinism begins to take the place of Marxism as the guiding philosophical framework.

5. The Tides and the Moon

What has Franco Moretti written about? What is the overarching theme of his work? It seems to me that his oeuvre can be understood as a sustained interpretation of modernity conducted through literature: the emergence of a secular idea of sovereignty, the rise of the continental and British bourgeoisie, the unravelling of its moral compromises and perceptual structures between the late nineteenth and early twentieth centuries, the expansion of cultural spaces, and the rise of mass society – global in scope but locally rooted – that is, in part, the heir of the historical bourgeoisie and, in other respects, a new and regressive force.

In the first phase of this project (*The Way of the World*, *Modern Epic*, *The Bourgeois*, *Far Country*), the reflection proceeds from exemplary texts (modern tragedy, *Robinson Crusoe*, the great nineteenth-century novels, major works of Anglophone modernism and American literature, the world epics) and expands outward to the context, to the historical moment that produced them. This Moretti also acts as a critic of culture, revealing the contradictions between what the bourgeoisie promises and its failure to deliver, the tension between the supposed universality of its values and the reality of its practices. The second Moretti pursues the same project by relinquishing his own canons and adopting a new method. Distant reading is an attempt to respond by other means to the same conditions that gave rise to New Historicism and Cultural Studies. Among literary critics, Moretti – together with Pascale Casanova – has done the most to interpret *world literature*, and he is the one who has most rigorously addressed the challenge of developing a literary theory adequate to the digital archive.

If the sharpest critiques of the first Moretti were formulated by the second Moretti, the theories of world literature and distant reading from the later phase have, in turn, become the subject of extensive debate – much of which is thoroughly examined in other essays in this volume. To my mind, the geopolitical model of literature that Moretti proposed – centre, semi-periphery, periphery; the notion that the centre exports forms which the semi-periphery and periphery then hybridise with local materials – remains compelling. Equally convincing are some of the Stanford Literary Lab's attempts to map the other axis along which human space extends: the social. The first part of the collective essay 'Canon/Archive', for example, is an interesting effort to quantify literary prestige, reconstructing the social field of the English novel between 1770 and 1830 – essentially replicating Bourdieu through numerical data.[28] The second part is more open to criticism: it is valuable for the data it generates, but it fails to offer an explanatory model that goes beyond those already provided – very effectively – by Bourdieu, and later Casanova. The essay's conclusions acknowledge this difficulty: quantitative analysis cannot establish a correlation between morphology and a text's social prestige, or between morphology and aesthetic complexity.

---

28 The same attempt is made by some of the pamphlets of the Literary Lab. See Ed Finn, 'Becoming Yourself: The Afterlife of Reception', *Pamphlet* 3 of the Stanford Literary Lab, at litlab.stanford.edu (2011).

In the end, it confirms what was already known: the texts that endure are those that, at a given moment, align with the preferences of elite cultural niches – those still capable of transforming their tastes into canon. In this second phase, Moretti assumes the role of observer, of scientist; the critical-negative impulse, which was always central in the earlier phase, is now largely confined to the awareness that cultural exchange is structurally unequal, and to analysis of the mechanisms that sustain that inequality.[29]

In a passage of his reply to Prendergast, discussing the two facets of his work, Moretti cites a metaphor by Marc Bloch:

> 'Tides are certainly connected to the phases of the moon', wrote Marc Bloch in *The Historian's Craft*, 'but in order to know it for sure one had first to independently determine the ones and the others.' The fact that *Distant Reading* is published alongside *The Bourgeois* – a book that couldn't be more unlike it in spirit and execution – makes me think that I prefer studying tides and the moon independently of each other. Whether or not a synthesis will follow, remains to be seen.[30]

Those who study the movements of the moon relativise the tides, seeing them as the effect of a cause. Those who study the moon's movements are also alienated, uprooted – people who regard the tides as shadows, not material things. In the latest stages of modernity, the globalisation of culture and the explosion of archives have unsettled what we in our niches have always taken for granted. At the same time, what we have always taken for granted are also our real problems – the things that truly belong to us, whatever content we associate with the pronoun 'we'. Reconciling the two sides, bridging books like *Distant Reading* and *The Bourgeois*, is objectively difficult. This is also because world literature is a mechanical, not an organic, unity: it gathers together cultures that largely ignore each other, since they do not know each other's languages; they know a few trees, not the forest, and understand others through

29 Roberto Schwarz noted this as well – cited in Moretti, *Distant Reading*, p. 50.

30 Moretti, *Distant Reading*, p. 138.

stereotypes. And since the politics of translation, like culture more generally, is increasingly shaped by the market, it becomes ever harder to take seriously the image we have of other literatures, as is made evident by the distorted images other national cultures hold of our own. The world expands, but individual literatures are far more vernacular and far more unknown than they might seem; and a title like *Far Country* is, in the end, appropriate for nearly any international exchange. Likewise, the problems that interest us are more regional than our cosmopolitan sensibility is ready to admit. A region may span a continent, but it is still bounded. Ours will not be the generations to inhabit a world culture with anything like the internal coherence – still fragile – achieved by Western literatures over the past few centuries. Comparative literature remains more a project than a discipline.

5

Morphology in America: Evolutionary Theory as an Experiment in Radical Sociology

Andrea Miconi

1. Forms

On an abstract level, at least, matters have been clear for some time. 'The sociological consideration of art falls down above all when, in analysing the content of artistic creations, it attempts to draw a straight line between that content and particular economic relations. The social element of literature is instead its form.'[1]

Form as the social element of literature: a major insight, and one on which the humanities have built surprisingly little in the century since the young Lukács first formulated it. For while there have been many studies on artistic morphology, some of them outstanding, one must look beyond literary theory to find them. A striking example is Max Weber's analysis (representative of that Wilhelmine sociology which was so attuned to form, as Moretti has noted) of the relationship between tonal music and the rationalisation of the world.[2] That rationalisation, Weber explains, was made possible only through harmonic intervals built on prime numbers lower than seven, unlike in medieval or Byzantine

1 Georg Lukács, 'Entwicklungsgeschichte des modernen Dramas', *Werke*, vol. 15 (Darmstadt: Neuwied, 1981 [1911]). Lukács expressed the same concept in *Die Seele und die Formen.* See Georg Lukács, *Soul and Form*, transl. Anna Bostock (New York: Columbia University Press, 2010 [1916]).

2 Franco Moretti, *Far Country: Scenes from American Culture* (London/New York: Verso, 2019), p. 11.

music.[3] His analysis thus goes extraordinarily deep, pointing towards what Moretti would later call 'sociological formalism' (which, incidentally, is not at all the oxymoron it might seem).

Literary theory, by contrast, has offered far fewer histories of form. On the one hand, criticism has rarely freed itself from a normative orientation; on the other, it must be said honestly that sociology has not done much better, contenting itself with loose analogies or vague references to context, without ever fully confronting the object of study.

As we know, it is precisely literary morphology to which Moretti has devoted much of his intellectual energy, along a trajectory that can ideally be condensed into three main assumptions: the initial investigation of forms as abstractions of social relations (as seen in some of the essays collected in *Signs Taken for Wonders*); the now-legendary metaphor of the centaur-critic that shapes the middle period of *Modern Epic*, situated at the confluence of close reading and evolutionary theory; and finally, his work on abstract models, which will occupy the bulk of the pages that follow, and which constitutes the penultimate stage of his research before the computational turn.

It must be said, if we are to be honest, that a fully developed theory of literary morphology lies beyond the scope of this essay, and perhaps beyond my own expertise. Still, it seems clear to me that 'form' is often used to refer to quite different things, ranging from genre theory to narratology, stylistics and textual linguistics. For this reason, I will focus on a more oblique aspect of Moretti's reflection, one that is, in its own way, broadly Weberian: namely, the methodological separation between the *real object* – a given novel, or a specific work – and the *object of knowledge*, understood as the abstract plane on which one can analyse the constants and variables of literary history.

Hence the three main morphological studies proposed by Moretti: polyphony in the macro-text of modern epic; free indirect style in the nineteenth- and twentieth-century novel; and the clue in the structure of detective fiction. Although not initially mapped as a diagram, the trajectory of polyphony forms the central thread of *Modern Epic*: a stylistic

---

3 Max Weber, *The Rational and Social Foundations of Music* (Carbondale, IL: Southern Illinois Press, 1958 [1921]).

score that first emerges in the archetype of modern epic – *Faust*, especially in the Walpurgisnacht scene – and then takes an unusual path.[4] Throughout the nineteenth century, polyphonic writing – rather than reappearing in the pure dialogism that Bakhtin identifies as the epochal exception of Dostoevsky – is absorbed into narrative structures that are capable of both amplifying and constraining it. In *Moby-Dick*, for instance, it is filtered through Ishmael's narrative voice, which brings the myriad languages of Ahab's crew under control.

In Whitman, it takes the form of rhetorical questions that simulate an interlocutor who is in fact absent – an artifice that makes *Leaves of Grass* the ideal symbolic form of modern democracy, in which the popular perspective is solicited but not truly heard, subsumed instead into the abstract space of public discourse. In *Bouvard et Pécuchet*, polyphony gives way to the impersonal viewpoint, a cultural trait of mass democracy reduced to the dull mediocrity of common sense. In the twentieth century, polyphony erupts anew in the fluid languages of *Ulysses* ('the first six chapters dominated by the stream of consciousness', Moretti writes, 'the last seven by polyphony').[5] But just as the fabric of narrative appears permanently torn, the pendulum of history swings back. In *The Waste Land*, multilingualism is reabsorbed into the depth of myth through the invocation of archetypes, marked by the use of definite articles. *One Hundred Years of Solitude*, finally, offers Western culture what it can no longer produce on its own: the purity of a radically monologic narrative, which contains the disorder of the world-system within the enchanted voice of an omnipotent narrator. As evolutionary theory tells us, geographic discontinuity is the key to morphological variation; in the

---

4 *Modern Epic* does in fact contain another vaguely Darwinian study – the one on the evolution of the stream of consciousness. See Franco Moretti, *Modern Epic: The World System from Goethe to García Márquez* (London: Verso, 1996), pp. 168–80. However, this concerns a technique that does not recur throughout the macro-text, and seems to me to characterise not modern epic as such, but certain variants of it, such as the metropolitan one. In contrast, polyphony, by directly shaping the linguistic plurality of the world-system, seems to me a temptation inherent to the genre (because what Moretti is proposing here is in fact the existence of a new genre, even if not everyone has noticed it).

5 Moretti, *Modern Epic*, p. 183.

same way, as a literary technique moves across regions, it undergoes divergent re-functionalisations – but, in the case of modern epic, it also encounters resistance to its capacity for speciation.

Beneath the surface, the struggle plays out between the rationalising impulse of the bourgeois novel and the modernist passion for polyphony, driven by a crisis of anthropocentrism – until the epic temptation rewinds the reel of history, revealing the reactionary nature of Faust's project to master the world.[6]

The tree of free indirect style likewise begins with a classic case, that of Jane Austen, and branches out around a major bifurcation: on one side, the orientation towards the individual, introspection, and the first person; on the other, towards the second person, the collective, and the spoken word.[7] If free indirect discourse expresses the encounter between the individual and the social planes, its spectrum of variations – its leaning more towards one or the other – measures the tone of the mediation achieved, and reveals the particular compromise through which each form of civilisation responds to the great dilemma of modernity.

So it is with Austen and the invention of the socialised individual: those young women coming of age who narrate themselves in the third person because they have so thoroughly internalised the gaze directed at them. And so it is with Flaubert's characters: condemned to speak in the words of others, so deeply has the mechanism of *doxa* taken hold of their patterns of perception. And so it is, on the opposite side of the tree, with the village murmurings in Verga, or the echoes of the working class in Zola: cases of the collective voice, which show how the same technique may serve divergent functions depending on the symbolic demands it encounters along its migratory path.

Thus, while nineteenth-century mimesis bends free indirect discourse towards the communal viewpoint, the cooler bourgeois narration of the twentieth century – with Proust, Mann and Woolf – returns it to the service of individual subjectivity, gradually moving away from the historical compromise embodied in the Bildungsroman. And it is beyond the boundaries of European culture that free indirect style undergoes

6 Ibid., p. 228.

7 Franco Moretti, *Graphs, Maps, Trees* (London: Verso, 2005), pp. 81–8.

its most radical variations: first in Dostoevsky's dialogic second person, and then, in a different and opposite semi-periphery, in the dominant first-person ego of the Latin American dictator novel – a voice that absorbs everything around it like a collapsing star. Here, Moretti explicitly embraces a Darwinian framework, invoking in particular Ernst Mayr's concept of 'allopatric speciation': 'A new species (or at any rate a new formal arrangement), arising when a population migrates into a new homeland, must quickly change in order to survive. Just like free indirect style when it moves into Petersburg, Aci Trezza, Dublin, Ciudad Trujillo . . .[8]

2. Diagrams

Displacement as the key to random morphological variation, and then the survival of the fittest as the non-random criterion of natural selection: it is on this second aspect that the most successful of Moretti's trees is constructed, the one devoted to the role of the clue in the crime novel. In this case, Moretti immediately identifies the decisive element – the clue – and then maps its range of variation in an evolutionary diagram that explains, with crystalline clarity, the canonisation of the Sherlock Holmes cycle.[9] With one bifurcation after another, Conan Doyle's competitors fall away: some because they do not use clues at all, others because they grasp their necessity but fail to understand how to use them, merely having characters mention them or burying them in inaccessible corners of the plot. That even part of Conan Doyle's own output ends up on the 'wrong' side of the tree, where clues are invisible or indecipherable, confirms that literary history is shaped more by imperfection than by intelligent design. Conan Doyle simply

8 Ibid., p. 90.

9 Identifying the decisive element from the outset is a move that may be open to criticism, such as that voiced by Christopher Prendergast in 'Evolution and Literary History', *New Left Review* II/34 (2005). Prendergast's essay, however, disappoints, as it merely argues that many other factors could explain Conan Doyle's success (which is true), without offering any alternative hypothesis – rendering the argument entirely futile.

used clues better than the rest – but not perfectly, and certainly not systematically.[10] Of course, Conan Doyle's success might have other explanations. For instance, to start with a simple hypothesis: publishing in a more popular magazine offers a considerable advantage over the competition.

To test this objection, Moretti repeats the experiment on all the detective stories published in *The Strand*, and produces a perfectly symmetrical tree: since almost all the other works have disappeared despite the magazine's prestige, the explanation must lie within the literary field itself, in the morphology of the texts.[11] Hypothesis, experimental verification, falsification of the hypothesis: scientifically watertight.

Implicit and almost unconscious in *Modern Epic*, and explicitly foregrounded later, the evolutionary model seems to offer something genuinely new: an explanation for why one form proves more effective than another – the canonisation of Shklovsky's cadet branch, with something more: namely, an account of the process, the *how* and the *why*. Which suddenly reminds us of an old friend: 'To do it justice, a centaur-like critic would be required: half formalist, to deal with the how; half sociologist, to deal with the why. *Nota bene*: half and half. Not some reasonable compromise, but Jekyll and Hyde.'[12] Darwinian theory now appears to give real substance to that long-pursued project of literary history as comparative morphology: first, the random variation unleashed by narrative production, and then the canonisation of those variants best suited to solving problems. A cultural history without authors – and, in some respects, even without works – where the true protagonist is form, which, like Richard Dawkins's 'selfish gene', uses the organism of the novel to reproduce itself, tracing the submerged path of evolution.[13] A modest renunciation, perhaps, of the longstanding habit of reflecting on the moral and human meaning of literary poetics, in exchange for a significant gain: the possibility of objective, repeatable and comparable analysis. In other words, the fulfilment of the project of

10 Franco Moretti, *Distant Reading* (London: Verso, 2013), p. 72.

11 Ibid., pp. 73–4.

12 Moretti, *Modern Epic*, p. 6.

13 Richard Dawkins, *The Selfish Gene* (Oxford: Oxford University Press, 1976).

a 'falsifiable criticism', made up of 'univocal and potentially complete – and thus refutable – analyses.'[14]

As to why one might invoke the natural sciences rather than the social sciences – with all the epistemological challenges that entails – one could debate endlessly; for reasons of space, I will limit myself to a single observation. In short, the sociology of culture has failed to provide suitable models, settling instead for interpretations of the world based on literary metaphors, rather than recognising that it should be doing the opposite: analysing works of art on the basis of the socio-historical context in which they become canonised. Strictly speaking, I do not believe there exists a sociology of literature in the proper sense of the term – not in the same way, that is, as there exists a sociology of religion or a sociology of work.

So, Moretti's model must be perfect, then? Of course not, because there are no perfect models, and applying the laws of the natural sciences to the field of culture brings with it significant complications, which in this specific case I will reduce to four main issues.

In the first place, while Darwin's tree – that single, 'odd looking' tree that appears in the *Origin of Species* – measures generational intervals over the course of evolution, the branching points fixed by Moretti are not separated by regular temporal intervals.[15] They represent, therefore, a spectrum of variation – almost in a synchronic sense – rather than a truly phylogenetic process. We are perhaps closer to the kind of trees 'without roots' which, by definition, 'do not provide any indication about origins – i.e. the initial subdivisions or branching'.[16] What relationship they might have with the moment of origin of the literary technique under examination thus remains entirely to be clarified.

Secondly, with regard to the specifics of literary history, it is a fact that Moretti's trees operate on various analytical levels, ranging from morphology to stylistics, from the grammar of free indirect speech to the

---

14 Franco Moretti, *Signs Taken for Wonders: Essays in the Sociology of Literary Forms*, transl. Susan Fisher, David Forgacs and D. A. Miller (London: Verso, 1997 [1983], 2nd edn 1988), p. 23.

15 Moretti, *Graphs, Maps, Trees*, p. 67.

16 Luigi Luca Cavalli-Sforza, Paolo Menozzi and Alberto Piazza, *Storia e geografia dei geni umani* (Milan: Adelphi, 1997), p. 59.

narratological plane of clues. The evolutionary trajectory of the different forms may follow the same principle – character divergence; but it remains unclear what the ultimate unit of variation over time actually is. This is one of the most delicate issues within the broader research agenda of cultural evolution. As Luca Cavalli-Sforza has noted, we are in a situation somewhat analogous to the early phase of Darwinian theory, which was developed before the discovery of the laws of genetics – that is, before the identification of the key player in the process: the gene.[17]

Thirdly, as Alberto Piazza has noted in his commentary on Moretti's work, in evolutionary biology trees, the branches progressively diverge with no possibility of reconnecting, just as in the major model of the tree of human languages.[18] By contrast, literary forms continue to contaminate one another, and can re-converge even after having split apart. This opens up, as we will see, a critical issue: the role of convergence in the history of culture.

Finally, especially with regard to the study of clues in detective fiction, the fact that all the bifurcations are rendered as binary seems at odds with the principle of imperfection that should underpin Darwinian thinking. There is, after all, no reason to assume that evolution unfolds through differences reducible to dichotomous variables. And, given Moretti's premises, this may well be the most serious flaw in the entire approach.

Methodologically improvable and theoretically open to debate, the Darwinian model nonetheless offered a major analytical advantage: it offered what every researcher has always dreamed of – a rational explanation of historical processes. Moretti's approach also seemed to me a unique opportunity to free ourselves, in one stroke, from the major vices of academic work. First and foremost, there is literary criticism's highbrow tautology, which explains every text in terms of its uniqueness and always starts anew, as if cultural history were composed of a constellation

---

17 Luigi Luca Cavalli-Sforza, *L'evoluzione della cultura. Proposte concrete per studi futuri* (Turin: Codice, 2004), pp. 67–8.

18 Alberto Piazza, 'Evolution at Close Range', afterword to Moretti, *Graphs, Maps, Trees*, pp. 95–113; Cavalli-Sforza, Menozzi and Piazza, *Storia e geografia*, pp. 190–2.

of masterpieces rather than a dense dialogue between canonical and non-canonical forms. Second, the Hegelian historiographical schema, because here the animating force of literary production is not the interplay between author and zeitgeist – or between soul and form – but a messy, competitive, triangular relationship between the symbolic needs of a historical moment and the various responses available on the market. And, while we're at it, also poststructuralist doctrine, with its hunt for original sin and its obsession with expanding the canon: because even if there is a large degree of contingency in how authors seek a path through the space of forms, Moretti's analysis suggests that there is very little arbitrariness in the superior effectiveness of some over others – so much so that Conan Doyle, for example, objectively outperformed his contemporaries in responding to the challenges posed by modern complexity.[19]

More than the 'spirit of the age', we have come to speak, in Moretti's words, of 'all rhetorical forms [that] aspire to *become* the "Spirit of the Age"', and of their struggle for survival: a method that is repeatable, immediately useful and, I would go so far as to say, *simple*, in the noblest sense of the term, for subjecting literary history to a scientific mode of inquiry.[20] It is the same feeling I had, in my own small way, when I applied Moretti's model to a sample of 140 twentieth-century Latin American novels. The diagram, first of all, made sense of the symbolic division of labour between metropolitan narratives steeped in realism and formal experimentation, and those set in imagined places or remote territories, which were tasked with reviving the stylistic features of myth.

Within this latter cycle, the model also helped explain why so many authors, like Conan Doyle's rivals, ended up making the wrong choices – reducing the

---

19 I imagine that for a far-left intellectual like Moretti, this result – that the canonised forms are the ones that work best – is not particularly gratifying, as emerges in his reflections on the critiques by Christopher Prendergast and Roberto Schwarz (see Moretti, *Distant Reading*, pp. 137–58). In some ways, it is the same discomfort one feels when studying the role of Hollywood in the symbolic economy of the twentieth century: a tool of cultural imperialism, but also an extraordinary site of creative production and stylistic innovation. At the very least, this is something I hope I have learned from Moretti's work: if we don't like what we find, as researchers we can't just pretend we didn't find it.

20 Moretti, *Signs Taken for Wonders*, p. 25.

magical to an anomalous event, isolating it in a single deviant character, or confining it within the bounds of direct speech – as opposed to the few who made it an everyday reality, the very fabric of the quotidian, and who aligned almost perfectly with the epicentre of the *real maravilloso*.[21]

An elegant framework, designed to withstand the fire of infinite tests: again, it seemed we might finally be able to arrive at answers – debatable and certainly partial ones, but something clear for once. A golden opportunity, and one we promptly let slip through our fingers. We would hear no more of evolutionary trees or the space of literary forms: for it is precisely here that Moretti's research comes to a halt, just when the challenge of constructing a falsifiable scientific method seemed within reach. And since I have never quite understood why Moretti abandoned such an effective model, I will venture a few hypotheses. I believe there are two main considerations that might explain the withdrawal from the Darwinian model, beyond the more contingent circumstances that may also have played a role: first, the relationship between divergence and convergence in literary forms; and, second, the difficulty of extending morphological analysis to the large numbers of ordinary literature. These two critical factors will be the focus of the following sections.

3. Branches

The first complication arises from the suspicion that the vital mechanism of evolution – divergence – can only explain part of literary history. Moretti, who is of course aware of this, takes up the challenge by reproducing Kroeber and Basalla's tree of culture, whose branches, in addition to diverging, sometimes end up intertwining.[22] The history of literature, then, ought to be seen as an alternation between phases of divergence and convergence: proportional relationship between the two cycles remains to be determined; but since no model can claim universal scope, the compromise seems, all in all, acceptable.

---

21 Andrea Miconi, 'Dal *real maravilloso* al realismo magico. Approccio evolutivo alla formazione di un genere', *Paragrafo* 2 (2006), pp. 27–48.

22 Moretti, *Graphs, Maps, Trees*, pp. 78–88.

Divergence, to be explained according to the laws of evolution, is followed by a phase of convergence, which will obviously require the application of different models. This objection, in itself, would not be all that damaging, if it did not carry with it something more troubling: namely, the ability, I believe, to summon some old ghosts.

A form is always the result of the action of a force, Moretti has repeatedly stated over the years, quoting his favourite line from D'Arcy Thompson: '. . . in the comparison of kindred forms . . . we discern the magnitude and the direction of the forces which have sufficed to convert the one form into another'.[23] And I fear this is the crux of the matter: coming to terms with the force behind the drive towards convergence. The cardinal sin of literary theory has a precise name, Moretti once wrote, and it 'is named Georg Wilhelm Friedrich Hegel' – for what it is worth, I agree.[24] The zeitgeist: this is the old ghost I am talking about. A sociologically flimsy concept, since every historical epoch is marked by cultural currents that are diverse – by alternative and conflicting 'world volitions' (*Weltvollen*), as Karl Mannheim famously insisted – and yet so deeply ingrained that it inexorably resurfaces, generation after generation, to exert its influence.[25]

And as far as we are concerned, while we expect the space of forms to open itself to infinite mutation – expecting, in the Darwinian sense, that quantity will generate variety – a contrary force seems to act upon the course of history: the eternal return of the same figures, the obsessive repetition of stylistic formulas, the pressure to conform to a canon, the countless novels that all tell the same story.[26] This is a problem Moretti, in a way, eventually embraces, with that passion for elementary questions that is the mark of great thinkers: why the novel is written in prose; why

---

23 D'Arcy Wentworth Thompson, *On Growth and Form*, new edn (Cambridge: CUP, 1942), p. 1027, cited in Moretti, *Graphs, Maps, Trees*, p. 63 (which incorrectly cites the shorter first edition of 1917).

24 Moretti, *Signs Taken for Wonders*, p. 25.

25 Karl Mannheim, 'The Problem of Generations', in *Essays on the Sociology of Knowledge*, transl. Paul Kecskemeti (Oxford: Oxford University Press, 1952 [1928]), pp. 276–322.

26 Charles Darwin, *On the Origin of Species* (London: John Murray, 1859). For the reason that quantity does not always produce variety in the world of culture, I fear that it will be necessary to return to reading Adorno.

it tends towards a certain length; why it so often contains plots of adventure; why novel titles grow increasingly similar – and so on.[27]

Confronting the dark mass produced by literary convergence is, above all, the aim of the 'other' Moretti, the one who reflects on the great dominant structures of the serious century, the *Bildungsroman*, or bourgeois fiction: where a particular formal or rhetorical feature becomes so central, so hegemonic, that it emerges as the defining matrix of an epoch.

In this context, the risk of making concessions to the zeitgeist – to the so-called serious century – is genuinely high, and for that very reason must be firmly resisted. Hegel's limitation, as Lukács already pointed out, was in failing to recognise fully – indeed, often misrecognising – the fact that 'the causes of the prose of modern life are rooted in the capitalist division of labour'.[28] And it is precisely here, in the moment of primitive accumulation, that the rupture between the individual and society is located: 'The unity of public and private life in the earliest stages of ancient society is the foundation of the pathos of ancient poetry, that immediate bond between individual passion, realistically portrayed, and the fundamental problems of social existence. This bond is absent in the reality of capitalist society'.[29] The organisation of production, rather than the sacred flame of the zeitgeist, is the true force acting behind the convergence of forms.

This is presumably why Moretti is drawn to Marxist theorists like Fredric Jameson and Roberto Schwarz, who help to explain the world through the major shifts in material history: the enclosure of common land, the transition from ancient regimes to modern state structures, the configuration of urban spaces, the capitalist division of labour.

Naturally, the problem with the notion of zeitgeist is not that dominant cultural logics do not exist, but rather that such dominance is the *result* of canonisation – unpredictable and contested – not a philosophical precondition of artistic production.

---

27 Moretti, *Distant Reading*, pp. 159–78, 179–210.

28 Georg Lukács, 'Problemy teorii romana', *Literaturnyj kritik* 2 (1935), pp. 214–49. [Miconi cites the Italian translation in Vittorio Strada, ed., *Problemi di teoria del romanzo*, transl. Clara Strada Janovič (Turin: Einaudi, 1976), pp. 6–7.]

29 Ibid.

And here, for once, a bit of sociology proves helpful: I am thinking especially of Pierre Bourdieu's concept of the 'field', already adapted in a similar way by Pascale Casanova, or Howard Becker's model of 'worlds of art', which both offer compelling accounts of the power relations out of which structures of aesthetic value are forged.[30] To redeem the theme of convergence from the burden of idealism, in short, there is only one way forward: a materialist historiography of culture, which brings into focus the concrete agents at work behind the processes of canonisation. The history of forms, after all, is also the history of the vectors that distribute them, of the institutions that bring them to market, and of the contexts that select them: schools, publishers, readers, and then agents, tastemakers, mass media, and so on. The task, as Moretti wrote halfway through the *Atlas*, was to build 'a bridge between two lines of research: book history – and the history of forms. They seem very distant; they *are* very distant. And that's why the bridge is useful.'[31]

And of course, once again, we took care not to build it.

4. Numbers

Expanding the framework of discourse to a broader scale – the centuries of the *longue durée*, the world-system of *Weltliteratur*, the archives of normal literature – requires the adoption of increasingly abstract concepts, as Moretti repeatedly observes; and he is right. Over time, his models come to seem almost rarefied: from the narration of the city in the words of great novelists to the geographic maps of the *Atlas*, and from there to their further abstraction in the form of diagrams – ideal narrative geometries now detached from any direct connection with physical place.[32] It is along this trajectory, I believe, that Moretti's recent turn towards computational analysis can be understood: because nothing is

30 Pierre Bourdieu, 'Champ du pouvoir, champ intellectuel et habitus de classe', *Scolies* 1 (1971); Pascale Casanova, *La République mondiale des lettres* (Paris: Seuil, 1999); Howard S. Becker, *Art Worlds* (Berkeley/Los Angeles: University of California Press, 1984).

31 Franco Moretti, *Atlas of the European Novel* (London: Verso, 1998), p. 143.

32 Moretti, *Graphs, Maps, Trees*, pp. 56–64.

more abstract than numbers, and the promise of big data, on the surface at least, seemed to be the most coherent conclusion to the entire arc of his research.

> While I was studying evolution . . . Ernst Mayr's theory of speciation made me aware of the role of geography in the generation of new forms; so I turned to cartography, to make literary maps; but maps need homogeneous data, so I started to extract small series from novels (beginnings and endings in Austen, Balzac's young men in Paris) . . . Evolution, geography, maps, series, diagrams . . . One step led to the next; one step *asked* for the next. And one day I realized that the study of morphological *evolution* had itself morphed into the analysis of quantitative data.[33]

And yet this is not how things went. Ideally, the progression laid out by Moretti makes perfect sense; in practice, however, computational analysis led him far from his earlier models, into a neutral terrain still untilled by theory – as commonly happens in the early stages of exploratory research. This was for countless reasons of various kinds, no doubt, but also due to to a highly technical issue that forms the missing link between the era of the first distant reading and that of the Literary Lab: multivariate analysis.

As I have noted, evolutionary theory provides a remarkably clear explanatory model, but only on the condition that we accept that divergence in the space of forms is not always as radical as we might like. More often than not, it comes down to minimal but decisive variations: whether a clue is decodable or not (which really is a matter of nuance); how much *doxa* is embedded in just a few words of free indirect style – and so on. Not dramatic bifurcations, but rather shades, details that demand the care and patience of very close analysis – and thus, again, the selection of a relatively small sample. Paradoxical as it may seem, the kind of analysis Moretti conducted on clues can require even more time than traditional close reading.

As a result, the method proves extraordinarily useful for in-depth textual analysis, but of limited applicability to the large-scale archives of

33 Moretti, *Distant Reading*, p. 179.

'normal literature', or what Margaret Cohen has called the 'great unread' – everything we have never read and likely never will.[34]

Unless, of course, we find a different solution. And indeed, there is a technique capable of automatically querying a large sample of texts across multiple dimensions simultaneously – a technique used, not accidentally, for frequency distribution in evolutionary studies: factor analysis, or multivariate analysis. Yet, after an initial attempt made by Moretti and his team in 2011 – to generate computerised clusters of Shakespeare's works and then of novelistic genres – we hear little more about it.[35] And unfortunately, I think, for good reason. As a researcher, I know all too well the lingering sense of unfulfilled promise that multivariate analysis tends to leave behind: an advanced technique still in search of a theoretical framework robust enough to guide it, and one that rarely yields results equal to expectations. In the case of breaking down literary works, the issue boils down to a problem as intuitive as it is difficult to solve in practice: translating the concepts of morphology (or of textual linguistics, or narratology) into unambiguous variables, and then quantifying them. Without the intermediate step of operational definition, theory and analysis fall apart: the computational software spits out a vast mass of data that answers no question – and pure computation, because of the times we live in, inevitably takes centre stage.

Personally, I am a great enthusiast of quantitative history, while for a range of reasons – reasons that would require a separate discussion – I remain sceptical of computational analysis (which is obviously not the same thing). That said, I do not agree with many of the criticisms levelled at Moretti's most recent work: in particular, I do not share the accusation that he produces trivial results despite substantial research efforts.

---

34 Margaret Cohen, *The Sentimental Education of the Novel* (Princeton NJ: Princeton University Press, 1999), p. 23.

35 Sarah Allison, Ryan Heuser, Matthew Jockers, Franco Moretti and Michael Witmore, 'Quantitative Formalism: An Experiment', *Pamphlet 1* of the Stanford Literary Lab, 2011, at litlab.stanford.edu; also published in *n+1* 13 (2012). Even if technically successful, the Lab's first experiment already contained the seeds of the problems to come: the software worked well (in my view, quite inexplicably) in terms of genre classification, but it wasn't actually answering any question that it hadn't raised on its own.

Perhaps it is because, as a sociologist, I am more accustomed than literary critics to the sophisticated dullness of data; or perhaps it is because I remember the day at Sapienza University of Rome, when we discovered the work of Paul Lazarsfeld, one of the founders of quantitative research.

It was 1949 when Lazarsfeld presented the findings of a study on the lives of American soldiers, based on an astonishing 600,000 interviews. An enormous undertaking, yes, but with results that seemed modest and largely predictable: essentially, white soldiers showed more ambition for career advancement than African American ones – something that at the time surprised no one (to the point that Lazarsfeld could conclude that 'the lack of ambition among Negroes is almost proverbial'); better-educated servicemen exhibited more signs of psychological disturbance, as did educated people in general; and men from rural areas adjusted more easily to the front than those from cities.[36] These were, indeed, predictable results, Lazarsfeld noted: after all, country people are more used to getting by, to living outdoors, and to enduring the discomforts of weather, so it was normal that they fared better away from civilisation. But if the answers are 'so obvious' that they align with common sense, Lazarsfeld explicitly asks, why spend 'so much money and so much energy for results of this kind?' Indeed, what was the point?

Except that Lazarsfeld was brazenly bluffing – in order to deliver one of the greatest lessons in the history of methodology. The actual results were, in fact, exactly the opposite of the (false) ones he had just listed: African Americans were by no means unambitious, and it was men from the cities – not rural recruits – who adapted better to life on the front. And even that, strange as it may seem, is easy to explain: urban residents were mostly factory workers, and thus more accustomed to the division of labour and the regimentation required by military life. Two opposing outcomes, yet both seem 'obvious' – because in the humanities, every answer feels obvious once we have learned it. The purpose of research, let's face it, is rarely to uncover hidden truths, and far more often to bring order or establish a hierarchy among equally plausible hypotheses. If the English novel had been the hegemonic form of the nineteenth century,

---

36 Paul Lazarsfeld, 'The American Soldier: An Expository Review', *Public Opinion Quarterly* 13: 3 (1949), p. 380.

for instance, we would consider it a self-evident fact, and we could easily draw a historical analogy with Hollywood: after all, Britain was the dominant imperial power at the time, and global rule has always required instruments of soft power. But we know instead that it was the French novel that captured the European public's imagination – and that too, in retrospect, we can just as easily explain in terms of the autonomy of the cultural field, at the intersection between Bourdieu's sociology and Braudel's historical geography. Likewise, it is easy to scoff when network analysis reveals that the central character in *Hamlet* is, well, Hamlet.[37] But to me, it is more worthwhile to reflect on the distinction between genres in which a work's protagonist also functions as the primary connector, and those in which the symbolic core of the story does *not* correspond to the graph's central node. I doubt that *Dracula*, or even *Père Goriot*, would be geometrically central in the network of character relationships – and once again, we might find that so easy to explain that it ends up seeming obvious.

I will end this digression to make clear that I am not questioning the value of computational analysis per se, though I have my opinions, but rather registering the discontinuity it marks, specifically, with respect to Franco Moretti's earlier work. This is where the myth of the centaur-critic breaks down, and the dialogue between analysis and theory comes to a halt: a fact vividly illustrated by the simultaneous publication of two books, *Distant Reading* and *The Bourgeois*, which stand in stark opposition to one another.

Of Moretti's methodological revolution – introducing a research protocol based on empirical observation into a disciplinary field where everyone is 'free to do as they like' – little now seems to remain, perhaps for a practical reason as well.[38] In truth, the distant reading project met with only modest success, and we have seen relatively few maps, graphs or trees make the rounds (I gave it a try myself, but being a dilettante in

37 I am obviously referring here to the criticism received by the work presented in 'Network Theory, Plot Analysis', which Moretti himself recognises as being only partially successful (Moretti, *Distant Reading*, pp. 211ff). The overall conclusions are far more complex than this, however, even if there is not the space to discuss them here.

38 Moretti, *Signs Taken for Wonders*, p. 24.

literary studies, it is no surprise that no one noticed). In the end, was the proposal of the field's most celebrated theorist, the 'great iconoclast' of literary studies, no more than a drop in the ocean?[39] To some extent, yes, I think, because academia is a peculiar place, where one can cite an author endlessly without really taking them seriously, let alone attempting to apply their models.

A final remark. If comparative morphology and material history never gained a foothold in the humanities – a fact which we can only regret – computational analysis, on the other hand, is thriving, becoming dominant in departments across the globe, and opening up a sea of possibilities. I know: this is a rather crude and partial explanation for Moretti's final turn. But the sociology of science, especially in the 'strong programme' iteration, has long emphasised how the material conditions of intellectual labour shape the research protocols developed in the lab.[40] And so, this is where a long path has led: to that same big-data paradigm that is steadily taking control of the world. It would seem, in the end, that the spirit of the age has had its revenge on its most resolute adversary.

---

39 John Sutherland, 'The Ideas Interview: Franco Moretti', *Guardian*, 9 January 2006.

40 David Bloor, 'The Strengths of the Strong Programme', *Philosophy of the Social Sciences* II/2 (1981), pp. 199–213.

6

Towards a More Rational Literary History

Patricia McManus

> *To deprive the bourgeoisie not of its art but of its concept of art, this is the precondition of a revolutionary argument.*
>
> Hans Hess, *Pictures as Arguments*

The above is not a sentence one could imagine Franco Moretti writing. His literary-historical work does not take the style of a political intervention even when the thrust of his argument is polemical – the rewriting of the task of literary history, for example. If his work is addressed to the future, to being part of what creates that future, it addresses itself only to improving the specialised future of literary history itself. Though he responds to his critics – especially when he agrees with them – these responses are rarely the object of his attention for long, but are treated more as an opportunity for adjustment or refinement, detailed but brief, before a return to the main object of enquiry: the past. The gaze of his work is typically turned to the material – to what it throws up to confound extant approaches to itself, to how methods from other fields can lend themselves to the project of making visible or legible – new or newly meaningful – reworked or hitherto undiscovered aspects of that material. His own style is not primarily argumentative but inquiring, exploratory and speculative – and explanatory, making deft use of empirical work, the digging out of patterns, firstly to indicate the need for theoretical models from other fields, which are then adapted to posit and to test hypotheses to explain phenomena in the literary field. He is a careful reader of other historians' work, but he does not argue with them so much as use them to flesh out or to illustrate the need for his own – he is a champion user of quotations for this purpose.[1]

And yet Moretti's work has done much to disenchant the mode of literary history that the bourgeois concept of art needed: the mode of literary history as '*histoire* évenementielle, where the "events" are great works or great individuals'.[2] In Moretti's hands, literature promised to become genre, pattern and repetition, the series and its mutations – a player in the force-field contributing to the 'petrifying' of existence, the 'wearing out of forms', a 'regulative' and 'coercive' power.

Locked into or onto its object, and pursuing the goal only of making the field of that object 'longer, wider, deeper', Moretti's work is hugely ambitious and energetic, joyful (at times) in its ecumenical approach to the methods, models, traditions which will push the project of mapping and understanding a little further down the road. And it is meticulously materialist in that it will never knowingly succumb to idealism, but at the same time animated with a tremendous sense of the importance of the work, of a better – a more accurate – literary history.[3]

His is work, however, which seems curiously timeless if its time is taken as its own, immune to 'theory wars', to disciplinary shifts – even as it was itself the source of them – and to the whole catastrophic world

---

1 There are exceptions. One in particular deserves to be mentioned for the speed with which it is dismissed: Moretti's disagreement with Edward Said's reading that the Bertrams of Mansfield Park received material support from the slave trade, sugar and work on colonial plantations. No, says Moretti, the economic role of the British Empire was important but not 'indispensable' in the economic life of the landowners of the early nineteenth century, as well as in the Bertrams' financial affairs. The presence of colonial fortunes in the 'sentimental novels at the turn of the century' must be motivated by factors other than 'realism'. See Franco Moretti, *Atlas of the European Novel* (London: Verso, 1998), pp. 24–7.

2 Franco Moretti, *Signs Taken for Wonders: Essays in the Sociology of Literary Forms*, transl. Susan Fisher, David Forgacs and D. A. Miller (London: Verso, 1997 [1983], 2nd edn 1988), p. 13.

3 Moretti's work includes explorations of tragedy and other forms of drama, film, and some initial work on the language used by non-literary genres, including the annual reports of the World Bank. I will concentrate on the novel and its history in this essay.

outside the discipline. 'Now', any sense of existing in a 'now' is missing from his writing. This is something I will return to in my conclusion.

There is not space enough in this essay to do the work of situating Moretti fully within the Marxist literary traditions from which he emerged. His own work is punctuated by moments of self-reflection which, though brief, are informative enough about how he himself sees his beginnings and the trajectory he traced from them. What is needed is a more thorough and historicising interrogation of how and why the ensemble of Marxist literary-historical methods he tested and found wanting survives in altered form (or does not) in the landscape Moretti has opened up.

Such a task must await a longer work, but I hope to indicate here that it would be one worth completing. The governing question in this essay is: What is a Marxist literary history for? It is a crude question, but perhaps inevitably so, given the scope and sharpness of the challenges to extant understandings that Moretti's work has thrown down. The job of the question is to give focus to what follows: a brief sketch of literary history as Moretti saw it in the studies he produced before both 'Conjectures on World Literature' (2000) and *Graphs, Maps, Trees* (2005); a description of the promise of a richer literary history held out by that later work; and, finally, a conclusion which suggests that the projects inadequately described under the rubric of 'distant reading', while not in themselves Marxist, are ones a Marxist literary history must absorb into its own project of a political a formalism organised around questions of genre, a formalism newly attuned to questions of how, as well as to the older questions of why.

1. Before the Beginning: Souls and Forms

'Forme is power' runs the epigraph from *Leviathan* used by Moretti in 'The Soul and the Harpy', the essay introducing the several pieces of work that make up *Signs Taken For Wonders* (1983). Almost four decades later, in the opening essay of *Far Country* (2019), it is still form that is the hinge of his work, and form is still a shaping power: form operates as an '*agonistic* process: *anti*-chaotic . . . the *Realpolitik* of form: the gray zone where beauty comes into contact with power, and even with violence.'[4]

The identification of 'form' as the key category for a Marxist literary theory was by the 1980s a given: the formal patterns organising a text or genre, and the stylistic work done by those patterns, were the place where the imprint of historical forces and tensions could be accessed not only at their most acute, but also in ways that indicated the importance of culture to the successes and defeats of social reproduction. This was not a reduction of form to history, but rather a way of opening up a reading of what the text had made of history, how it had made itself look as if it was not historical at all, how it had *formed* itself.

The first essay after the important introduction in *Signs Taken for Wonders,* 'The Great Eclipse: Tragic Form as the De-consecration of Sovereignty', sets itself the task of examining how English tragedy of the early modern period prefigured the draining of legitimacy from the body and role of the absolute sovereign. For Moretti, the English tragedies have an especially freighted relationship with power, and a historiographically useful difference from the modern novel, the central genre of the world that would usurp that of the tragedies.

Written to be performed within the shade of absolutism, these plays dramatise a 'universe in which everything has its origin in the decision of the king'.[5] The fault lines of absolutism as a political system were structural and social, but involved also a conflict of ideas within which the plays operate. The imbrication of the political and the symbolic, or the articulation of the political as the symbolic, marks the

> crucial pertinence of the ideological field here. In the political system of absolutism, the relation between culture and power differs considerably from that obtaining in other kinds of society, capitalism in particular. In the latter, social power finds its legitimacy from the very beginning in the simple fact that it exists . . . [With absolutism] the legitimacy of social power derives from a form of divine investiture. Power is founded in a

4 Franco Moretti, 'Teaching in America', in *Far Country: Scenes from American Culture* (London/New York: Verso, 2019), p. 10.

5 Moretti, *Signs Taken for Wonders*, p. 43.

> transcendent design, in an intentional and significant order. Accordingly, political relations have the right to exist only in so far as they reproduce that order symbolically. In a word, if bourgeois property can have a meaning because it exists, absolute monarchy can exist because it has a meaning.[6]

A power legitimated through 'cultural' processes is extremely vulnerable to being delegitimated by those same forces. The tragic form has as its material the values or self-image of absolutism, complete with the internal frailties or pressure points of that self-image. Tragedy 'stages not the institutions of absolutism, but its culture, its values, its ideology'.[7]

Here, then, is a structural concept of tragedy, one 'capable of simultaneously defining a syntagmatic axis (plot) and a paradigmatic axis (values), and of clarifying the unique relation that obtains between them in tragedy', put to work to 'read' the situation of tragedy – its meanings – as a historical situation. It is a particularly ambitious and imaginative version of historical materialism: English tragedy is read as a form tightly entwined with – illegible without – the dissolution of the symbolic forms that had, briefly, been part of what had made absolutism possible.[8] The historical reading is one that proceeds from within the text, laying open by reading – by interpreting – its patterns and their mutations across political time.

In 'Dialectic of Fear', Moretti enters into the historical age and social sensibility where he would go on to spend most of his time: the expansive nineteenth century and its mover and shaker, the equally expansive but also frightened bourgeoisie. The essay takes as its object the social meanings of horror – what the forms of the 'modern monster' mean, and why or how they are desired and repulsed. Mary Shelley's *Frankenstein* (1818) and Bram Stoker's *Dracula* (1897) bookend the historical moment. Again Moretti proceeds immanently, taking a

6 Ibid., p. 44.

7 Ibid., p. 43.

8 There is a characteristically brief but persuasive critique of the failures of the thesis of the 'Elizabethan World picture', a thesis which prevents sight of what is precisely distinctive about that 'world picture', the 'dynamic of destruction' at work in its tragedies. See Moretti, *Signs Taken for Wonders*, pp. 48–9.

textual figure and elaborating its shades and patterns, positioning it in relation to the narrative system of which it is a part, and pursuing what happens as that system moves to its end, all the while understanding the work of the narrative as work done in response to – to figure and to quell – historical fears. The readings here are more abstract than in the earlier essay; they move too quickly to read textual formations as metaphors for historical situations perhaps – but how else to move when tracing the presence of what is irreducibly abstract and yet materially forceful, capitalism as capital and as system? There is no figure of the Crown left to make textually concrete power and its work, so any understanding of the modern monster must proceed by way of a certain de-concretisation or de-textualisation. This style, an explanatory one, is relatively abstract historically; its agents are categories rather than events, or even local processes: capitalism, America, the proletariat, the family. Yet because it reads the novels as articulating fears about the coherence of these categories, struggling at times to keep their fears in order, it is an explanatory style capable of moments of a descriptive precision that is exhilarating in its scope while remaining embedded in and illuminative of the literary text.

But the arguments put forward in the three books after *Signs Taken for Wonders* all betray, or are powered by, an increasing impatience with the extant categories and procedures of literary-historical traditions: inadequate canons, incoherent categories, insufficient or no attention paid to genre patterns to which a dependence on close reading leaves scholarship blind. Even as *The Way of the World* (1987), *Modern Epic* (1996) and *Atlas of the European Novel* (1998) continue the work of what Moretti calls 'the "formalist" version of political criticism', rather than departing to either a historicism or a sociology of literature, the impatience of each of these books with the limits of what they are doing is tangible.[9] If there was a Marxist tradition in those dark days of the 1980s and 1990s, then Moretti was a part of it even if its threads were unravelling – or, if that phrase retrospectively imposes too much

9 Franco Moretti, 'Preface' (2000), in *The Way of the World: The* Bildungsroman *in European Culture* (London: Verso, 2000 [1987]), p. xiii.

coherence on the late hey-day of Althusserian Marxism, at least failing to cohere.[10]

It is tempting here to ask: What happened? Why did Moretti appear to veer so definitely away from what I will not call 'close reading', but historical reading, or, after Carolyn Lesjak, 'dialectical reading' of historical forms?[11] To put the question in that way is to suggest, however, that he has veered 'away', that he has left the field of the problematic of how to read form historically. He has not, I think, but he has moved that field to a point where its abstraction needs to be yanked back down to history if form is again to be made meaningful as power.

2. Speaking of Countless Novels

The brief 'Foreword' to each of the two English-language volumes of *The Novel* (2005) names the interruption precisely: 'Countless are the novels of the world. So how can we speak of them?' The problem to be grappled with was now also an empirical one, or one discoverable by empirical methods. Interpretation might remain a player, but not at the level of the individual text; it was now explanation that was sought, and explanation

---

10 It should be noted that Francis Mulhern includes Moretti in *Contemporary Marxist Literary Criticism* (Harlow: Longman, 1992), a collection of eleven essays gathered to illustrate the diversity and the continuity of the Marxist tradition. In the slightly later collection, *Marxist Literary Theory* (London: Blackwell, 1996), edited by Terry Eagleton and Drew Milne, there was nothing from Moretti. The more explicitly theoretical bent of the later collection may explain this: prior to 'Conjectures on World Literature', Moretti had seemed to distance himself from 'theory' even as he thought theoretically (see, for example, the 'sketchy' reply offered to 'the inevitable question, "Would you mind explaining what exactly is a literary failure?"' in the Appendix to *The Way of the World*, pp. 243–4). But the absence of Moretti still seems unlikely, and a more ambitious exploration of the place of Marxist literary history in the overall assemblage of Marxist work on culture would need to consider the ways in which Moretti's reaching for new methods diverges from the main threads of that history even as early as the mid-1990s.

11 Carolyn Lesjak, 'Reading Dialectically', *Criticism* 55: 2 (Spring 2013), pp. 233–77.

that had to work at various levels, both those smaller than greater than the text. The causes and conditions of meanings and their mutations are now sought where those mutations or alterations in a genre's shape could only be read at a distance, when the reader became not a reader of texts but of their transubstantiation in – or by the methods and hypotheses borrowed from – world-systems theory, from quantitative history, and from evolutionary theory.

Here is Moretti describing his problematic in 1983:

> Literary texts are *historical* products organised according to *rhetorical* criteria. The main problem of a literary criticism that aims to be in all respects *a historical discipline* is to do justice to both aspects of its objects: to work out a system of concepts which are both historiographic and rhetorical . . . To a large extent, such a theoretical apparatus already exists. It is centred on the concept of 'literary genre'.[12]

'Genre' here already involved a scaling up, a recognition of the deficiencies of the model of reading which asked an individual text – or the canon they comprised – to do the explanatory work, the heavy lifting of speaking historically about the moment they occupied and the pressures within it that they responded to or resisted. The lure of Hegel (fatal for 'empirical solidity') is pinpointed as the source or 'secret cause' of the 'universalising immodesty' that 'follows literary historiography about like a shadow' when the scholar moves from her rhetorical analysis to 'social history'.[13] But the scholar need not succumb to generalisations or the 'zeitgeist fallacy'. Keep in mind that the aim of rhetoric – to persuade, to elicit allegiance – requires division to be its founding soil: no 'zeitgeist' will obtain without the battle it does with similar pretenders to the status of necessary value. If the scholar respects instead the 'specificity of each individual form', something only achievable by recognising its differences from other forms, this will be her best guarantee of restraint in the claims made about that form's wider social meanings: 'The more one

12 Moretti, *Signs Taken for Wonders*, p. 9.

13 Ibid., p. 25.

manages to differentiate a given form from "rival" forms, the more social and ideological connections one will find are prohibited. The advantages of this both for historical concreteness and empirical testability are obvious.'[14]

Back in the early 1980s, Moretti described this 'historical project', one that would revivify work on form through a return to work on genre, as lying 'almost entirely in the future', and its existence as possibly even 'just a little personal utopia'. The work done under the rubric of 'distant reading' continues to be adamant about the need for such a literary history and its potential achievability.

In the later work, the impatience with established methods, and the ambition to use new methods to rewrite the very field itself, take over and become the new task. It is at this moment that the term 'distant reading' is dwelt upon to signify a decisive move away not from any one older interpretive method, but from the medium of them all – reading:

> Perhaps it's too much, tackling the world and the unread at the same time. But I actually think that it's our greatest chance, because the sheer enormity of the task makes it clear that world literature cannot be literature, bigger; what we are already doing, but more of it. It has to be different. The *categories* have to be different . . . world literature is not an object, it's a *problem*, and a problem that asks for a new critical method: and no one has ever found a method by just reading more texts.[15]

I do not want to engage here with any of the critiques already mounted against the project of 'distant reading', or those variations of computational criticism that are arguably one development of that project. There is not time to do justice to any of them, and, arguably, the most expansive or noisy of those critiques (those in defence of 'close reading' because of the immanent value of reading) are not relevant here. I want to stick with the main thread: the question of what Marxist literary history is for. If its

---

14 Ibid., p. 26.

15 Franco Moretti, 'Conjectures on World Literature' (2000), in *Distant Reading* (London: Verso, 2013), p. 46.

job is the production of a historical-materialist understanding of literary forms, can it still be possible when its object or problematic is stretched – and transformed by being so stretched – to encompass all the (surviving) novels of the world, the multitude of novels across the world-system in all their variety? When faced with such volume, there is no question of an adequate or competent knowledge – a knowledge specialised enough to be sensitive to the historical continuities and discontinuities in any one formal feature, yet a knowledge also capacious enough to trace that formal feature across geopolitical space while seeing its mutations or metamorphoses as meaningful in terms of that 'morphospace'. But what use is the morphospace to history if its insights, the knowledge it is composed of and generates, cannot be returned to the work of reading the relative specificity of located forms? Reading them now with a better sense, a more accurate understanding of that specificity but still with a need to know what those forms did in any particular moment in which they gathered themselves to a point to address a historical reader.

First in 'Conjectures on World Literature', then in the essays later collected in *Graphs, Maps, Trees*, in *Distant Reading*, and in some of the pamphlets that have emerged from the Stanford Literary Lab, Moretti has put to work or tested new models for literary history. These have all been presented as experimental models, borrowed from other disciplines to do exploratory or open-ended work, to change the field, and to illuminate how it changes once it is considered through a very different conceptual lens. If the novels of the world are countless, these were the theoretical models that might be repurposed to allow us to speak of them, to ask questions of them (where these forms came from, how and why) – even as we did not read them.

'Perhaps it's too much, tackling the world and the unread at the same time': Moretti's response to his own objection or anxiety was at once determined, committed even: we have no choice, 'world literature cannot be literature, bigger; what we are already doing, just more of it. It has to be different'.[16] And it was equally open, adventurous, excited. The increase in scale, and the depth and density of what that scale could hold,

16 Ibid.

means that literary history has lost its object. There is no longer a novel or its history there. There is now a problem – whether the problem of world-literature, or that of the network of micro-units, formal devices, or stylistic moves that comprise any one moment or layer of its own history. Problems require new critical methods, and 'no-one has ever found a method by just reading more texts. That's not how theories come into being; they need a leap, a wager, a hypothesis, to get started.'[17]

The specific analyses carried out in 'Conjectures' and the experimental premises they tested have been subjected to a number of critiques, the most useful of which Moretti responded to in 'More Conjectures' (2003). The models put forward in *Graphs, Maps, Trees* likewise received their share of responses, some more helpful than others. I want to pause here on one moment in an exchange generated by one of the most useful of those responses: Christopher Prendergast's unfolding of some of the explanatory weaknesses generated when a model drawn from evolutionary theory is used to shape an understanding of literary-historical movement.[18]

Moretti's work in the essay 'Trees' had found that the detective stories that competed with Conan Doyle's for the attention of late-nineteenth-century readers had failed to outlive their moment, because they either did not use clues or used them only superficially or opportunistically: just 'another awkward attempt to smuggle [clues] into a text that does not really need them'.[19] The use of clues, then, 'their absence, presence, visibility', becomes in 'Trees' a test case of how evolutionary theory can push literary history into a more comprehensive, objective and repeatable direction, one no longer rooted in and dependent on the reading of texts that 'typify' or even 'represent' a genre, and now rooted in the identification and explanation of patterns: 'The very small, and the very large; these are the forces that shape literary history. Devices and genres; not

17 Ibid.

18 Christopher Prendergast, 'Evolution and Literary History', *New Left Review* II/34 (July–August 2005).

19 Franco Moretti, 'Trees' (2004), in *Graphs, Maps, Trees: Abstract Models for Literary History* (London: Verso, 2005), p. 75. 'Trees' built on the earlier work presented in 'The Slaughterhouse of Literature' (2000).

texts. Texts are certainly the real objects of literature . . . but are not the right *objects of knowledge* for literary history.'[20] The pressures of the market, conceptualised and brought to bear on a genre's 'space-of-forms', where the latter is visualised as a tree of divergences, enables historical change to become visible. All those now forgotten stories that once jostled for attention with Conan Doyle's get to speak again when resolved into the abstract model of an evolutionary tree. Instead of 'reiterating the verdict of the market', the silence of 'extinction', 'these trees take the lost 99 per cent of the archive and reintegrate it into the fabric of literary history, allowing us to finally "see" it'.[21]

Prendergast's response to *Graphs, Maps, Trees* focuses on the third essay, 'Trees', partly because of the longer history of Moretti's interest in evolutionary theory, and partly because that essay 'operates at a higher level of theoretical synthesis . . . addressed to the general principles and underlying assumptions of his project'.[22] For Prendergast, Moretti takes 'two indisputable facts, one social, one literary: Doyle's popularity and his use of clues', and relates them causally to confirm his hypothesis that the literary marketplace is a site of 'ruthless competition, hinging on form'.[23] Moretti had argued that readers of late-nineteenth-century detective stories had discovered that 'they like a certain device, and if a story doesn't seem to include it, they simply don't read it (and the story becomes extinct)'.[24] Prendergast takes Moretti's formulation too literarily, questioning how these readers can 'know that a given detective novel does not contain the device if they have not read it'.[25] This mistakes the 'Great Unread' (a phrase which needs to be retired) for the 'never read', the formal device for the text it would have belonged to (but not uniquely), and the space of time necessary for the popularity of clues to 'take off' – something that did not happen in the 1890s, a time of formal innovation or even desperation for mystery writers in the *Strand* magazine, but took

20 Moretti, *Graphs, Maps, Trees*, p. 76.
21 Ibid., p. 77.
22 Prendergast, 'Evolution and Literary History', p. 41.
23 Ibid., p. 49; Moretti, *Graphs, Maps, Trees*, p. 72.
24 Moretti, *Graphs, Maps, Trees*, p. 72.
25 Prendergast, 'Evolution and Literary History', p. 50.

a generation, as writers moulded in the older paradigm were replaced with those who did not need to unlearn how to write mystery stories without clues.[26]

Nevertheless, if the exact detail of Prendergast's objections cannot be accepted, the basis of them can be: How can we know not only that readers liked clues (so much so that variants that neglected to use them substantively failed), but *why* they liked clues? An answer to the first part of this question may deploy 'text-independent verification'; but the second part throws us back into the old problematic of literary history: Why (and not only how) do we have what we have? The point made by Prendergast is the use of 'what readers like'.[27] That is,

---

26 Prendergast is too careful and precise a critic to have made 'mistakes': it seems rather as if he was using a tactical misreading to condense and highlight a weakness. However, the work done in 'The Slaughterhouse of Literature' – the work 'Trees' refers readers back to – does make explicit both that Moretti's sample of mystery stories includes those published in the *Strand* during the first Holmes decade, a total of 108. The non-clue-using or only-superficially-clue-using stories would have been read alongside those of Conan Doyle. It is not until the next generation that those former stories (or their negative formal distinction of not using clues) pushes them into the realm of the no-longer-imitated or no-longer-read. Likewise, Moretti makes it clear too, I think – though perhaps does not dwell on it as much as his argument needed – that the example of clues used in 'Trees' to illustrate one level of the explanatory productivity of an evolutionary model may be misleading, as it uses a 'process of selection determined by a *single character* [which] is almost certainly atypical [since as] a rule, literary trees will have to be based on a multiplicity of morphological traits'. Moretti, *Graphs, Maps, Trees*, p. 72, emphasis in original.

27 Also, arguably, in 'Slaughterhouse' where the markets again select the (social) canon. Moretti quotes Arthur De Vany and W. David Walls's essay on the economic forces of the film industry: '"Film audiences make hits or flops . . . not by revealing preferences they already have, but by discovering what they like".' Arthur De Vany and W. David Walls, 'Bose-Einstein Dynamics and Adaptive Contracting in the Motion Picture Industry', *Economic Journal*, November 1996, cited in Moretti, 'Slaughterhouse of Literature', p. 69). This formulation only restates the problem; it brings us no nearer to understanding either those preferences or how the cultural artefacts that evoke them come about. The same could be said for the longer, data-driven version of the same formula tracked in Jodie Archer and Matthew L. Jockers, *The Bestseller Code: Anatomy of the Blockbuster Novel* (New York: St Martin's, 2016), a perhaps predictable use of computational methods and digitisation to create a 'Bestseller-ometer'.

> as the equivalent – or analogue – of 'environment' in evolutionary thinking, the milieu that provides either favourable or unfavourable conditions of 'adaptation': a 'liking' for certain kinds of clues assures the survival of one variant of the genre, while the absence of that feature in other variants condemns them to extinction.[28]

At the point where the tracing of the mutations of the formal device – the initial divergences in how clues were put to use, the later convergence and spread of one mode of use – becomes thick and rich with detail, abstracted detail, the point opened up by 'distant reading', simultaneously the historicity of the reader or of the reading public thins out, becomes less material, shrinks to resemble the poor legibility of market-mediated likes and dislikes. This is where Prendergast's objection hits home:

> If, on further inspection, the necessary evidence were indeed forthcoming, then the preference itself would need to be explained. *Why* did readers come to 'like' this sort of thing? But the answer to that question would require 'interpretation' . . . But it is just this kind of interpretive inquiry that is bracketed out, and it leaves a gaping hole in Moretti's explanatory apparatus.[29]

3. Conclusion

At one level, Moretti remains committed to the priority of form as the analytic moment in which text, history and ideology do most work together. In his response to Prendergast's critique, 'The End of the Beginning' (2006), Moretti makes explicit an assumption buried in 'Trees': the old idea that 'literary genres are problem-solving devices', formal resolutions of 'a contradiction in their environment'.[30] Forms address readers: the 'pleasure provided by that formal organisation is

28 Prendergast, 'Evolution and Literary History', p. 50.
29 Ibid., p. 51, emphasis in original.
30 Moretti, *Distant Reading*, p. 141.

therefore more than just pleasure – it is the vehicle through which a larger symbolic statement is shaped and assimilated'.[31] But what happens to form when it is disassembled and reassembled so that what is studied is its abstract representation, or more precisely an abstract description of one of its morphological aspects as it appears or fails to appear across a wide corpus of texts? The row between Moretti and Prendergast is an important one, as it identifies a problem that cannot be solved by more data, or by devising more precisely formulated ways to represent the data, as it has to do with the methods by which the data is made meaningful. It has to do with readers, both historically and in their role in formal change.

Prendergast's objections went beyond the failure of Moretti's formula to deliver a 'demonstrable causal explanation' of why clues might be the ground or variable involved in Doyle's popularity. He sketched his own suggestive explanation for why Doyle's contemporary and later readers might have liked clues, asking in effect for Moretti to return to the problems of interpretation: Why do readers like what they like? How are those preferences present as determinants in the choice made about what gets written next, what gets published next, whether it gets reviewed or not, and how – and whether it is elevated to commercial success or to the prestigious but pleasure-poor afterlife of inclusion on state-sponsored school or university curricula?

Moretti has never ceased, it seems to me, to depend on the type of interpretive work Prendergast suggests, but he does at times seem to have stopped working towards it.[32] In his response to Prendergast, he

31 Ibid.

32 It is too early by far to see how the work taking place under the aegis of computational criticism will enable a richer understanding of why and how we have the forms of fiction we do. The Stanford Literary Lab pamphlets authored or co-authored by Moretti suggest that he envisions the sharper, deeper, more expansive map of form enabling us, at some point, to '*reverse the direction*, and return from abstraction to literary history.' Even here, however, the literary history to be returned to is still too abstract: form, Moretti writes, 'will *never* explain a single text, and is the *only* thing that can explain a series of them.' Sometimes we need to understand individual texts (most urgently in teaching them), and when we do we have nothing but form with which to give them a historical life. Moretti, 'Patterns and Interpretation,' *Stanford Literary Lab* 15 (September 2017), p. 8. Emphases in original.

interprets readers' liking for clues in familiar terms: 'because the structure provided by clues makes them feel that the world is fully understandable, and rationalisation can be reconciled with adventure, and individuality is a great but dangerous thing . . .'[33]

The ellipsis speaks of a frustration: this is ground already well-trodden, work already done. But it speaks arguably also of a shrunken attention: we know what forms and genres do, so we do not need to follow them in any one particular moment or place where readers encounter them. The attention granted to social history and to readers as part of that history shrinks, even as our knowledge of how their reading – their 'choices' – altered the shape and work of those forms and genres grows in the abstract.

It seems as if the more form itself is materialised, the more the features of the morphospace become thick or rich, and the more history itself becomes dematerialised, made visible in its most legible mode as success or failure, commercial popularity or obscurity. If it shows up there, then it can be explored further. But what shows up there is not a liking for this book or that, or even for this genre or that, but for one or several of their component features separate from the book or from the genre itself.

Taking up a question put by Steven Johnson to *Graphs, Maps, Trees* – that of how the reader, or the reader's 'mind', is influenced by form – Moretti acknowledges an absence or '"black box" right in the middle of the argument': 'I think that my reasoning must have proceeded like this: given the centrality of clues in detective fiction, and Doyle's success with its early readers, there must be a way in which his use of clues was perceived by those readers. "There must be": that's the black box.'[34] In the version of his comments published later, Johnson suggests that the literary system cannot be analysed 'purely from the bird's eye view of distant reading. You need to zoom in as much as you need to zoom out: all the way to the human brain itself.'[35]

---

33 Moretti, *Distant Reading*, p. 141, Moretti's ellipsis.

34 Ibid., pp. 143–4.

35 Steven Berlin Johnson, 'Distant Reading Minds', in Jonathan Goodwin and John Holbo, eds, *Reading Graphs, Maps, Trees* (Anderson, SC: Parlor, 2011), p. 75.

But the 'black box' in Moretti's argument is not the reader's mind – still less the 'human brain'; it is the text as it addresses its desired reader in time: not the reader who buys, borrows or steals the text, but the one the text wants to 'get it' – to realise its meanings and to admire them.

It is not much – books compared to readers. But when it comes to the role of readers – all the social, commercial and domestic apparatus of reading in the dance between explanation and interpretation – it is what we have: the traces of readers left behind in what the text imagined or desired the reader to be. The work of Moretti, and of his critics and collaborators, has indeed given us a new object, a new field or problematic called literary history – one wider, deeper and longer; one in which the unknowing collectivities of form and genre have sharper borders, more distinct tasks, as well as rivals and winners and losers.

But what to do with this field but work it? How does a Marxist literary history go to work on this? By returning to the level Moretti or one part of Moretti seems keen to move away from. Quoting Krzysztor Pomian's *L'Ordre du temps*, Moretti likens the objects traced within *Graphs, Maps, Trees* to the 'invisible objects' invoked by Pomian as the things contemporary historians work with. These are 'constructed objects [which] are also invisible objects, in the sense that no-one has ever seen them, could ever have seen them . . . thanks to seriation, and the use of long stretches of time, historians conjure up objects that have no equivalent within lived experience'.[36] Moretti: 'Objects that have no equivalent within lived experience: this is what *Graphs, Maps, Trees* is made of.'[37]

Fictions, however, are also objects with no equivalent in lived experience. They have a form which fits them, a created form, whereas life or lived experience does not:

> Austen's England; what an invention. And I say invention deliberately, because today the spatial scope of her novels may strike us as obvious, but historically it wasn't obvious at all. Readers needed a symbolic form

36 Krzystof Pomian, *L'Ordre du temps* (Paris: Gallimard, 1984), cited in Moretti, 'The End of the Beginning', in *Distant Reading*, p. 157.

37 Ibid.

> capable of making sense of the nation-state . . . but, before Austen, no one had really come up with it.[38]

The way in which a fictional form addresses its reader – its narrative style or mode of address – is the dialectical point between the past (all the already existing genre conventions open to or possible for that mode of address, and all the sedimented existences buried in it) and the present of that text (what it chooses to work with, to make both its own novelty and its recognisability compelling in the right proportions). We may now have a hugely enriched archive, and an enriched knowledge of how a particular formal device, isolated from the texts in which it does its work, is changed in its travels across time and space, and we will hopefully soon have a similarly enriched knowledge of how those units greater-than-any-individual-text, the sub-genres that constitute the novel, also work across time and space.

But now that knowledge does need to be brought back to forms and genres in history, to change how we read the texts that comprise them at any one moment, to change the questions we ask of them. There are two reasons for this. First, our vocabulary of form and genre is still too thin; by and large, it is still a vocabulary drawn from the practices of those literary histories (including the Marxist ones) that took shape under the sign of the 'exceptional' or even 'typical' novels.[39] To enlarge it, we need to go back and read the no-longer-read work of the past, and the 'best-sellers' and their imitators of the last century. No, it is not possible to read

38 Moretti, *Atlas of the European Novel*, p. 20. See also the Samuel Delaney anecdote on how, 'for the tale of Elizabeth and Darcy to unfold as it does in *Pride and Prejudice*, one must assume a world quite different from that in which Jane Austen actually lived.' Paul K. Alkon, '*Gulliver* and the Origins of Science Fiction', in Frederik N. Smith, ed., *The Genres of 'Gulliver's Travels'* (Newark, DE: University of Delaware Press, 1990), p. 163.

39 'Weber, Simmel, the early Lukács, Russian formalism, Benjamin, Spitzer, Adorno: these pages could (almost) have been written a hundred years ago', writes Moretti when leading up to stressing the continuity of his interest in form – and it is true, but it is a problem. The theoretical and historical language used to identify and analyse formal and generic features and properties still does not encompass or take its cue from the 'great unread'; rather the latter are read through structures generated by the canonically read. Moretti, *Far Country*, p. 10.

all of them, but it was 'close reading' that gave us our vocabulary of form in the first place: if it is agreed that form, in all its petrified work, remains the dynamic force of fiction, the shaping and organising element, the interface between history and story, then we need to learn more about how form operates once its historicising and analytic expanse is opened to more of the 'great unread'.

Second, form is a unity, or conceptually posits a unity, the language a narrative form organises – badly or well – or pulls into shape is so pulled to address a reader. You can isolate a formal or stylistic device and track it beyond the scope of any one text to access the history of that device or cluster of devices. But the meaning of a novel will not be that history, but its own – a meaning that will mutate as it is read past its own moment, but will always bear within it some trace of how it desired to be read, some instance of its own self-image. To engage with that text's own moment is to catch it at the moment where critique or the work of political criticism happens most potently.

In *Aesthetic Theory*, Adorno writes of the impossibility for aesthetics of evading value:

> The diremption of understanding and value is a scientific institution: without values nothing is understood aesthetically and vice versa. In art, more than in any other sphere, it is right to speak of value. Like a mime, every work says: 'I'm good, no?'; to which what responds is a comportment that knows to value.[40]

If we do a certain damage to Adorno, if we treat all novels – those of the culture industry as much as those struggling for a formal autonomy – as involving both the compulsion if not to be admired then to be understood, and also as involving the 'comportment that knows to value' which that compulsion asks from its readers, which it must teach its readers, then the place where the literary historian must, at some point, dig is the individual text. Moretti's work means that digging is now to be done with concepts much more expansive, much more acutely attuned to

40 Theodor W. Adorno, *Aesthetic Theory*, transl. Robert Hullot-Kentor (New York/London: Bloomsbury, 2013 [1970]), p. 356.

the before and after of the text's own moment; but what the text makes of its own moment, and how it does so, is still the way into history offered by the study of the novel. If we do not take the offer, we may gain a better understanding of the novel as a global form, but only at the expense of the historical, and hence political, work novels do.

7

Moretti and the Sociology of Literature: Bridging Distant/Close Reading and Field Theory

Gisèle Sapiro

Franco Moretti's work has profoundly reshaped literary history, and made a significant contribution to the sociology of literature. In his various research projects he has to bridge the gap between the Marxist approach, more focused on content (and above all on representations of the social world in literary works), and the formalistic approach that had begun to develop with the Russian formalists and continued with structuralism (and which tended to neglect this social dimension). His research programme can be defined as a materialist history of literary forms. This programme has developed in two different directions: close reading and distant reading. Here I will focus on distant reading, but I will also give some examples of his methodology of close reading – although, as he himself explained in a talk at the Wissenschaftskolleg in May 2019, they do not operate at the same level of analysis. I will first show how Moretti's approach to distant reading makes an important contribution to the historical sociology of literature. In the second part of the essay, I will discuss the functionalist explanatory frameworks from the standpoint of historical sociology, and more specifically Bourdieu's theory of social transformation and his field theory. In the conclusion, I will suggest that distant reading and field theory can be complementary: while field theory can help connect distant and close reading, distant reading resituates different states of the literary field in the broader context of the book market and the evolution of literary forms.

1. Reading Literary History Through Sociological Patterns: Time and Space

Franco Moretti's notion of 'distant reading' is a method for grasping literary evolution on a broader temporal and spatial scale. Furthermore, the method aims to reintegrate the tiny portion of literary works that have 'survived' the test of history into the wider production of their time. Drawing from evolutionary theory in biology – which offers a system for identifying constants within contingent changes – Moretti hypothesises that the diachronic and geographic structures of literary evolution are not random. For example, in Ernst Mayr's *Systematics and Origins of Species*, he found a concept that links evolution through time and space: that of 'allopatric speciation', which explains the 'genesis of new species by their movement into new spaces'.[1]

Using basic quantitative methods to explore the intermediate level between the *longue durée* and micro-history, Moretti shows that literary evolution is structured around cycles. Comparing the rise of the novel in various countries, similar curves are observed at different historical moments.[2] Furthermore, genres and subgenres are characterised by a cyclical evolution even within the same cultural space: the historical novel followed the gothic novel, which followed the epistolary novel; and the rise of each genre corresponds to the decline of the previous one.[3] A distant quantitative approach also challenges views of supposedly linear processes such as 'feminisation', revealing a cyclical alternation between the predominance of male and female authors, and their related genres (domestic or sentimental versus historical or military novels).[4] Moretti

1 Franco Moretti, *Distant Reading* (London: Verso, 2013), p. 1.

2 Franco Moretti, *Graphs, Maps, Trees: Abstract Models for Literary History* (London: Verso, 2005), p. 6, fig. 1.

3 Ibid., pp. 15–16, figs 7 and 8.

4 Ibid., p. 27.

suggests that these cycles correspond to generational cycles. They also reflect the logic of the market, as we will see.

However, form circulates through different channels: Darwin's trees here become an inspiration for representing the morphology of literary evolution, in the same way that Cavalli-Sforza, Menozzi and Piazza had used them in *History and Geography of Human Genes* to measure the distance between linguistic groups.[5] Moretti illustrates this divergent morphology through two examples: clues in the detective novel, and free indirect speech.

Going beyond the comparative method, Moretti is also interested in the structure of literary space, and proposes a geography of the circulation of literary forms between centre and periphery, using Wallerstein's world-systems analysis and Even-Zohar's polysystem theory. He observes that most European countries import from abroad more than half of the novels they publish, whereas France and Great Britain import a much smaller percentage.[6] These two countries produce many novels, and thus do not need to import as many, he argues.

The cycles observed are the result of what Franco Moretti has called 'Jameson's law', after Fredric Jameson's analysis of Japanese and Indian novels as hybrids of Western forms and local realities: 'in cultures that belong to the periphery of the literary system (which means: almost all cultures, inside and outside Europe), the modern novel first arises not as an autonomous development but as a compromise between a western formal influence (usually French or English) and local materials'.[7]

This combination of diachrony and geographical comparison leads him to describe a historical process: that of the growing centralisation of the market at both national and international levels. This is an observation confirmed by socio-historical works, which also show that this asymmetrical structure has remained stable over time, through the twentieth century and into the twenty-first, with the substantial modification of the rise of New York as a dominant centre and the

5 Ibid., p. 70.

6 Franco Moretti, *Atlas of the European Novel* (London: Verso, 1998), p. 151.

7 Franco Moretti, 'Conjectures on World Literature', *New Left Review* I/1 (January–February 2000), p. 58.

relative decline of Paris – which nevertheless remains an important centre.[8]

Furthermore, comparing the two central countries, France and the United Kingdom, Moretti observes that, in France, the share of foreign novels increased from 10 per cent to more than 25 per cent between 1750 and 1816, dropping slightly to 20 per cent in 1850, whereas in the UK, their share has progressively declined from 20 per cent to just over 5 per cent.[9] Using the world-systems model that contrasts centre and periphery, Heilbron has described the asymmetric circulation of translations across different languages: he demonstrated, using the UNESCO Index Translationum online database, that in the 1980s central languages exported more than they imported, while peripheral languages imported more than they exported.[10] This pattern of asymmetric circulation also applies between town and country, and seems related to the concentration of publishing.[11] Comparing the share of foreign novels in France and the UK over time may therefore indicate the beginning of the (slow) decline of Paris's position at the centre of the 'World Republic of Letters', and the concomitant rise of London, in turn overtaken by New York in the 1970s.[12] But more data would be needed to confirm this hypothesis.

A closer analysis may help us refine this first hypothesis: the large share of foreign novels (mainly English) translated and published in France in 1816 was fostered by the liberalisation of the press (by Article 8 of the Charter of 1814), but also by interest in a genre that was not yet very widespread in France. In French book production at the time, reprints still far outnumbered new titles, and the category of 'belles-lettres'

8 Gisèle Sapiro, *Translatio. Le marché de la traduction en France à l'ère de la mondialisation* (Paris: CNRS, 2008), pp. 418–39; Gisèle Sapiro, 'De l'internationalisation à la mondialisation: les grandes tendances du marché de la traduction en France XXe siècle', in Y. Chevrel and B. Banoun, eds, *Histoire des traductions en langue française* (Paris: Verdier, 2019), pp. 1–124.

9 Moretti, *Atlas of the European Novel*, pp. 152–3.

10 Johan Heilbron, 'Towards a Sociology of Translation: Book Translations as a Cultural World System', *European Journal of Social Theory* 2: 4 (1999), pp. 429–44.

11 Gisèle Sapiro, 'Globalization and Cultural Diversity in the Book Market: The Case of Translations in the US and in France', *Poetics* 38: 4 (2010), pp. 419–39.

12 Pascale Casanova, *The World Republic of Letters*, transl. Malcolm DeBevoise (Cambridge, MA: Harvard University Press, 2004).

accounted for only a third of titles and a quarter of book print-runs.[13] In 1828, Philarète Chasle counted 267 novels, far fewer than history books (736), books on religious topics (708), poetry (463), drama (308) and jurisprudence (286); but more than books on politics and administration (264), education (260) or medicine (220) (at the time, books on philosophy barely reached 100 per year).[14] The expansion of the book trade during this period, thanks to its liberalisation, rising literacy rates and the industrialisation of printing (the mechanised process so well described in Balzac's *Illusions perdues*), helps to explain the importation of foreign novels. Representative of this importation, the great success of Walter Scott's historical novels during the Restoration period is related both to these favourable material conditions and to the interest in history that emerged after the Revolution.[15] Their translation helped legitimise a genre that was still regarded as lowbrow.

French authors began to imitate Scott: Alfred de Vigny published *Cinq-mars* (1826), Honoré de Balzac *Les Chouans* (1829), Mérimée *Chronique du règne de Charles IX* (1829), Victor Hugo – who had written reviews of Scott as a teenager, starting in 1819 – *Notre-Dame-de-Paris* (the publication of which was delayed to 1831).[16] The domestic production of novels in French grew after the liberal revolution of 1830, and especially after the success of serial novels, which offered writers an opportunity to live off their pens: Balzac's *La Vieille fille* was first released in the new daily *La Presse* in 1836. Authors like Balzac and Sue elevated the status of the novel, asserting its function as a tool of social investigation.[17] The growth

13 Isabelle Conihout, 'La Restauration: contrôle et liberté', in R. Chartier and H.-J. Martin, *Histoire de l'édition française*, vol. 2, *Le Livre triomphant (1660–1830)* (Paris: Fayard/Promodis, 1990), pp. 694–718; Martyn Lyons, *Le Triomphe du livre. Une histoire sociologique de la lecture dans la France du XIXe siècle* (Paris: Promodis/Éditions du Cercle de la librairie, 1987).

14 Philarète Chasles, 'Statistique littéraire et intellectuelle de la France', *Revue de Paris*, 1829, in Chartier and Martin, *Le Livre triomphant*, pp. 739–40.

15 Martyn Lyons, 'The Audience for Romanticism: Walter Scott in France, 1815–51', *European History Quarterly* 14 (1984), pp. 21–46.

16 Anne-Marie Thiesse, *La Fabrique de l'écrivain national. Entre littérature et politique* (Paris: Gallimard, 2019), p. 118.

17 Judith Lyon-Caen, *La Lecture et la Vie. Les Usages du roman au temps de Balzac* (Paris: Tallandier, 2006).

of domestic production explains the fall in the share of foreign novels to 20 per cent in 1850 (though in absolute numbers imports of translated novels must have increased). The rise of the novel therefore seems to be correlated to the expansion of the publishing market, and the success of the genre encouraged publishers (and local writers) to invest in it. A similar evolutionary pattern can also be observed elsewhere, in relation with the construction of national identities and the codification of a national language (in contrast, the peripheries of linguistic areas, especially in colonial or postcolonial settings, are very dependent for imports and exports on the centres where publishing is concentrated).

At the national level, based on the English and Italian cases, Moretti observes the growing centralisation around cultural capitals.[18] Moreover, he finds evidence of the formation of a national market and a national literary canon by analysing British libraries. He notes that, by the end of the nineteenth century, in the provinces the novel had become the dominant genre, and practically the only one (constituting between 70 and 90 per cent of books), replacing religious reading, while in London novels accounted for only a third of books. A look at the titles available in circulating libraries reveals the exclusion of foreign novels and concentration on a small number of popular authors, such as Jane Austen. The logic of market concentration reinforced the formation of a national space, as Benedict Anderson has observed.[19] This closure is typical of dominant centres of the World Republic of Letters: it is probable that, in other countries, foreign novels could be found in libraries, including provincial ones, and this would indicate the formation of a world literary canon, already attested through translations.[20]

Not only is the novel the dominant genre, it is also the symbolic form of the nation-state, contends Moretti (thereby rectifying the Marxist doxa which had emphasised the relationship between the novel and capitalism): the novel stages the tensions and conflicts generated by the

---

18 Moretti, *Atlas of the European Novel*, pp. 164–71.

19 Benedict Anderson, *Imagined Communities: Reflections on the Origin and Spread of Nationalism* (London: Verso, 1983).

20 Casanova, *World Republic of Letters*; Gisèle Sapiro, 'How Do Literary Texts Cross Borders (or Not)? A Sociological Approach to World Literature', *Journal of World Literature* 1: 1 (2016), pp. 81–96.

unification of the nation-state, geographically (between the countryside and urban centres, the provinces and the capital) and socially (especially between the bourgeoisie and the aristocracy, as Lukács noted).[21] In *Atlas of the European Novel* (1997), Moretti explores the inner geography of the novel with the help of maps, illustrating these tensions between provinces and cities, a topic also central to French novels from Stendhal's *The Red and the Black* to Balzac's *Lost Illusions* and Barrès's *Les Déracinés.*

In his previous book on the *Bildungsroman*, Moretti had analysed this genre using the method of close reading. Interested in the conflicting dimensions symbolised by this same form, he argued that the *Bildungsroman* focuses not only on the borders between periods, as suggested by Bakhtin, but also on those between different classes, especially between the bourgeoisie and the aristocracy – the two competing dominant classes. The *Bildungsroman* deals with social mobility. It emphasises the attraction exerted by the aristocratic lifestyle and ethos on the *Bildungsburgertüm*, the bourgeoisie endowed with or having accumulated cultural capital – of which *Bildungsroman* heroes such as Wilhelm Meister, Julien Sorel, Lucien de Rubempré and Frédéric Moreau are representative – an attraction that contrasts with their rejection of the vulgar economic bourgeoisie. Moretti also highlights the differences between the European novel, which takes place within an unregulated space, and the British novel, where the rules are always observed and the legal system plays a significant role – suggesting a relationship with the fact that the English Revolution is the only revolution that grounded its legitimacy in law.

To his close reading of these novels, Moretti adds Marxist approaches, referring to Max Weber, Albert Hirschmann and various political theorists, thus deepening our sociological understanding of fictional representations of economic, sociocultural and political changes, and our interpretation of a character's behaviour. These references invite a comparison between sociological and literary interpretations of social change, but also a reflection on how literary representations have nourished sociological understandings of these changes and of human behaviour under capitalism.

21 Moretti, *Atlas of the European Novel*, p. 17

Thus, Moretti makes a very significant contribution to the historical sociology of literature, developing invaluable experimental methods and tools for studying *longue durée* and medium-term developments, in parallel with the profound interpretations of the sociological meaning of the novel. These methods and tools are descriptive; but at the same time they suggest some explanatory frameworks that deserve to be discussed.

2. Explanatory Frameworks

While Moretti has produced groundbreaking analyses of literary evolution, I would like now to discuss the explanatory frameworks from the standpoint of historical sociology. Market analyses tend to adopt functionalist explanations spontaneously: the British literary market didn't need to translate novels, as it produced enough of them for the market, whereas other markets did not. To a certain extent, these explanations seem to work.

However, I would like to challenge functionalist explanatory models. Robert Merton's critique of these models provides a first level of objection: while functionalism advantageously replaces essentialist approaches, it still carries the risk of postulating (instead of interrogating) the equilibrium of the system as static rather than dynamic, and of confusing elements with their functions.[22] More sophisticated versions of functionalism – such as the one developed by Merton himself – avoid these biases. Marxism introduced dynamics and struggle, and did not confuse them with functions. Drawing from the Russian formalists, polysystem theory provides the most elaborate and heuristically sophisticated version of functionalism in the field of literary studies.[23]

But even if one overcomes these risks, functionalist models still often appear insufficient to explain transformations of the social structure – all the more so those of markets in symbolic goods, to use Bourdieu's

---

22 Robert Merton, 'Paradigm for Functionalist Analysis in Sociology', in *On Social Structure and Science* (Chicago: University of Chicago Press, 1996), Chapter 6.

23 Itamar Even-Zohar, 'Polysystem Studies', *Poetics Today* 11: 1 (1990).

expression.[24] The first reason for this is that the functionalist method draws explanations from the system itself rather than from its agents. The second is that markets in symbolic goods are not demand markets, but supply markets. Readers do not 'need' that peculiar book. Furthermore, they are markets of prototypes, in the sense that, beyond a specific work (which itself changes in translation, and even in different editions), demand is never for the same product, even within the most codified genres, such as the detective or sentimental novel. In this sense, Moretti's use of evolutionary theory to describe morphological differentiation in the form of 'trees' (the third tool of distant reading) is much more adequate for describing literary evolution than the supply-and-demand framework, which he also uses to understand 'literary survival'.[25] But 'trees' are descriptive: they describe the form, the morphology of evolution, while the mechanism of supply-and-demand is an explanatory framework.

Whereas economists tend to explain the formation of value in these markets on the basis of demand – or more recently on the basis of the notion of 'preference', which sounds less functionalist and is close to the notion of 'taste' used by literary historians such as Moretti – their explanations tend to obscure the role of intermediaries in the market. Sociologists have become increasingly interested in this category of 'tastemakers', to use Bourdieu's phrase. Moretti takes up Bourdieu's interpretation of *L'Education sentimentale*, according to which the novel expressed the social indeterminacy that characterises the moment preceding the choice of an artistic vocation by the young educated bourgeoisie, and the maps Bourdieu draws of the social space of the novel. He also uses Bourdieu's concept of 'field' and its polarisation of large-scale and small-scale production to account for the gap between mass-market and modern literature.[26] But he does not introduce authors' and publishers' strategies to understand literary evolution – although, as I will try to show, it would fit and complement his approach.

---

24 Pierre Bourdieu, 'The Market of Symbolic Goods', *Poetics: Journal of Empirical Research on Literature, the Media, and the Arts* 14: 1–2 (1984), pp. 13–44.

25 Moretti, *Graphs, Maps, Trees*, pp. 70–4.

26 Moretti, *The Bourgeois: Between History and Literature* (London: Verso, 2013), pp. 31–2.

Introducing agency and practices into the explanatory framework draws us away from functionalist explanation towards power relations and struggles, as Marx and Engels showed. The book market obeys the laws of capitalistic markets: accumulation, competition and concentration of capital – an analysis that fits with Moretti's description, and that he himself mobilises in many places, as we saw in the first section. For instance, in his study on 7,000 titles of British novels between 1740 and 1860, Moretti observes, using large data sets, that titles' length decreased between 1770 and 1790, and explains this observation in terms of market competition.[27] However, this change was neither automatic nor organic: it was mediated by publishers' and authors' 'survival' strategies in the growing book market, and it would be interesting, from a socio-historical standpoint, to study how such practices changed (we could check, for instance, whether publishers participated in choosing the titles, as often happens; for instance, it was Sartre's editor, Jean Paulhan, who suggested the title of *La Nausée*, instead of *Melancholia*, proposed by the author).

Publishers' strategies may also create constraints for authors: such constraints exert mechanical causality. Here 'mechanical' refers to an outside cause, in Cartesian terms, as opposed to expressive causality, which draws from Leibniz, and was applied to literature by Georg Lukács and Lucien Goldmann through the notion of worldview (Moretti adopts this approach in his study of the bourgeois worldview, for instance), and to Louis Althusser's structural causality, which refers to Spinoza's immanent cause. Banned by Althusser, mechanical causality was rehabilitated at a local level by Fredric Jameson. To illustrate the local validity of mechanical causality, Jameson gives the example of the change in the book form at the end of the nineteenth century, which affects the novel's inner form: 'There seems, for instance, to have been an unquestionable causal relationship between the admittedly extrinsic fact of the crisis in late-nineteenth-century publishing, during which the dominant three-decker lending library novel was replaced by a cheaper one-volume format, and the modification of the "inner form" of the novel itself.'[28]

27 Ibid., pp. 179–210.

28 Fredric Jameson, *The Political Unconscious: Narrative as a Socially Symbolic Act* (Ithaca: Cornell University Press, 1981), p. 25.

Another example is the growing presence of dialogues in serial novels, because the authors were paid by line. So cultural intermediaries impose material constraints that exert a mechanical causality on literary forms (this is also true of other cultural forms, such as the duration of a play or a film). Some of these constraints result from anticipation by these intermediaries of the audience's preferences, but some are not (such as remuneration by line).

The mediation of market constraints (or retranslation of the public's alleged preferences into publishing strategies) by publishers of course also applies to genre. Moretti has observed the quasi-exclusion of poetry from the British book market since the beginning of the nineteenth century, which resulted from such 'survival' strategies, and has affected authors' strategies and careers. In France the novel became dominant by the end of the century, and authors who used to start with poetry and then move to theatre – the highest genre in the hierarchy – would now opt increasingly for the novelistic genre from the beginning.[29] Still, as Bourdieu notes, some publishers, like Auguste Poulet-Malassis, who published Baudelaire, invented a new position, creating a circuit of small-scale production for upmarket literature, including poetry.[30]

The process of concentration accelerated in the last two decades of the twentieth century, the sale and acquisition of firms by large conglomerates leading to a market structure described by economists as an 'oligopoly with fringes'.[31] Bourdieu dedicated his last empirical study to the concentration of the French publishing field in the 1990s.[32] Again, this process is not mechanical, but is the result of the more or less

29 Christophe Charle, *La Crise littéraire à l'époque du naturalisme: roman, théâtre et politique. Essai d'histoire sociale des groupes et des genres littéraires* (Paris: Presse de l'École normale supérieure, 1979).

30 Pierre Bourdieu, *The Rules of Art: Genesis and Structure of the Literary Field*, transl. S. Emanuel (Cambridge: Polity, 1996).

31 Bénédicte Reynaud-Cressent, 'La dynamique d'un oligopole avec frange: Le cas de la branche d'édition de livres en France', *Revue d'Economie Industrielle* 22 (1982), pp. 61–71.

32 Pierre Bourdieu, 'The Social Conditions of the International Circulation of Ideas', in Richard Shusterman, ed., *Bourdieu: A Critical Reader* (Oxford: Blackwell, 1999), pp. 220–8.

successful strategies of publishers as capitalist players, and conditions the structures that enable career opportunities. One should also introduce the role of literary agents who have become major players in the Anglo-American market.[33]

Social agents do not, of course, control the consequences of their acts and decisions; for instance, they mostly cannot predict the success of a book. But they sometimes deploy successful strategies, and compete harshly on the market by various means, some of which can be judged unfair (such as buying prominent spaces in bookstores, such as beside the till – common in the United States nowadays). Thus, the supply readers are exposed to is already a selected portion of, resulting from power relations among intermediaries. Consequently, the selection cannot be merely interpreted as resulting from readers' taste (though, of course, strong sellers are far from entirely predictable).

Regarding the spatial relations between centre and periphery that have been adapted to Marxist theory by Wallerstein and Harvey, one should rather interpret the unequal power relations and the concentration process as a result of aggressive strategies by dominant publishers, backed by copyright laws and by the capacity to impose contract law.[34] While the novel as a literary form existed before the eighteenth century (Moretti analyses the case of Chinese novels in the sixteenth and seventeenth centuries), its circulation and the dominant position it has acquired in most countries is the result of the capitalistic expansion of Western publishing and the progressive unification of a world literary marketplace, which has culminated in the era of globalisation, with its proliferation of international book fairs.[35] This explanatory framework fits very well Moretti's accurate description of this expansion. In his article 'Evolution, World-Systems, *Weltliteratur*', he acknowledges the homogenising effect of the market: 'Here, the crucial mechanism by

---

33 John B. Thompson, *Merchants of Culture: The Publishing Business in the Twenty-First Century* (Cambridge: Polity, 2010).

34 Sapiro, 'How Do Literary Texts Cross Borders (or Not)?'

35 Moretti, *Distant Reading*, pp. 172–8; Sapiro, 'French Literature in the World System of Translation', in Christie McDonald and Susan Suleiman, eds, *French Global: A New Approach to Literary History* (New York: Columbia University Press, 2010), pp. 298–319.

which the market operated was that of *diffusion*: books from the core were incessantly exported into the semi-periphery and the periphery, where they were read, admired, imitated, turned into models – thus drawing those literatures into the orbit of core ones, and indeed "interfering" with their autonomous development.'[36]

But this imperialistic model needs to be given more nuance. First, according to Bourdieu, fields circumscribe spaces of specific struggles and competition, which do not obey the laws of the market, but rather specific rules and interests. Profit is not the only motivation of agents in the field, and some are even ready to lose money because they share the characteristic *illusio* of the field: the belief in specific aesthetic values, which are assessed by peers and by literary critics. This movement of autonomisation of the field from the market occurred, according to Bourdieu, at the very moment of the triumph of the novel in the book market: it is not by chance that Flaubert tried to renew the genre by overcoming the opposition between romanticism and realism (while taking some ironic distance from both currents), and to legitimise it from an aesthetic standpoint. Bourdieu also describes Baudelaire as a 'nomothete', and his publisher, Poulet-Malassis, as inventing a new position in the publishing field, that of small-scale production for the educated elite of aesthetes. This strategy proved successful: Baudelaire's poetry 'survived' in the long term, and became a classic.

Thus market forces are counterbalanced by literary forces, as Moretti acknowledges.[37] This is also true of international circulation. Some translators and publishers invest in translations without expecting any economic profit. Moreover, dominated players may develop opposing strategies that can prove successful, as suggested by the example of the founder of Actes Sud, Hubert Nyssen, a Belgian publisher who decided in 1979 to establish his publishing house in Arles rather than in Paris, and to accumulate capital through translations. The success of his firm had an impact on the translation market in France by fostering greater linguistic and cultural diversity.[38]

---

36 Moretti, *Distant Reading*, p. 127.

37 Ibid., pp. 31–2.

38 Sapiro, 'How Do Literary Texts Cross Borders (or Not)?'

Second, political and ideological motivations also intervene in the circulation of literary forms. Moretti underscores such motivations when he mentions, for instance, the rejection of French novels in Great Britain after the Revolution.[39] Ioana Popa's work on the importation of eastern European literature in France during the communist period illustrates these political stakes and struggles: socialist realism, officially promoted by the Communist governments, was challenged by literatures of dissent.[40] Religious forces have also tried to control the market, and to prevent or foster the circulation of certain products – through censorship on the one hand, and the publication of specific book collections on the other, but also through criticism. In a similar way, while they definitely played a role in the capitalistic expansion of the novel, nation-states also acted as a counterbalancing force: not only through censorship, but also through diplomacy and state export policies, in order to promote literatures from the semi-peripheries or even from the peripheries.[41] In the same way, in some countries, such as France, book policies helped support small-scale production.[42]

Third, circulation processes cannot be reduced to mere imitation. Moretti was wrongly accused of promoting such an interpretation of the wide circulation of the novel.[43] In his formulation of what he calls the Jameson law, Moretti clearly describes the final product of this process as a hybrid combining an imported form and local materials.[44] Moreover,

---

39 Moretti, *Atlas of the Europeran Novel*, p. 154.

40 Ioana Popa, *Traduire sous contraintes. Littérature et communisme (1947–1989)* (Paris: CNRS, 2010).

41 On Italy, see Christopher Rundle, *Publishing Translations in Fascist Italy* (Oxford: Peter Lang, 2010). On the cases of the Netherlands and Israel, see Johan Heilbron and Gisèle Sapiro, 'Politics of Translation: How States Shape Cultural Transfers', in R. Meyerlarts and D. Roig-Sanz, eds, *Literary Translation and Cultural Mediators in 'Peripheral' Cultures: Custom Officers or Smugglers?* (London: Palgrave Macmillan, 2018), pp. 183–210.

42 See Gisèle Sapiro, 'The Literary Field Between the State and the Market', *Poetics* 31: 5–6 (2003), pp. 441–61.

43 Joseph R. Slaughter, 'Locations of Comparisons', *Cambridge Journal of Postcolonial Literary Inquiry* 5: 2 (April 2018), pp 209–26.

44 Responding to former critiques from Jale Parla and Jonathan Arac, Moretti acknowledged that even 'early English novels were written, in Fielding's

when studying the circulation of free indirect discourse to Russia, he emphasises the divergence, which fits his morphological model of differentiation (trees).[45] Rather than mere imitation, the operations that lead to such a product should be characterised as appropriation, as anthropologists and book historians have suggested from different perspectives.[46] Moreover, as both Even-Zohar and Bourdieu have underscored, the importation process has to be understood from the standpoint of the field of reception rather than that of the original field.[47] Bourdieu highlights three crucial operations by importers: selection, marking and interpretation. This framework closely fits Moretti's model of evolution through selection and differentiation, in which the model or the product becomes something different to adjust to another milieu. But here lies the major difference with the evolutionary model in biology: these operations and strategies are carried out by people and social forces with agency, and not by mechanical or organic processes. These strategies can be studied both qualitatively and quantitatively, differentiating the channels and selection strategies used by publishers from those used by other intermediaries.[48]

In relation to the circulation of works and models, acknowledgement of the circulation of the form of the novel from Great Britain, and to a lesser extent France, certainly conforms to the center–periphery model. However,

---

words, "after the manner of Cervantes" (or of someone else), thus making clear that a compromise between local and foreign forms occurred there as well'. Moretti, *Distant Reading*, p. 116.

45 Moretti, *Graphs, Maps, Trees*, pp. 83–5.

46 Arjun Appadurai, *Modernity at Large: Cultural Dimensions of Globalization* (Minneapolis, MN: University of Minnesota Press, 1996); Roger Chartier, *Les Origines culturelles de la Révolution française* (Paris: Seuil, 1990).

47 Even-Zohar, 'Polysystem Studies'; Bourdieu, 'Social Conditions of the International Circulation of Ideas'.

48 See the examples of the importation of Eastern European literary works in France during the communist period: Ioana Popa, 'Translation Channels: A Primer on Politicized Literary Transfer', *Target* 18: 2 (2006), pp. 205–28; and of translations of French literature in the United States in the 1990s; Gisèle Sapiro, 'Translation and Symbolic Capital in the Era of Globalization: French Literature in the United States', *Cultural Sociology* 9: 3 (2015), pp. 320–46.

a) this model is not normative but descriptive, outlining flows of translations and the circulation of models;
b) it is not unidirectional: whereas most of the translations circulate from the centres to the peripheries, where they contribute to the construction of a local market, there are also works circulating in translation from the peripheries to the centre. Some scholars have argued that these flows may more or less reflect the scale of production, which is debatable, as this is a functionalist explanation that obscures political and cultural motivations and forces.[49] Similarly, literary models from peripheries or semi-peripheries, like the haiku, can be appropriated in the centre (often by avant-garde or experimental authors), but these borrowings are often obscured.[50]
c) when translated novels arrive in the peripheries, they contribute to the creation of a book market in the national language and establish both a corpus of printed text in that language and a literary repertoire.[51] Consequently, they participate in the process of the construction of national literatures and cultures. However, this does not mean that there was no literary tradition there already, whether oral (folk tales, poetry) or written (classical texts), and these are precisely the 'local materials' that are incorporated into the modern form of the novel, as Ahmadou Kourouma's work has shown.[52] Moretti rightly distinguishes plot, which circulates more easily, from style (or language), which is more

49 Anthony Pym and Grzegorz Chrupala, 'The Quantitative Analysis of Translation Flows in the Age of an International Language', in Albert Branchadell Albert and Lovell Margaret West, eds, *Less Translated Languages* (Amsterdam/Philadelphia, PA: J. Benjamins, 2005), pp. 27–38. See also Sapiro, 'How Do Literary Texts Cross Borders (or Not).'

50 As Moretti also notes in his response to critics of 'Conjectures of World Literature'. Moretti, *Distant Reading*, p. 115 n. 12.

51 Even-Zohar, 'Polysystem Studies'.

52 Both Claire Ducournau, *La Fabrique des classiques africains. Ecrivains d'Afrique subsaharienne francophone* (Paris: CNRS, 2015) and Tristan Leperlier, *Algérie. Les écrivains dans la décennie noire* (Paris: CNRS, 2018) show the evolution of genre production in postcolonial configurations – sub-Saharan countries in the first case, Algeria in the second – and they both identify the later rise of the novel compared to poetry and drama, just as in 1830 France.

> likely to be informed by so-called 'local materials' through the process of translation.[53]

We can conclude that the logic of the market does not spread in a homogeneous way, but encounters resistance; and imitation is never mechanical, but is always to a some extent appropriation and differentiation (plagiarism being the borderline case). Moretti distinguishes two evolutionary models: waves and trees. These models apply to the history of literature, and they can be explained by reference to two contrasting processes: isomorphism and differentiation.[54] Neo-institutional sociological theory analyses isomorphism as resulting from three types of mechanism: constraint, imitation and professional norms.[55] We can apply these mechanisms to the production of cultural goods. While constraint acts as the main homogenising instrument in authoritarian regimes (as the canon of socialist realism illustrates) or under religious control (trough censorship and the labelling of recommended texts), imitation is typical of competitive free markets: publishers will give preference to successful genres (as Moretti shows in relation to the cyclical waves of subgenres in the nineteenth century), and to works already selected by their peers in other countries in order to reduce uncertainty.[56] Professional norms were established at a national level through authors' societies, and spread around the world through professional organisations, such as the Association Littéraire et Artistique, founded in 1878 to promote literary and artistic property; the Publishers' International Union, founded in 1896, which is tied to national publishers' unions; and the PEN Club, established in 1921, and which has local branches in each country. Nowadays, literary agents also contribute to

53 Moretti, *Distant Reading*, pp. 132–3.

54 Sapiro, 'How Do Literary Texts Cross Borders (or Not)?'

55 Paul J. DiMaggio and Walter W. Powell, 'The Iron Cage Revisited: Institutional Isomorphism and Collective Rationality in Organizational Fields', *American Sociological Review* 48 (1983), pp. 147–60.

56 Thomas Franssen and Giselinde Kuipers, 'Coping with Uncertainty, Abundance and Strife: Decision-Making Processes of Dutch Acquisition Editors in the Global Market for Translations', *Poetics* 41: 1 (2013), pp. 48–74.

harmonisation of the professional norms of national publishing fields. Some of these norms vary within the field of publishing, from country to country, but also between the poles of large-scale and small-scale circulation: for example, the norms of faithfulness to the original work and direct translation, which prevail in upmarket publishing, do not apply in commercial genres, which produces a strong divergence between the original and the translation in this market segment – but ensures that the final product more closely resembles its domestic equivalents.

Whereas isomorphism prevails at the pole of large-scale production, originality, which has been the norm in upmarket publishing since romanticism, is a principle of differentiation that counterbalances the tendency to isomorphism in the creative industries. This norm applies both for authors – who have to distinguish and make a name for themselves – and for publishers, who also need to maintain a distinctive brand identity in order to occupy an identifiable position in the book market. Charpentier established himself as an editor of the naturalist writers, as did Éditions de Minuit in relation to Samuel Beckett and the nouveau roman. Their name embodies their symbolic capital – that is to say, their catalogue and list of renowned authors. The theory of isomorphism by imitation does not answer the question of who imitates whom, and why. As a matter of fact, imitation is neither mechanical nor random, but mediated by agency and more or less conscious strategies. Publishers choose to follow the decisions of certain of their foreign counterparts rather than others. Elective affinities express identities, and thereby distinction.[57] Nation-states have also claimed, since the nineteenth century, that their literature embodies their cultural identity, and the national brand still works as a distinctive label on the globalised book market.[58] Differentiation also applies to the 'postcolonial exotic', defined by Graham Huggan as the 'global "spectacularization" of cultural differences'.[59] Finally, appropriation

57 Bourdieu, 'Market of Symbolic Goods'.

58 Anne-Marie Thiesse, *La Création des identités nationales. Europe XVIIIe-XXe siècle* (Paris: Seuil, 2001 [1999]).

59 Graham Huggan, *The Postcolonial Exotic: Marketing the Margins* (London: Routledge, 2001), p. 15.

also introduces differentiation through the hybridisation of genres and cultural traditions.[60]

3. Conclusion

These remarks are meant to show how complementary Moretti's distant/close reading and field theory can be, and thus what would be the gains of bridging them. Field theory can help connect the two levels of analysis developed by Moretti, distant and close reading, through the study of writers' strategies in the space of possibilities offered within a certain configuration of the field and of the book market. Moretti's distant reading helps us situate this space of possibilities within the broader market and in the historical evolution of literary forms.

Regarding this evolution, an analysis of the strategies of individual and collective agents – that is to say writers, publishers, critics, literary magazines, literary prize juries, state representatives and other intermediaries who control access to publishing and to the book market, such as literary agents today – would contribute to the understanding of the mechanisms of 'literary survival' described by Moretti – even though they do not, of course, entirely explain success and popularity. (Still, a work that has not been promoted and circulated has very little chance of survival, Kafka's manuscripts being an exception that also reveals the importance of mediators.) At the level of close reading, Moretti provides a method for comparative analyses of literary works from different periods and places. Field theory, combined with a study of authors' trajectories and dispositions, could help to illuminate how models circulated and were appropriated by them.

Finally, I have tried to show that, whereas the mechanisms fostering isomorphism translate into homogenising waves in book production, the logics of differentiation engender offshoots that shape trees. Appropriation enables us to account for both differentiation and hybridisation, a process rightly cited by critics of Moretti's work (especially Christopher

60 Appadurai, *Modernity at Large*; Lawrence Venuti, *The Scandals of Translation: Towards an Ethics of Difference* (London: Routledge, 1998), p. 159.

Prendergast) as common in cultural evolution but not in biological evolution.[61] Sociological forces can indeed account – better than functionalist explanations – for the waves and trees of literary evolution so well described by Moretti, as well as for the struggles that he wishes to reintroduce: if form can be framed as a struggle, it is because it is the product of social struggles.[62]

61 Moretti, *Distant Reading*, pp. 149–50.
62 Ibid., p. 134.

8

The Moon and the Tides: Franco Moretti as Literary Theorist

Federico Bertoni

1. Blindness and Vision

I would like to begin by clarifying the meaning of my title, especially in a critical landscape where theory has long fallen from grace. I think that Franco Moretti fully embraces the role of literary theorist, even if in his occasional critical self-portraits he prefers – like Auerbach before him – to describe himself instead as a historian, or even as a 'history professor'.[1] Of course, to loosely paraphrase Wittgenstein, it all depends on what you mean by 'theory'. So let's try to understand that first.

Obviously, there is a long history behind this terrible word, which I can't go through in any detail here. Above all, there are the enormous social, economic, cultural and technological transformations that have swept through Western societies in recent decades, radically changing the conditions of intellectual labour, scientific research, and teaching, far beyond the narrow misfortunes of literary studies. In this context, the shipwreck of theory may serve as a warning sign for a much broader intellectual catastrophe. The shipwreck was perhaps inevitable, and if in some ways even salutary, it nevertheless produced side effects that have been too costly to ignore, ones that would be unthinkable in other academic disciplines: scientific regression, unchecked empiricism, impressionistic analysis, methodological opportunism. And so we sail

1 Franco Moretti, *The Bourgeois: Between History and Literature* (London: Verso, 2013), p. 23.

among the wreckage: the remnants of the great theoretical era we have left behind are now recycled as trade goods, consumer products, cognitive tools completely de-historicised and reified, taken off the shelves of what Remo Ceserani once called 'the supermarket of critical methods'.[2]

In truth, this instrumental banalisation was already embedded in the historical trajectory, and arguably the very design, of theory (or rather, as we will see, of a certain kind of theory). Perhaps it was the hubris of its most brilliant minds, driven by the utopian ambition to forge a *mathesis universalis* of literary knowledge – the final spark of the grand Enlightenment project. Or perhaps it emerged from the sterile dogmatism of its most zealous functionaries, preoccupied only with defining, abstracting, classifying. Either way, twentieth-century literary theory ultimately died of boredom and repetition: undone by the technical reproducibility of its easiest formulas, and by the reduction of innovative and radical proposals to mere 'methods' – instruction manuals, recipes to be followed without asking too many questions. As Mario Lavagetto writes, 'those which had originally been new theoretical proposals, and as such carried a bracing power of intellectual provocation, gradually degenerated into epigonal routines repeated thousands of times, tools of a slow, unconscious suicide carried out without witnesses.'[3] The prime example is the pedagogical flattening of narratology and structural analysis, once ambitious and complex cognitive tools, degraded by their own success into 'instruments for knowledge control', aimed solely at perpetuating orthodoxy and transferring competencies.[4]

It is this descriptive and nomenclatural conception that fuels theory's bad reputation and the labels that circulate in everyday *doxa*: rigid, dogmatic, abstract, extreme, difficult, pedantic; abstruse language, specialised jargon, overcomplicated taxonomies, verbose declarations of

2 Remo Ceserani, *Treni di carta. L'immaginario in ferrovia: l'irruzione del treno nella letteratura moderna* (Genoa: Marietti, 1993), pp. xix–xx.

3 Mario Lavagetto, *La cicatrice di Montaigne. Sulla bugia in letteratura* (Turin: Einaudi, 1992), p. 39.

4 Jean-Marie Schaeffer, *Petite écologie des études littéraires. Pourquoi et comment étudier la littérature,* (Vincennes: Éditions Thierry Marchaisse, 2011).

methods and results. But, as so often happens, the cure can be worse than the disease: once theory is pronounced dead – once that 'demon' has been exorcised – its sworn enemy returns in triumph: common sense.[5] This has re-legitimised empty chatter, impressionistic criticism, and what Lavagetto has called 'the spontaneous anthropology of literary critics', 'that strange mixture of reflections on human beings, half-philosophical and half-moralistic, that leads . . . to converting discourse on literature into the most generic and improbable of discourses on the world – or, worse, on the supposedly universal human experience of the world'.[6] The risks here are obvious, and they affect not only narrowly literary questions, but also, and more broadly, political ones: when we discard a project of Enlightenment ambition like twentieth-century theory, 'we expose ourselves to an outright restoration – in our case . . . we expose ourselves too much to the return of a criticism made up of idle talk, with an idealist or, worse still, a neo-mystical bent'.[7]

Now, as Michel Charles wrote in a sophisticated and unfashionable book, there is a major misunderstanding about theory, 'because literary theory is not a system of reading, but the very foundation of any rigorous reading':

> Few, in fact, will deny the necessity of asking what kind of object we, as 'literary scholars', actually study; but this agreement is only superficial, and most, after conceding this necessity, return to their work without acknowledging that, as I said, one must ask this fundamental question at every moment and, above all, that it informs every single analysis at every moment.[8]

The misunderstanding lies, in short, in the bad faith of common sense: in reducing a general label (literary theory) to a specific domain

5 Antoine Compagnon, *Le Démon de la théorie. Littérature et sens commun*, (Paris: Seuil, 1998).

6 Mario Lavagetto, *Lavorare con piccoli indizi* (Turin: Bollati Boringhieri, 2003), p. 52.

7 Raul Mordenti, *L'altra critica. La nuova critica della letteratura tra studi culturali, didattica e informatica* (Rome: Meltemi, 2007), pp. 121–2.

8 Michael Charles, *Introduction à l'étude des textes* (Paris: Seuil, 1995), p. 5.

(structuralism, or rather a simplified popular caricature of it). This leads to calling 'theory' what is really a particular manifestation of it, developed mainly in France during the 1960s and '70s, and specialising in extreme hypotheses (reality is a construct, the author is dead, every act of writing is in fact rewriting, and so on) – as if someone were to call 'biology' the study of chlorophyll photosynthesis, or 'astrophysics' the study of solar wind. And it was, indeed, a spectacular revenge of common sense to identify theory – which Roland Barthes defined as 'the subversive weapon par excellence' – with one of its narrow, dogmatic versions, which later degenerated into a method or a recipe.[9]

Franco Moretti has navigated the complex phases of this retreat from theory as a leading figure. He has done so with tireless enthusiasm and a healthy sense of restlessness, driven by the kind of intellectual curiosity that led him to explore uncharted paths, to defamiliarise perspectives, shift methods and paradigms, and sharpen new critical tools to ask what still remains to be done. In this relentless, often empirical, and perhaps somewhat thankless work – combing through bibliographies, compiling lists, analysing quantitative data – he has always underscored the importance of abstraction, conceptual synthesis and methodological precision, rightly 'convinced that empirical research is impossible without a guiding theoretical framework'.[10]

This is the true spirit of modern science, the cognitive wager that rolls the dice of hypothesis: 'What is, however, important is to prefix a theoretical aim, for this is the life-blood of all real research. *On s'engage*: and then we will see.'[11]

It hardly matters whether the problems are difficult or even unsolvable, because the cognitive gain lies precisely in the question – in the propulsive force of those 'why?'s that so often punctuate Moretti's argumentative rhetoric: 'problems without a solution are exactly what we

9 Roland Barthes, *The Grain of the Voice: Interviews 1962–1980*, transl. Linda Coverdale (Oakland, CA: University of California Press, 1991), p. 153.

10 Franco Moretti, *Signs Taken for Wonders: Essays in the Sociology of Literary Forms*, transl. Susan Fisher, David Forgacs and D. A. Miller (London: Verso, 1997 [1983], 2nd edn 1988), p. 1.

11 Ibid., p. 132.

need in a field like ours, where we are used to asking only those questions for which we already have an answer.'[12] However, recalling criticism to a model of rational knowledge – insisting that even complex and polysemous objects like literary texts can be subjected to 'univocal and potentially complete' analyses – does not mean turning theory into an abstract, self-contained entity, a kind of metaphysical exercise locked within the flawless logic of its own system.[13] On the contrary, the materialist foundations of Moretti's intellectual training underpin the entirety of his research. What guides him, in his own words, is 'a somewhat pragmatic – if not instrumental – view of theoretical knowledge (theory of the kind that a historian likes, let's say). "Theories are nets", Novalis wrote, "and only he who casts will catch." Yes, theories are nets, and we should evaluate them, not as ends in themselves, but for how they *concretely change the way we work.*'[14]

This is, then, a deeply secular idea of literature and literary study – already hinted at in the title of Moretti's first book in English, *Signs Taken for Wonders* (1983): literary works are not 'prodigal', but concrete, earthly objects, 'prosaic sociocultural "signs" '; and literary study is not the rarefied auscultation of aesthetic vibrations or – worse still – 'a retrograde personality cult', but rational knowledge, technical analysis, scientific labour in which one formulates theses, analyses data, and tests hypotheses that are either confirmed or disproved.[15] Experimental criticism, in other words, as captured by the apt phrase that gives this volume its title.

There is a fine essay by Stevenson called 'On Some Technical Elements of Style in Literature', where that author – so often dismissed as 'simple' or 'naive' (never was a prejudice more mistaken) – sets out to explore 'the springs and mechanisms of any art', tricks and devices that may seem crude but 'if we had the power to trace them to their springs [would

---

12 Franco Moretti, *Graphs, Maps, Trees: Abstract Models for a Literary History* (London: Verso, 2005), p. 26.

13 Moretti, *Signs Taken for Wonders*, p. 22.

14 Franco Moretti, *Graphs, Maps, Trees*, p. 91.

15 Franco Moretti, *Far Country: Scenes from American Culture* (London/New York: Verso, 2019), p. 21.

show] indications of a delicacy of the sense finer than we conceive, and hints of ancient harmonies in nature'.[16]

I believe Moretti shares both the method and spirit of Stevenson's remarks, because even today – or rather, especially today – we need a 'literary history interested in explaining, in analyzing – in understanding, rather than judging': a 'truly profane' literary history, in other words.[17] And also because, at some point – or perhaps right away – the technical labour gives way to the pure pleasure of knowledge:

> A materialist history of literary forms is too splendid a challenge to intelligence to be let slip. To see clearly – and understand – how they function, those complicated things that humans enjoy reading: in all honesty, I know of nothing better, for anyone concerned with literature. But it is an irrational pleasure, which I shall try not in any way to justify.[18]

Let's focus on this phrase 'to see clearly', one of the many allusions Moretti makes to the visual sphere: a perceptual transcription of his idea (and, for what it's worth, mine too) of theoretical knowledge, not too far from what Proust called style, which is not a matter of technique but 'a visual quality'.[19] We are very far here from the normative, classificatory sense of theory, from that taxonomic demon that ultimately gave twentieth-century theory its bad name. Because the true function of theoretical work is not descriptive, but heuristic: not so much to catalogue, classify and label phenomena with arcane and meticulous terminology, but rather *to go and see*, in keeping with one of the etymological roots of the word 'theory'. To devise optical tools that allow us to see something we otherwise would not:

> Theorizing – whose etymology suggests that it is at once about 'contemplating a spectacle,' 'proceeding in a delegation,' and 'speculating with eyes closed' – consists in going to see . . . Far from limiting itself to the

---

16 Robert Louis Stevenson, *Essays and Criticism* (Boston: Herbert & Turner, 1904), p. 178.

17 Franco Moretti, *Il romanzo di formazione* (Turin: Einaudi, 1999), p. xxi.

18 Franco Moretti, *Modern Epic: The World System from Goethe to García Márquez* (London: Verso, 1996), pp. 5–6.

19 Marcel Proust, *Contre Sainte-Beuve* (Paris: Gallimard, 1971 [1954]), p. 559.

> taxonomic inflation that ended up giving 'literary theory' a bad name, the effort of theorization points primarily to adventure and exploration . . . according to a movement that invites us to go (to see) as far as possible, while also leaving us the option to turn back.[20]

I don't know whether Moretti is familiar with this passage by Yves Citton, but I believe the link between theory and vision is deeply in tune with his approach, especially in the dynamic sense (the double movement, outward and back) that Citton evokes.

First movement: *going to see* – which means exploring, taking risks, practising a kind of criticism as estrangement, in which a shift in perspective jams habitual mechanisms, strips the film of the obvious, refuses to recognise phenomena automatically, and forces us to see them as if for the first time.[21] That is how you become a comparatist, '*because you are convinced that that viewpoint is better.* It has greater explanatory power.'[22] Or you use abstract models because they 'place the literary field literally in front of our eyes – and show us how little we know about it', because 'they will possess "emerging" qualities, which were not visible at the lower level'.[23] For example, the circular structure of the world in *Our Village* had never been analysed 'because no one – in absence of a geographical map of the book – had ever managed to actually *see it*'.[24]

It is not enough, in short, to describe what is in the text or the context, as positivist philology or vulgar historicism tend to do. One must uncover what is there but not seen, through conceptual frameworks and analytical tools that let us grasp hidden things, those that elude ordinary perception (forms, patterns, structures, rhythms, relations): a little like putting literature through an X-ray.[25] And if you get it wrong, you can always turn back (second movement): adjust the aim, rethink the thesis,

20 Yves Citton, *Lire, interpréter, actualiser. Pourquoi les études littéraries?* (Paris: Editions Amsterdam, 2007), p. 35.

21 Federico Bertoni, *Realismo e letteratura. Una storia possibile* (Turin: Einaudi, 2018), pp. 283–4.

22 Franco Moretti, *Distant Reading* (London: Verso, 2013), p. 61.

23 Moretti, *Graphs, Maps, Trees*, pp. 3, 53.

24 Ibid., p. 53.

25 Moretti, *Distant Reading*, p. 218.

admit that a promising hypothesis has yielded little or been proved wrong.

The assertive, sometimes even apodictic tone of Moretti's theoretical statements is balanced by the intellectual honesty with which he acknowledges error or his own lack of knowledge on specific points – even to the extent of recently affirming the heuristic value of failed or inconclusive experiments: 'errors *throw a special light onto the whole process of research*'; 'By frustrating our expectations, failed experiments "estrange" our natural habits of thought, offering us a chance to transform them.'[26]

When Roland Barthes, in that extraordinary text *Criticism and Truth*, the manifesto of the French *nouvelle critique*, called for the advent of a new 'literary science' capable of subjecting the text 'to analyses which are *certain*', he simultaneously recognised that 'these analyses will leave aside an enormous residue', that which cannot be abstracted or categorised – perhaps precisely what we call *literature*.[27] This is what Paul de Man, in his posthumously published final book, called resistance to theory: theory's resistance to itself, but also the resistance of literary phenomena to any definitive or univocal solution – the exact opposite of the totalitarian project that common sense seeks to impose on it.[28] It is the resistance to any dogmatic rigidity, the endless dialogue with cultural objects that exist in ambiguity, dissonance, semantic overdetermination, and the simultaneous activation of multiple connotative potentials that no systematic reason can catalogue.

To paraphrase a reflection by Paolo Fabbri on semiotics, one could say that literary theory is inferior to the immense complexity of its

---

26 'In one respect, my observation was certainly wrong . . .': Moretti, *Distant Reading*, p. 152; '[T]he reason I kept "forgetting" geography for geometry was, first of all, ignorance: in order to write the *Atlas* I had studied some cartography, but had learned it only up to a point, and so I made mistakes': Moretti, *Graphs, Maps, Trees*, pp. 55–6; Franco Moretti, 'Literature, Measured', *Pamphlet 12* (2016) of the Stanford Literary Lab, p. 4 – at litlab.stanford.edu.

27 Roland Barthes, *Criticism and Truth* (London/New York: Bloomsbury, 2007 [1966]), p. 31.

28 Paul De Man, *The Resistance to Theory* (Manchester: Manchester University Press, 1986).

object – but, unlike in the past, it now fully knows this.[29] Franco Moretti is equally aware:

> If we want to understand a system in its entirety, we need to resign ourselves to losing something. There is always a price to pay for theoretical knowledge: reality is infinitely rich; concepts are abstract and poor. But it is precisely this 'poverty' that makes it possible to manage them, and thus to understand.[30]

Perhaps this is the price of any science or theory, a price as high as the object in question is vague, unstable and heterogeneous – as in the case of literature, an entity no one can define. But it is worth trying all the same.

2. An Inexact Science

Understanding the system in its entirety. Anyone who has seriously engaged with literary theory will recognise themselves in Moretti's critical predicament: the drive to expand the field, to master multiplicity, to bring heterogeneous classes of objects under synthetic concepts (the novel, the epic form, the bourgeois) and define their distinctive traits, morphological constants and salient qualities.

There is something vaguely Balzacian in this aspiration to totality – in the expansion of critical perspective to increasingly vast units of measurement that might asymptotically encompass the entire literary field; 'depicting all society, sketching it in the immensity of its turmoil'; 'describing truly the various phases of society': if we substitute 'society' for 'literary history,' we arrive at a fitting articulation of the ambition Moretti has pursued at various stages of his intellectual career – though always with a certain restlessness, a growing dissatisfaction with the

---

29 Paolo Fabbri, 'Il modello enunciativo', in Ugo Maria Olivieri, ed., *Le immagini della critica. Conversazioni di teoria letteraria* (Turin: Bollati Boringhieri, 2003), p. 17.

30 Moretti, *Distant Reading*, p. 49.

fragmentary nature of the results.[31] Unfortunately, there is no longer room for Balzacian titanism or the visionary dreams of the Romantic generations. What remains is a struggle far more akin to the twentieth-century neuroses of Gadda, convinced that every object 'necessarily leads us to admit the totality of objects', that 'the consideration of a finite object compels our mind to acknowledge the existence of all that is known, all that is conceivable, and more besides', casting us into the 'monstrous web of totality'.[32]

The somewhat anxious perception of the Great Unread is the perfect symptom of this: a vast Atlantis of literary history, a dark continent that highlights the partiality and irrelevance of our tiny store of knowledge – small islands in a mysterious ocean. Fair enough, writes Moretti in 'Conjectures on World Literature' (2000): let's say I work on nineteenth-century European fiction. But is that really true? In fact, 'I work on its canonical fraction, which is not even 1 per cent of published literature. And again, some people have read more, but the point is that there are thirty thousand nineteenth-century British novels out there, forty, fifty, sixty thousand – no one really knows, no one has read them, no one ever will. And then there are French novels, Chinese, Argentinian, American . . .'.[33] What is the truth status of our critical statements if our investigations routinely take place within a 'minimal fraction of the literary field', while the proportions at stake are 'the one per cent of the canon, and the ninety-nine of forgotten literature'?[34] This is why, he insists, one of the frontiers of literary history is 'the challenge of quantity – of the 99 per cent of all published literature that disappears from sight, and that nobody wants to revive'.[35] It is the stark but effective image of the slaughterhouse of literature, a process of 'decimating literary works' that selects the small fraction of the canon – the part we continue

31 Honoré de Balzac, 'Introduction' [1842] in *At the Sign of the Cat and the Racket,* transl. Clara Bell (London: J. M. Dent, 1895), pp. 9 and 11.

32 Carlo Emilio Gadda, *Scritti vari e postumi* (Milan: Garzanti, 1993), pp. 646, 822, 842.

33 Moretti, *Distant Reading*, p. 45.

34 Moretti, *Graphs, Maps, Trees*, pp. 2–3, 77.

35 Moretti, *Atlas of the European Novel*, p. 5.

to read and study – and suppresses the overwhelming majority of published literature, buried in a vast archive no human being could ever fully explore.[36]

Here too, anyone who has engaged theoretically with general questions (a genre, a morphological constant, a long-term theme, a section of literary history) knows very well the process of synthesis, selection and exclusion that risks invalidating any thesis, making it fragile and falsifiable. And I believe this also helps explain the appeal that quantitative methods and digital technologies have exerted on Moretti – not just as technical tools but as a kind of epistemological lens, in the sense once described by Benjamin (and later by many others). Technologies are transformative. They do not merely offer operational prostheses that enhance our powers of manipulation over reality; they change the very way we see, know and experience the world. In this sense, 'computation has theoretical consequences', and offers 'a unique chance to rethink the categories of literary study'.[37] The results may be debatable, but the theoretical choice is perfectly sound: the machine accelerates, multiplies, and vastly expands the horizon of the phenomena we can interrogate, and thus changes the very form of the object and the way we observe it. 'What do we have to gain?' Moretti asks in one of his methodological asides. 'What can quantitative methods *add* to the study of literature?'[38] First of all, he explains, new data and information, a richer context, and 'the related discovery of how *slowly* this territory changes, the discovery of "histoire immobile", as Braudel has polemically called it'.[39] But, above all, one gains a sense of literature in terms of totality – the possibility 'to come up with a new sense of the

---

36 Moretti, *Distant Reading*, pp. 63–89; Moretti, *La letteratura vista da lontano*, p. 90; transl. Mark Algee-Hewitt, Sarah Allison, Marissa Gemma, Ryan Heuser, Franco Moretti and Hannah Walser, 'Canon/Archive: Large-scale Dynamics in the Literary Field', *Pamphlet 11* of the Stanford Literary Lab (2016), pp. 1–2 – at litlab.stanford.edu.

37 Franco Moretti, '"Operationalizing": or, the Function of Measurement in Modern Literary Theory', *Pamphlet 6* of the Stanford Literary Lab (2013), pp. 9, 13 – at litlab.stanford.edu.

38 Moretti, *Atlas of the European Novel*, p. 149.

39 Ibid., p. 150.

literary field as a whole', 'throwing light on the literary field as a whole', even writing the 'total history of literature'.[40]

The provocative metaphor of 'distance', which has been widely debated, indeed expresses the cognitive posture induced by a certain set of technical tools (lists, databases, quantitative series, graphs, diagrams). But, more than that, it once again translates into optical-spatial terms a requirement that is intrinsic to any theory: to abstract, to generalise, to condense years of analysis into a day of synthesis, to grasp multiplicity without getting lost in the inventory of what Hegel called the 'bad infinity'. A 'fatal formula', as Moretti later described it in reference to the controversial essay on world literature, distant reading thus names a scale directly proportional to the mirage of totality: 'the more ambitious the project, the great must the distance be.'[41] In this sense, distance '*is a condition of knowledge*', not 'an obstacle, but *a specific form of knowledge:* fewer elements, hence a sharper sense of their overall interconnection. Shapes, relations, structures.' It is a little 'like having a telescope that makes you see entirely new galaxies'.[42]

An interdisciplinary scholar by vocation, Moretti draws from the natural sciences (mathematics, statistics, physics, geometry, biology, genetics, computer science, information theory) several operational paradigms that are still quite rare in the field of literary studies, especially after the retreat of theory and the general rejection of models based on abstract formalisation: to measure, to quantify, to operationalise. Thus, 'the operational approach . . . describes the process whereby concepts are transformed into a series of operations – which, in their turn, allow us to measure all sorts of objects', including literature.[43] Paraphrasing a well-known essay by Hans Robert Jauss, this is 'measurement as a challenge to literary theory'.[44] Not without reason, 'Literature, Measured' is the programmatic title of one of the Stanford Literary Lab pamphlets. To the

40 Moretti, *Distant Reading*, p. 67; Algee-Hewitt et al., 'Canon/Archive', pp. 12, 2.

41 Moretti, *Distant Reading*, pp. 44, 48.

42 Ibid.; Moretti, *Graphs, Maps, Trees*, p. 1; Algee-Hewitt et al., 'Canon/Archive', p. 1.

43 Moretti, '"Operationalizing"', p. 1.

44 Ibid., p. 9.

cynical, it may call to mind J. Evans Pritchard's joke at the beginning of *Dead Poets' Society* ('If the poem's score for perfection is plotted on the horizontal of a graph and its importance is plotted on the vertical, then calculating the total area of the poem yields the measure of its greatness') – but the pamphlet is based on entirely different methods and assumptions.[45] Measurement is important, Moretti argues, because 'it makes some concepts "actual" in the strong sense of the word', showing 'that, by following a series of steps, you can turn abstractions into a clear and, hopefully, unexpected elaboration of reality'.[46] Whether the results live up to the promise is, of course, never to be taken for granted. And while some analytical operations offer fresh and encouraging insights, others merely confirm by experimental means what literary critics had long intuited. But what matters is the symptomatic and programmatic value of this union between the formal and the quantitative ('formalism without close reading', as it has been called), including its profusion of charts, maps, graphs, diagrams, histograms, tables and webs – not always easy to decipher.[47] It is a project of introducing, *cum grano salis*, some healthy antibodies into a critical practice increasingly dominated by vagueness, approximation, empiricism, neo-contentism, simplified contextualism, and the dogmas of common sense.

I would interpret the misunderstanding Moretti recounts in one of his geo-literary essays according to the logic of the symptom: he presents as geographical maps what are in fact diagrams, as the geographer Claudio Cerreti objected in a review of *Atlas of the European Novel*; and thus he reads literature not through geography, but through geometry. Indeed, Moretti acknowledges as much: 'for me, *geometry "signifies" more than geography*. More, in the sense that a geometrical pattern is too orderly a shape to be the product of chance. It is a sign that something is at work here – that something has *made* the pattern the way it is.'[48]

45 Moretti, 'Literature, Measured'.

46 Moretti, '"Operationalizing"', p. 4.

47 Moretti, *Distant Reading*, pp. 65, 118, 180.

48 Moretti, *Graphs, Maps, Trees*, p. 56.

3. Norm and Exception

We can see here one of the critical points in Moretti's conceptual framework, one of those indispensable yet problematic junctures that offer his detractors a ready-made pretext to accuse him of determinism and mechanical causalism. It is the price to be paid by someone who has increasingly tried to prioritise the explanation of general structures over the interpretation of individual texts, if it is true that 'the real challenge lies . . . lies in the realm of causality and large-scale explanations'.[49] I would also argue that this need to investigate deep structures and formulate general laws belongs to Moretti's theoretical *habitus* as such, regardless of the later 'quantitative' development of his method. It is thus already clearly visible in *The Way of the World* and *Modern Epic*, where we find the inverse formula: not an inclusive method but an exclusive one, based on a narrow canon of exemplary texts through which to test foundational theses.[50]

This is an assertive, nomothetic tension that often comes through even in stylistic or typographic cues, such as syncopated, expressive punctuation, italics that underscore theses, or the adverb *always*, which generalises an axiom inevitably drawn from local information. The objects of this linguistic-conceptual elaboration vary. For instance, literature as such: 'Literary form is *always* a compromise between opposite forces.'[51] Or the spread of the European novel across a global chessboard: 'Four continents, 200 years, over 20 independent critical studies, and they all agreed: when a culture starts moving towards the modern novel, it's *always* as a compromise between foreign form and local materials.'[52] Or again, the determining connection between geographic location and

49 Moretti, *Distant Reading*, p. 155.

50 In *Modern Epic*, the choice is asserted, in order to isolate a new category (modern epic) from the generic and unusable *mare magnum* of modernism: 'the solution, therefore, lay in learning to omit – to restrict the field. The ambition of the historiographical hypothesis here coincided with its modesty. *Weniger ist mehr*, as Mies van der Rohe used to say; less is more.' Moretti, *Modern Epic*, p. 3.

51 Moretti, *Distant Reading*, p. 116.

52 Ibid., p. 52.

plot: 'in the sense that *each space determines, or at least encourages, its own kind of story*', with a corresponding complementary thesis: '*without a certain kind of space, a certain kind of story is simply impossible.* Without the Latin Quarter, I mean . . . we wouldn't have the wonder of the French *Bildungsroman.*'[53]

A typical expression of this nomothetic ambition is the paradigm of regularity, which informs many of Moretti's theses and often serves as connective tissue between subject and object, theory and history, analytical tools and observed phenomena. In an osmotic – or perhaps circular – logic, regularity can thus become the key to critical method, because it is already a fundamental characteristic of literary history, or at least of large portions of it. The lexical markers leave little doubt: *regular, normal, repetitive, quotidian, prosaic, average, boring* are key words that reflect Moretti's impatience with the most complacent practices of literary studies, in service of yet another change of course: reversing the hierarchical link between norm and exception, and thus weakening the status of the canon, the masterpiece, or the stylistic pinnacle in order to shift attention – following the lesson of the *Annales* historians – 'from the extraordinary to the everyday, from exceptional events to the large mass of facts'.[54]

Already in *Signs Taken for Wonders*, Moretti favoured the first term in the convention/innovation dyad, which has never truly become an object of knowledge in its own right, since the idea of 'normal literature' has no real standing in literary criticism.[55] In *The Way of the World*, he distanced himself from formalist theories that oppose laws to anomalies, 'precisely because it conceives of the story only as an exception and negation of a fixed paradigm: as the anomaly of a law, necessarily fortuitous or even inexplicable'.[56]

To test this thesis, he turned not to the unstable, 'Napoleonic' French (or Russian) case, but to the English *Bildungsroman*, the perfect example

---

53 Moretti, *Atlas of the European Novel*, pp. 70, 100.

54 Moretti, *Graphs, Maps, Trees*, p. 3.

55 Moretti, *Signs Taken for Wonders*, p. 15.

56 Moretti, *The Way of the World: The* Bildungsroman *in European Culture*, transl. Albert Sbragia (London: Verso, 2000 [1986]), p. 105.

of a narrative device that symbolically fuses form and ideology, plot and social structure, *homo fictus* and bourgeois: on the one hand, the 'peaceful normality of the hero'; on the other, 'a stable and well-classified world' – two planes that would remain conflict-free and ahistorical if not for the 'monstrous' intervention of a villain who provides the spark for the plot.[57] Even a decisive essay like 'Serious Century', Moretti's personal contribution to *Il romanzo*, later taken up in *The Bourgeois*, makes regularity the key concept through which to sum up an entire century and to grasp the systematic correlation between morphology and history. This rests on a long-standing, never-abandoned materialist conception of literary form – a sociological formalism – that sees forms as 'the abstract of social relations', or even 'as the most profoundly social aspect of literature: *form as force*'.[58] In this sense, Moretti comments, '*regularity*, not disequilibrium, was the great narrative invention of bourgeois Europe', because the European middle class expected from fiction a symbolic satisfaction consistent with its values – seriousness, stability, normality, everyday routine.[59]

This alone explains the widespread diffusion of one of the formal constants of the nineteenth-century novel: the *filler*, elements with little narrative function that narratologists call satellites or catalyses – an equivalent, Moretti writes, to 'the good manners so dear to nineteenth-century novelists . . . a mechanism designed to keep the "narrativity" of life under control; to give it a regularity, a "style"'.[60] In other words, the secret to the success of fillers must be sought outside the literary field, 'in the sphere of . . . private life', 'because they offer *the kind of narrative pleasure compatible with the new regularity of bourgeois life*'; 'fillers *rationalize the novelistic universe*, turning it into a world of few surprises, fewer adventures, and no miracles at all. They are a great bourgeois invention . . . because through them the logic of rationalization pervades *the very rhythm of the novel*.'[61]

57 Ibid., pp. 199–202.

58 Moretti, *Distant Reading*, pp. 59, 117, 157; Moretti, *Graphs, Maps, Trees*, p. 92.

59 Moretti, *The Bourgeois*, p. 15.

60 Ibid., p. 72.

61 Ibid., pp. 80–1.

When Moretti later embraces computational criticism, he also transfers the paradigm of regularity to the methodological level: the serial operations performed by machines process vast amounts of data to identify constants, cycles, recurring structures and long-term processes:

> This is what quantitative methods have to offer to the historian of literature: a reversal of the hierarchy between the exception and the series, where the latter becomes – as it is – the true protagonist of cultural life. A history of literature as history of *norms*, then: a less innovative, much 'flatter' configuration than the one we are used to; repetitive, slow – boring, even. But this is exactly what most of life is like, and instead of redeeming literature from its prosaic features we should learn to recognize them and understand what they mean. Just as most science is 'normal' science . . . so *most literature is normal literature*.[62]

This is the osmotic or circular logic I was speaking about before: the method relies on an operational principle that is already assumed a priori in literary history, whose rhythm is not so much marked by breakthroughs, ruptures or exceptions, but by 'a kind of secret metronome' – cycles, alternations, repetitions.[63]

Thus we see that the paradigm of regularity operates on multiple interconnected levels: micro-formal constants (fillers), the logic of the plot (backgrounds, details, controlled surprises), ideological configurations (stability, normality, bourgeois rationalism), the design of literary history (cycles, *longue durée*, normal literature), analytical methods (schemes, abstract models, quantitative series). The problem is obviously how to account for the inevitable exceptions – especially when their names are, say, Pushkin or Stendhal:

> Like their heroes, these authors are not in the least interested in the laws of social life, but only in their violation . . . To use a conceptual pair similar to that of law and anomaly, Pushkin and Stendhal are far more interested in 'foreground' than in 'background' . . . Plot becomes a

---

62 Moretti, *Atlas of the European Novel*, p. 150.

63 Moretti, *Graphs, Maps, Trees*, pp. 26–30.

> sequence of *arbitrary acts*: precisely what the bourgeois desire for predictability aimed to do away with . . .[64]

The challenge, once again, is how to account for the pervasive conflict, the deep dissonance (a key term in Moretti's critical lexicon) that literature cultivates as its distinctive hallmark. Even a quick look at the tradition of the so-called realist novel reveals that the orderly, rational, and sometimes rather dull prose of the world is constantly disrupted by anti-mimetic currents, narrative detritus, imaginative compromises and smuggled-in elements that fracture the ideological coherence of the most emblematic symbolic form of bourgeois rationalism. Everyday realism, subdued passions, regular rhythms, prose of the world – true. But how many exceptions are there to that rule? Convinced that conflict is 'the key mechanism behind literary history', Moretti knows that forms are unstable compounds, hybrid and contaminated structures in which opposing forces not only coexist, clash and interact but, most importantly, produce meaning.[65] Literature, he rightly says, is a kind of bricolage, not the blueprint of an engineer.

The novel, then, is a spurious, imperfect conglomerate, often shaped by chance, in which historically outdated forms like the *romance* (that is, adventure, unpredictability, arbitrariness, irrationality, the incredible) resurface from archaic layers and are reactivated, in compromised form, in the heart of bourgeois rationality. This is true even at the very centre of the 'serious century', structured by a principle of ambivalence that runs through nearly all the novels labelled as realist.[66] Not only Pushkin and Stendhal, but also Balzac, Dickens, Zola, Fontane, Thackeray, George Eliot and even Manzoni. Perhaps only Flaubert succeeded in purging the novel of any romantic temptation, reducing it to parody and *bêtise*, or at most confining it to the free zone of lavish, visionary texts. And perhaps only the Flaubert of *Sentimental Education* fully realises – in the

64 Moretti, *Way of the World*, p. 105.

65 Moretti, *Far Country*, p. 7.

66 See Bertoni, *Realismo e letteratura*, pp. 152–4; Federico Bertoni, 'Nascita e metamorfosi del romanzo', in Piero Boitani and Massimo Fusillo, eds, *Letteratura europea*, vol. 2 (Turin: UTET, 2014), pp. 133–4.

implacable osmosis of form and ideology – the narrative regularity of a bourgeois world that is uniform, inescapable, without rupture or reprieve, where everything is kneaded from the same dough and smoothed to the homogeneous consistency that Proust recognised in his style. But Flaubert is unique, thankfully, with his genius and his cruel lucidity.

More broadly, Moretti's totalising ambition must contend with the ungovernable multiplicity of the literary field. He argues, for example, that the proliferation of novelistic subgenres renders the great theories of the novel obsolete, as they have 'reduced the novel to one basic form only', whereas what is needed is 'a theory, not so much of "the" novel, but of *a whole family of novelistic forms.* A theory – of diversity.'[67] Similarly, attempts to funnel early-twentieth-century literature under the catch-all label of modernism are doomed to fail, since it is a 'multiplicity of disconnected phenomena' without 'any common denominator'. 'It's a Big Bang of European literature: a sudden liberation of energies giving life to the most disparate forms.'[68] Not to mention the Great Unread, a forest teeming with strange and varied creatures, which even suggests a hypothetical, counterfactual version of literary history – a web of possibilities in which only one thread has been selected and actualised, at the expense of countless alternative worlds: in other words, 'literary history *could be different from what it is*'.[69]

Perhaps it is an arbitrary suggestion, but I believe Franco Moretti's critical utopia aims to formulate an impossible equation between two values that Italo Calvino hoped to pass on to the next (that is, our) millennium: exactness and multiplicity. In other words, to provide a precise, accurate, scientifically verifiable description of a fractal-like object that proliferates in every direction – but that, unlike a fractal, is not generated by an algorithm. Naturally, as already in Calvino, this provides ample fuel for more than one kind of neurosis. 'We look for patterns', Moretti admits, 'because they reveal some kind of order, and we *want* to find order, especially when we are confronted with large masses of

---

67 Moretti, *Graphs, Maps, Trees*, p. 30. See the non-structural structure of *Il romanzo*, a true monument to plurality.

68 Moretti, *Modern Epic*, p. 200.

69 Moretti, *Distant Reading*, p. 88.

data.'[70] And yet, 'once we have seen the pattern, we can take off the blinders, and then, it's impossible not to notice how *small* the region of order actually is. Form is everywhere encircled by noise: a maelstrom of semantic options that have kept whirling around, without ever crystallizing into stable structures.'[71]

Order and chaos, form and flux, crystal and vortex. Calvino's words inevitably come to mind, when he writes that 'the literary work is one of those minimal portions in which existence crystallizes into a form, acquires a meaning – not fixed, not definitive, not frozen in mineral immobility, but alive like an organism'.[72] On one side: synthesis, the model, the abstraction of forms understood as the regular recurrence of patterns and relations ('the form is precisely *the repeatable element of literature*', Moretti writes tirelessly).[73] On the other: analysis, the endless computation, the acquisition of ever larger and more heterogeneous data sets, in that 'Balzacian' drive towards the totality of the real that forces one to widen the horizon, to increase distance and scale – making the details and the 'real' things disappear.

With his vigilant methodological self-awareness, Moretti often reminds us that models are not real things but abstractions – artificial objects, images that no one has ever seen, something not found in nature but constructed through a deliberate process of reduction, abstraction and quantification: 'And this, of course, is what makes quantitative methods so repugnant to literary critics: the fear that they may suppress the uniqueness of texts. Which indeed they do. But as I don't believe in the epistemological value of the unique, its suppression doesn't really bother me.'[74]

In reality, behind the somewhat swaggering tone, this is only one side of the coin. His journey along the 'narrow bridge' of theory – borrowing an image from Virginia Woolf – advances precariously between exception

---

70 Franco Moretti, 'Patterns and Interpretation', *Pamphlet 15* of the Stanford Literary Lab (2017), p. 9 – at litlab.stanford.edu.

71 Ibid., p. 10.

72 Italo Calvino, *Saggi 1945–1985*, vol. 1 (Milan: Mondadori, 1995), p. 688.

73 Moretti, *Distant Reading*, pp. 86, 142; Moretti, 'Literature, Measured', p. 6; Moretti, 'Patterns and Interpretation', pp. 6, 8.

74 Moretti, *Atlas of the European Novel*, p. 143.

and norm, the individual case and the general law, 'the chaos of empirical data and the clarity of conceptual form'.[75] Not by accident, one of the key methodological issues in his work is the problem of scale: the challenge of calibrating effective units of measurement for observing and processing data, an updated equivalent of what formalist and structuralist criticism once called 'levels of description'. Thus, when faced with the vastness of the manifold (the novel, the literary field, the world-system), 'the solution lies in multiple layers of description and explanation, linked together by a chain of successfully analysed "details" . . . God lies in the detail – perhaps. Our understanding of culture certainly does.'[76] It is no accident that, over time, Moretti has increased the tension between extremes, embracing a 'mix of the micro and the macro', which he traces back to Leo Spitzer's *Stilkritik*, for whom 'all that mattered were the "detail" and the "whole"'.[77] 'The very small and the very large; these are the forces that shape literary history.'[78]

A familiar concept from the Russian formalists, the device, thus ends up collaborating with a very old category that modernity has now rendered unstable, but certainly not obsolete: the *literary genre*. The result is a bifocal gaze – microscope and telescope – that sidelines the middle term, the *text*, much to the dismay of current efforts towards philological restoration. 'Devices and genres; not texts. Texts are certainly the *real objects* of literature . . . but they are not the right *objects of knowledge* of literary history.'[79] For this reason, with a provocative irony Moretti insists we must learn *not to read* texts:

> Look at them from a distance, dismantled into their smallest units (figures, themes, episodes, stylistic recurrences), or merged into vast groupings (genres, literary systems). Between the very small and the very large, the 'measure' of the text will indeed be lost – but something

---

75 Moretti, 'Patterns and Interpretation', p. 9.

76 Moretti, *Distant Reading*, p. 105.

77 Mark Algee-Hewitt, Ryan Heuser and Franco Moretti, 'On Paragraphs. Scale, Themes, and Narrative Form', *Pamphlet 10* of the Stanford Literary Lab (2015), pp. 1, 4 – at litlab.stanford.edu.

78 Moretti, *Graphs, Maps, Trees*, p. 76.

79 Ibid.

> else may finally become visible: the outline, the grammar of literary history as a whole.[80]

Philological fetishism aside, this is of course a point on which one may disagree – especially if one aims to recompose the three elements that recent critical practice has tended to separate: theory, criticism and interpretation.[81] Personally, I remain convinced that theory, as a science of literature's general conditions, also contributes to the understanding of individual texts – though this relationship is flexible and inherently unstable, and must be renegotiated each time (which makes it epistemologically costly). There is no science without laws; but there is no literature without exceptions. Perhaps no one experienced this more viscerally than Barthes, who, within just a few years, went from the dream of a 'science of literature' to the explosion of the text in its difference, and finally to the 'desperate resistance to any reductive system' he invoked in *Camera Lucida*: 'why mightn't there be, somehow, a new science for each object? A *mathesis singularis* (and no longer *universalis*)?'[82]

Between the titanic hubris of the universal and the sceptical drift of the singular, there may be a narrow passage – a thin causeway: 'out and out one went, further and further, until at last one seemed to be on a narrow plank, perfectly alone, over the sea'.[83] In truth, Moretti tries to keep these two sides distinct: on the one hand, 'the "nomothetic" attempt to discover general laws'; and on the other, 'the "idiographic" desire to account for the specificity of individual cases'.[84] That the tide is caused by the phases of the moon, to borrow from Bloch's *The Historian's Craft*, cannot be assumed in advance: before establishing any relationship, one must study the movement of the tides and the lunar phases separately. This is why, Moretti continues, 'I prefer studying tides and moon independently of each other. Whether or not a synthesis will follow, remains

---

80 Moretti, *Il romanzo di formazione*, p. xxi.

81 See Federico Bertoni, 'La resistenza alla teoria', *Ermeneutica letteraria* 14 (2018), pp. 277, 283.

82 Roland Barthes, *Camera Lucida: Reflections on Photography*, transl. Richard Howard (New York: Hill & Wang, 1981), p. 8.

83 Virgina Woolf, *To the Lighthouse* (London: Hogarth, 1927), p. 265.

84 Moretti, *Distant Reading*, p. 152.

to be seen.'[85] Still, the attempt must be made, if only to rescue literary studies from the opposing currents presently driving it off course: specialisation and dilettantism, neopositivism and impressionism, scientistic reductionism and the *bêtise* of common sense. In any case, Moretti is right: much remains to be done. So let us start over again.

---

85 An outward confirmation of this dual requirement, Moretti notes, is the simultaneous publication of *Distant Reading* and *The Bourgeois*, two books that could not be more different in spirit and execution. Moretti, *Distant Reading*, p. 138.

9

Serious Experiments

Mads Rosendahl Thomsen

Franco Moretti's highly influential article from 2000, 'Conjectures on World Literature', contains a lot to unpack in a few pages.[1] There is a discussion of the future of literary studies, juxtaposing comparative studies and the study of national literature. Each field has its merits, yet Moretti appears to find it more worthwhile to take up the challenge, adopting a perspective focused on the study of global waves of influence, rather than concentrating on the leaves and branches of the great tree of literary history. There is a sketch of a model of influence in which foreign forms are imported into literary cultures and used locally, in a way that pushes the evolution of literatures forward through an encounter between the local and the foreign, in terms of both form and content. This is a bold claim, and although the model of foreign form, foreign content and local form is difficult to formalise in a robust way, there is substantial empirical support for it. The thesis of 'Conjectures' is supported not only by the numerous internal references within the article, but also by Moretti's edited multi-volume work *The Novel*, which includes essays analysing, for example, the arrival of the novel in Japan and Nigeria.

Then there is the concept of 'distant reading', which has become a staple in digital humanities to describe the goal of applying computational methods to the study of texts – even though some critics see it as a problematic term that implies a technocratic relationship with literature. However, if one applies *close reading* to Moretti's article, it becomes clear

1 Franco Moretti, 'Conjectures on World Literature,' *New Left Review* II/1 (January–February 2000).

that what is at stake is the production of knowledge – and sometimes a knowledge that cannot be attained without stepping beyond traditional close-reading practices. Interestingly, while the article has become a landmark in digital literary studies, it does not mention any use of computational methods. Rather, it merely suggests that certain models might serve to integrate the knowledge produced by numerous scholars working in diverse ways and throw new light on, for example, the development of a genre across nations and languages. Moretti's development of a computational approach came later, through the Stanford Literary Lab, and has more broadly taken off with a new generation of researchers working at the intersection of computer science and literary studies.

All the interest in the above somewhat explains why there has been much less attention given to a bold suggestion – one that might initially seem like a throwaway idea, but which deserves more scrutiny:

> See the beauty of distant reading plus world literature: they go against the grain of national historiography. And they do so in the form of *an experiment*. You define a unit of analysis (like here, the formal compromise), and then follow its metamorphoses in a variety of environments – until, ideally, *all* of literary history becomes a long chain of related experiments.[2]

It is a challenging and daring idea. Instead of conceiving literary history as a well-organised assemblage of periods, genres, contexts, and so on – built on an ever-expanding base of knowledge that eliminates uncertainty – Moretti suggests that the 'long chain of related experiments' could be a model for a historiography of literature. Intuitively, this could be seen as an unserious mode of doing research: Should the end goal of literary history not be more than experiments? But one could also think of this as a more honest way of thinking about literary history that respects its complexity. Periods, genres and other categories never seem to hold up, anyway, whereas the seriously conducted experiment could reveal something that is difficult not to accept as a part of the puzzle. And if we accept that the puzzle can never be completed, maybe we are better off with empirically based pieces that we link together. The approach of

2 Ibid., pp. 61–2.

serious experimentation not only pertains to Moretti's model of literary history, but runs throughout his body of work, and it should also be connected to his notion of flawed masterpieces, first formulated in *Signs Taken for Wonders*. In this essay, I will first address literary historiography through the lens of the experiment, then proceed to argue that the concept of flaws and evolution in canonical works rests on a similar paradoxical poetics of literature – one that may nonetheless prove deeply meaningful – before concluding with a reflection on the relationship between evolution and teleology.

1. The Shape of Literary History

Literary history is an inherently complicated field, as it represents both a genre and the elusive idea of some external coherence that could be described. The genre itself has seen better days, and there is little excitement or willingness to produce multi-volume literary histories, even though such projects can be a useful way to encourage good research. In particular, scepticism towards national identities has taken away a good deal of the genre's credibility, while the reinvention of the genre in the many competent projects of the International Comparative Literature Association stands out because they commit to multiple strategies for presenting the history of, for example, a region (which again is an experiment, since regions are much less tightly knit than nations). Still, it remains a worthwhile task to consider how the parts and the whole in literary studies add up to some kind of history, and what the consequences should be for research. David Perkins's 1992 book *Is Literary History Possible?* is not optimistic about the existence of any firm foundation for literary history, although he concludes that, even if there is no intellectually honest way of writing literary histories, they remain useful and necessary. Perkins focuses in particular on the problem of achieving both complexity and coherence in literary history, and how different strategies tend to favour one or the other – both of being noble aims in principle. The encyclopaedic mode, which has been explored by *A New History of French Literature* and a number of successors to that volume, clearly opts for complexity: detail, overlapping narratives, and a blurring of the distinction between minor and major events. But Perkins is not convinced by the merits of this form, which sacrifices coherence for complexity, and often ends up being dull and unfocused. Embracing complexity and rhizomatic structures is tempting, but often mostly in theory. On the other hand, the more traditional approach to literary history, which narrates a succession of dominant periods, influences and borrowings among literatures, can be engaging but is not to be trusted in its pursuit of coherence. As Perkins puts it, 'We must perceive a past age as relatively unified if we are to write literary history; we must perceive it as highly diverse if what we write is to represent it plausibly.'[3] There is no winning concept – everything rests on trade-offs.

The sense of being overwhelmed by the complexity of literary history was also at the centre of Erich Auerbach's short article 'Reflections on World Literature', published in German in 1952.[4] Implicitly defending the approach Auerbach took in *Mimesis*, where the history of realism is told through a series of chapters – each opening with a lengthy quote from a literary work – he suggests one must find a point of departure, or *Ansatz*, and proceed from there, fully aware that the complexity of literature makes it impossible to master the whole field of investigation. Instead, one must trust that a non-arbitrary relationship exists between the fragments and the whole, and that meaningful connections can be drawn. One could argue that Moretti's recent book, *Far Country: Scenes from America Culture*, published after the ideas for this essay had taken shape, follows a similar logic of multiple points of departure, in the style of Auerbach. Sometimes this takes the form of juxtapositions between foreign and American artists – for example, Charles Baudelaire and Walt Whitman, and Jan Vermeer and Edward Hopper – and sometimes with a focus on single authors, like Ernest Hemingway and Arthur Miller. The analysis of the 'iceberg technique' in Hemingway's work offers an almost perfect analogy, albeit probably unintentional, with Auerbach's *Ansatz*.[5]

---

3 David Perkins, *Is Literary History Possible?* (Cambridge, MA: Harvard University Press, 1992), p. 27.

4 Erich Auerbach, 'Philology and "Weltliteratur"', transl. Edward Said and Maire Said, *Centennial Review* 13: 1 (Winter 1969 [1952]).

5 Franco Moretti, *Far Country: Scenes from American Culture* (London/New York: Verso, 2019), p. 51.

The alternative approach is to consider literary history not as a genre but as an ephemeral object – partly constructed, partly pre-existing. Without the desire to uncover layers as well as to build narratives, there would be little to worry about. Frank Kermode and Pierre Bourdieu, each in their own way, have contributed to the articulation of this analytical impulse. In his essay 'Canon and Period', Kermode suggests that there are two ways of organising the literary past: by creating canons, or by defining periods. In both cases, Kermode argues, these operations are also a way of modernising the past, by selecting from it what resonates with contemporary discourse.[6] However, he does not go so far as to investigate how canon formation might be studied, practically speaking.

The making of canons is not an individual project – even Harold Bloom's idiosyncratic selections end up restating the obvious or drawing criticism; it is the outcome of a long process of selection across different domains. Or, as Moretti has in 'The Slaughterhouse of Literature', the lay reader makes sure that Jane Austen stays in the canon, while poetry relies on professors and students.[7] Of course canons are made, but it is exactly the process in which they are made, or the inclusions and exclusions that take place over time, that is interesting. This process can be studied in a number of imperfect, yet certainly useful ways that, by going beyond mere construction, reveal the sum of millions of choices. When it comes to literary periods, the element of construction is more pronounced, and time and again literary historians struggle to slot works into available boxes. Ted Underwood, in his book *Why Literary Periods Mattered* (2013), and even more so in *Distant Horizons* (2019), tries to show that some of the conventional wisdoms regarding periodisation do not hold up. An experimental approach to literary history would allow, on the one hand, for a less constructed and more nuanced picture of canons, and, on the other, for the blurring of sharp divisions between periods into longer phases of transition.

If Kermode's reflections on canons and periods place a strong emphasis on the internal organisation of literary history, Pierre Bourdieu's

6 Frank Kermode, *History and Value* (Oxford: Clarendon, 1988), p. 123.

7 Franco Moretti, 'The Slaughterhouse of Literature', *Modern Language Quarterly* 61: (2000), p. 209n.

theory of art and literature centres on social structures.[8] He is certainly not alone in this, but the significance of his work is emblematic, and influenced Moretti in his *Atlas of the European Novel*. Moretti draws on Bourdieu in his attempt to formalise literary space by comparing it to the real world, even reproducing the French scholar's map of Flaubert's *Sentimental Education*. Naturally, from this perspective, literature becomes incredibly complex, as it is both representative and autonomous – a paradox Bourdieu himself acknowledges, even as he gives free rein to his inner Sainte-Beuve by asserting that the social structure of Flaubert's novel exactly fits its historical structure. The point is that the desire to forge historical or cultural connections has always been evident, but it remains enormously difficult to formalise. For a while, it seemed that New Historicism had struck gold with the lure of the anecdote and thick descriptions. Meanwhile, Hans Ulrich Gumbrecht offered a more credible portrayal of the complexity of just a single year in his book *In 1926: Living at the Edge of Time*, emphasising how the fundamental distinctions used to define a period would be undone by other texts, as he elegantly demonstrates in two sections titled 'Codes' and 'Collapsed Codes'. Coexisting with this series of experiments is integral to the book, which does more than suggest a method: it puts it into practice.

Some would of course beg to differ about what a good poetic or literary history should look like. Paul de Man – whose words, it must be stressed, should not be taken literally – once suggested that 'To become good literary historians, we must remember that what we usually call literary history has little or nothing to do with literature and that what we call literary interpretation – provided only it is good interpretation – is in fact literary history.'[9] Walter Benjamin had already warned us against a literary history that longed for totalities.[10] Yet the related experiments seem to challenge such criticisms without fully sharing their

8 Pierre Bourdieu, *The Rules of Art* (Stanford, CA: Stanford University Press, 1996).

9 Paul de Man, *Blindness and Insight: Essays in the Rhetoric of Contemporary Criticism* (London: Routledge, 1983 [1971]), p. 165.

10 Walter Benjamin, *Selected Writings*, vol. 2 (Cambridge, MA: Harvard University Press, 1999), p. 461.

standpoint. They are not without method, but they also cannot be written off as attempts to build a complete system.

What is distinctive about Moretti's approach, however, is his interest in creating a scaled model. He is not explicit about this, but one could argue that the idea of the experiment has to be related to some notion of scalability, and that the purpose of a limited focus is precisely its ability to operate at scale. This becomes especially clear in light of his later engagement with computational methods. But it is important to clarify what counts as an experiment – and as a serious experiment. For sure, it means formulating a hypothesis that can be formalised, verified and repeated. Experiments only matter if they are not one-offs, but instead help to draw one-to-one maps; otherwise, the result is a *mathesis singularis*, as Roland Barthes might put it.

Some of the most exciting work in computational literary studies comes from scholars a generation or two younger than Moretti, who clearly adopt this experimental approach – posing a problem and proceeding through trial and error in small-scale formalisation, before scaling up. For example, the work of Ted Underwood, David Bamman and Sabrina Lee on the notable decline of female voice representation in fiction is a powerful instance of a large-scale experiment.[11] It generates valuable insights that might have been reached otherwise, but with greater effort. And even if it had simply confirmed the intuitive hypothesis – that female characters gain narrative space as societies become more egalitarian – it would still have been a meaningful contribution. Similarly, Dennis Yi Tenen proposed methods to measure the presence of objects in literary discourse, while Andrew Piper used topic modelling to open new perspectives on several centuries of German literature – for example, by analysing the prominence of the theme of death in over 14,000 volumes.[12] Closer to the work done by Moretti in *Atlas of the European Novel* is the research by Matthew Wilkens on the geography of

11 Ted Underwood, David Bamman and Sabrina Lee, 'The Transformation of Gender in English-Language Fiction', *Journal of Cultural Analytics* 3: 2 (2018).

12 Dennis Yi Tenen, 'Toward a Computational Archaeology of Fictional Space', *New Literary History* 49: 1 (Winter 2018); Andrew Piper, 'Novel Devotions: Conversional Reading, Computational Modeling and the Modern Novel', *New Literary History* 46: 1 (Winter 2015).

literature, which uses place-name extraction across millions of texts to show, for example, the differences within the geographic imagination of London.[13]

'*All* of literary history becomes a chain of related experiments.' Is this overlooked metaphor of the 'chain' meant to contrast with the idea of the casual experiment – and leave no doubt as to the seriousness of the proposal? The question of seriousness runs like a red thread through all of Moretti's writings. The search for identity in the *Bildungsroman*, the fascination of the bourgeois with what Moretti termed 'the serious century', and the inclusion of science – especially evolutionary theory – among his reference points all suggest a way of thinking about literature and literary history in which experimentation and seriousness go hand in hand.[14] This is a pivotal concept in *The Bourgeois*, a study of the class whose rise to power coincided with the triumph of the novel: 'Serious may not be the same as tragic, true, but it does indicate something dark, cold, impassable, silent, heavy; an irrevocable detachment from the "carnivalesque" of the labouring classes. Serious, is the bourgeoisie on its way to being the ruling class.'[15]

However, method and subject need not always go hand in hand. An experimental poetics of literary history could be created without having any resemblance to the material it tries to explain. And yet it is striking how the same traits are often used to describe certain portions of literature studied by Moretti. One unusual and surprising feature of *Distant Reading* is the brief introductory commentaries preceding each essay, which often reflect retrospectively on a process of trial and error. The transparency of that process is, in many cases, admirable – and lends a certain colloquial authority to the work as a whole. These are serious experiments.

---

13 Matthew Wilkens, 'Genre, Computation, and the Varieties of Twentieth-Century US Fiction', *Journal of Cultural Analytics* 2: 2 (November 2016).

14 Franco Moretti, 'The Serious Century', in Moretti, ed., *The Novel, Volume 1: History, Geography, and Culture* (Princeton, NJ: Princeton University Press, 2006), pp. 364–400.

15 Franco Moretti, *The Bourgeois: Between History and Literature* (London: Verso, 2013), p. 74.

2. Flawed Masterpieces

The fascination with the imperfect and the open-ended is also evident in a spirited early conceptual innovation in *Signs Taken for Wonders*. Moretti suggests that T. S. Eliot's 'The Waste Land' and other modernist classics are 'flawed' in the sense that there is a discrepancy between a proposed mythical framework and its actual execution through a conspicuous bricolage that emphasises the contingency of the work, more in tune with their worldview.[16] Again, just as common sense would not suggest that literary history should be composed of experiments, it is also counterintuitive to think of masterpieces as imperfect – shouldn't they be flawless, with not a single word out of place? The hubris of creating riddles meant to keep literary scholars busy for 300 years, as James Joyce reportedly suggested of *Ulysses*, rests on the same conception of doing things *just right*. To think of a masterpiece in paradoxical terms is a simple yet powerful way to explain why certain works have exerted undeniable fascination across generations. Perhaps Shakespeare is hyper-canonical not in spite of the elements that cannot be described as flawless – or at least replaceable – but *because* of them. The overused concept of genius might thus be both dismantled and salvaged, if we think of it this way.

As might have been expected, the novel lends itself particularly well to this paradigm, being – as Bakhtin noted – a genre in constant evolution, one that continually draws on other genres and has no definitive end, but possesses a unique capacity for self-critique.[17] In his essay on literary evolution, the brief history of the novel traced by Moretti seems nearly to reach its conclusion in the nineteenth century: after the establishment of the modern novel in the eighteenth century, with its great variety of techniques and forms, the novel perhaps became too successful,

16 Franco Moretti, *Signs Taken for Wonders: Essays in the Sociology of Literary Forms*, transl. Susan Fisher, David Forgacs and D. A. Miller (London: Verso, 1997 [1983], 2nd edn 1988), p. 220.

17 M. M. Bakhtin, *The Dialogic Imagination* (Austin, TX: University of Texas Press, 1981), p. 6.

self-assured and dependent on the market in the nineteenth century, before being pushed again towards new limits at the beginning of the twentieth. The highly ambitious novels that Moretti studies in *Modern Epic*, or those Stefano Ercolino has called 'maximalist novels', cannot be comprehended in the paradigm of perfection. Ercolino describes the delicate balance of such works as being characterised by

> a more mobile polyphony, freer to expand. Even if, to be sure, it is never a question of complete freedom, but if anything of a 'guarded freedom,' since polyphony never degenerates into chaos in the maximalist novel. There will always be ordering criteria to the story . . . which serve to contain the rich maximalist polyphony within sustainable and 'audible' limits, thereby preventing deflagration and anarchy.[18]

In one of the most radical attempts to balance order and chaos, Georges Perec even had a list of errors to be made when writing what was clearly conceived as a candidate for a modern masterpiece of literature, *Life: A User's Manual.* Rather than praising genius, literary criticism has a much more interesting task: to understand why imperfection adds value to a category of works whose worth has been proved across generations. Naturally, the flawed masterpiece also has an impact on close reading, and on the notion that everything in a text is there for a reason – and that it is always the reader's fault if they fail to grasp it. Sometimes, individual details are not essential to the bigger picture, but the pattern formed by the sum of those details should still be of interest to us.

I would like to suggest two points that might contribute to the perspective proposed by Moretti at the outset: one concerning the question of subversion in culture, and the other relating to complexity in literary works. I have written elsewhere about 'subversive foundations', arguing that a number of Western literary texts – so canonical that they are considered foundational to national literatures, and even part of what could be called world literature due to their broad circulation and acclaim – are

18 Stefano Ercolino, *The Maximalist Novel: From Thomas Pynchon's* Gravity's Rainbow *to Roberto Bolaño's* 2666 (London/New York:: Bloomsbury, 2014), p. 62.

actually far from affirming the cultures they are said to represent.[19] Rabelais, Montaigne, Cervantes, Shakespeare, and later Dostoevsky and the hyper-canon of early-twentieth-century novels – Joyce, Kafka, Musil – belong firmly to the literary tradition, yet remain deeply subversive in their critique of religion and morality, often also favouring stylistic play, layering and uninterpretability. It has even been suggested that the New Testament can be viewed as a subversive text, in that it gives human form to a distant and vengeful God. This ability to find cultural value at the margins of what is foundational – by denying those very foundations – is a marvellous paradox, and one that makes perfect sense in relation to the dynamics and evolution of Western literature in particular.

Secondly, on a much more formal level – one that reflects on findings in digitally supported research – there are grounds for speculation concerning the more or less optimal complexity of literary works. Moretti is one of the co-authors of the pamphlet 'Canon/Archive: Large-scale Dynamics in the Literary Field', which seeks to investigate, on a large scale, whether there are features that distinguish canonical from non-canonical works.[20] True to the spirit of the pamphlet series, the article openly discusses all the considerations and doubts regarding the ability to construct models capable of identifying significant and non-trivial differences between the two groups of texts. One of the most interesting findings is the less predictable use of word classes in canonical works compared to non-canonical ones. This might not come as a surprise, since variation is often a marker of creativity and writing quality; but it would not be possible to assert this without conducting such large-scale textual analysis.

In a study conducted by Gao Jianbo and Kristoffer Nielbo, the focus is not on types of words, but rather on the distribution of sentiment within a novel, with the aim of measuring predictability and variation

---

19 Mads Rosendahl Thomsen, 'Subversive Foundations: Renaissance Classics and the Imported Canon', ed. Dominique Jullien, *Foundational Texts of World Literature* (New York: Peter Lang, 2011).

20 Mark Algee-Hewitt et al., 'Canon/Archive: Large-scale Dynamics in the Literary Field', *Pamphlet 11* of the Stanford Literary Lab (2016) – at litlab.stanford.edu.

throughout a work.[21] The thesis of the model is that highly predictable works are unlikely to succeed artistically, while those that are radically unpredictable tend to be unreadable and uninteresting. By analysing more than 10,000 novels, the research reveals a significant distribution of works across the corpus, the majority of which fall into the domain of predictability and repetitiveness. More interestingly, many of the works considered to be of artistic merit cluster in a zone where there is a balance between repetition and change. While the research is not yet conclusive, it does provide another way of formalising a complex challenge for literary studies: understanding the differences between canonical works (those whose value has been affirmed over time by readers and critics) and non-canonical ones. Of course, this is not a method that closes the debate once and for all, but rather, in the best spirit suggested by Moretti, an experiment that yields results which – once brought to light – cannot be ignored.

From his earliest studies, Moretti showed an interest in natural evolution and the possible analogies it might offer for understanding the development of literary genres. He was not the first to propose that evolution could serve as a metaphor for literary development – Jules Huret and Jurij Tynjanov had already done so; but his perspective on genres and their gradual transformations gained strength through dialogue with Darwinian theory. Beyond the obvious analogy, in which successful genres are those capable of adapting to their social environment, Moretti has suggested that, just as nature sometimes finds new functions for organs or traits that were on the verge of becoming obsolete but instead acquire renewed relevance, something similar can occur in literature – though, he warns, the analogy must not be pushed too far.[22] After all, literary works are constructs, not living organisms, and they do not die. Even so, Moretti has rightly pointed out that the beloved figure of a belatedly recognised author – say, Melville or Stendhal – is more myth

---

21 Qiyue Hu, Bin Liu, Mads Rosendahl Thomsen, Jianbo Gao and Kristoffer Laigaard Nielbo, 'Dynamic Evolution of Sentiments in *Never Let Me Go*: 2 Insights from Multifractal Theory and Its Implications for Literary Analysis', *Digital Scholarship in the Humanities*, 2020.

22 Moretti, *Signs Taken for Wonders*, p. 274.

than reality. Their works were continuously reprinted throughout their supposed years of neglect, and could only 'flourish again' because they had never truly died.

3. Happy Endings?

It is often interesting to see if one can spot a hero in a body of critical work. In a large part of Moretti's work, the genre of the novel could be said to be the hero – a complex system of texts that continues to expand its influence across the world, gradually reducing the space left for other genres. But there are also references to conflicting models. Marxist theory might find its adversaries among advocates of open-ended development: specifically, on the one hand Charles Darwin, on the other Karl Popper, both of whom would caution against ideas of finality and completion. Is it possible to reconcile the promise of a definitive social order with the continuous evolution of forms and structures? Probably not, and this pessimism is captured negatively in a well-known formulation by one of Moretti's contemporaries, Fredric Jameson, who claimed that it is easier to imagine the end of the world than the end of capitalism. Still, Moretti's latest large, book-length study does address the end of a particular adversary in Marxist thinking: the bourgeois, who has in fact ceased to exist in the way he did in Europe for centuries – although his decline was not brought about by a revolution against capitalism.

In his article, 'On Literary Evolution', Moretti cites Darwin's famous ending to *The Origin of Species*, where Darwin rightly remarks:

> There is grandeur in this view of life, with its several powers, having been originally breathed by the Creator into a few forms or into one; and that, whilst this planet has gone cycling on according to the fixed law of gravity, from so simple a beginning endless forms most beautiful and most wonderful have been and are being evolved.[23]

In Moretti's article this view is, of course, applied to literature by way of analogy. The question is whether it should also go for all kinds of history,

23 Ibid., p. 278.

including literary history. Art can do anything: there is no getting it wrong, though it can fail to be convincing. But literary criticism – particularly as a *Wissenschaft*, in the German sense – should aim to do its work correctly. What does that mean today? Accepted truths are often questionable, and criticism has the task of unmasking common beliefs, as Ted Underwood has done effectively in Moretti's wake. And what if the literary historian is like a character in a novel who takes things seriously, even when there is no objective reason to do so – except that the beauty of the experiment demands seriousness? Moretti has at times been a controversial figure in literary criticism over the past decades, but he is hard to ignore for the well-crafted provocations he brings to the discipline of literary studies – not least with the advent of digital humanities, of which Moretti himself has been far from uncritical. In many ways his work has been driven by a desire to push the discipline towards new forms of knowledge, in the hope not that new tools might produce something fundamentally different, but that serious experiments might shift our perspective.

10

Can the Digital Humanities Kill Their Own Theories?

Jérôme David

> *Scientists try to eliminate their false theories, they try to make them die in their stead. He who believes in them . . . perishes along with his false beliefs.*
>
> Karl Popper, *Objective Knowledge*

1.

Franco Moretti entered the field of digital humanities with the same experimental rigour and uncompromising approach that characterises his broader body of work. In addition to using actual algorithms to analyse cultural data produced by the Stanford Literary Lab, which he founded in 2010, he has been deeply engaged in examining how these new computational procedures might contribute to the study of literary history and theory. This reflexivity has taken the form of methodological essays focused on specific issues (such as power in tragedy, style, or genre in the novel) and epistemological commentary interwoven with accounts of ongoing experiments. The 'operationalisation' of concepts, to reprise a term coined by Moretti, develops on two levels simultaneously: on the one hand, through a mutual adaptation between notional components (features of 'style' as understood by Leo Spitzer, for example) and computational tools (such as Docuscope and Most Frequent Words); and, on the other, through an evaluation of the relevance or novelty of the 'results' in light of the knowledge already established by literary scholarship.[1]

1 Franco Moretti, 'Operationalizing', *New Left Review* II/84 (November–December 2013).

This trajectory of the digital humanities has been marked by rare surprises and numerous disappointments. The thrill of the challenge has given way to a persistent sense of perplexity, to the point where Moretti now appears more interested in understanding the failures – or rather, the false promises – of the digital humanities by analysing the underlying ideas about science, history and culture that guide research in this field, rather than blaming inadequate software, the gaps in a digital corpus, or the vagueness of a literary concept. His diagnosis does not stop at considerations on method, but engages with the philosophy of science and a broader debate on the logic of the social world.

From this perspective, Moretti's reflections on visualisations in the digital humanities are crucial, and they allow us to highlight the two levels of critical judgement he develops in his work. When visualisation is treated as evidence, it raises epistemological questions; when it is approached as a symptom of a cultivated imaginary, it sets off a political investigation. Moretti, however, develops these two evaluative frameworks by drawing on distinct intellectual genealogies – Popper for science, Marx for politics – whose combination is anything but straightforward.

2.

In his introduction to a collection of articles on the digital humanities, Moretti suggests that, within the framework of distant reading, close reading would consist of interpreting images produced by certain software programs with the same rigor one would apply to interpreting a passage from a literary classic: 'Images come first, in our pamphlets, because – by visualizing empirical findings – they constitute *the specific object of study of computational criticism*; they are our "text"; the counterpart to what a well-defined excerpt is to close reading.'[2] Deciphering point clouds and the vector connections that link them, paying attention to the unexpected 'noise' that makes certain areas of the image more obscure – all of this requires the same meticulous and systematic attention one would devote to the study of a poem.

2 Franco Moretti, 'Literature, Measured', *Pamphlet 12* (2016) of the Stanford Literary Lab, p. 3 – at litlab.stanford.edu.

This interpretation of the 'empirical data' made visible by software serves several purposes. It is not about uncovering meanings or processes, as one might do with a literary text. In the first instance, the analysis aims to evaluate the data obtained in relation to the knowledge already established within literary studies. Can we learn something new thanks to computational tools? In most cases, the visualisations simply confirm what we already know about tragedy or the novel. They offer '*more* clarity, rather than clarity of a different kind'.[3] For Moretti, this is already progress: if such different tools lead to the same conclusions, then the phenomena described must have truly existed. This confirmation through visualisation increases the truth value of scholars' hypotheses – hermeneutic intuition is corroborated by concrete demonstration.

Here we can recognise the scientific optimism of Karl Popper, whose epistemological reflections are consistently invoked by Moretti: an empirical test is meaningful because it increases the probability that a hypothesis is true, even if it does not lead to major breakthroughs. All the more so: the falsification of a hypothesis constitutes scientific progress, because it requires the formulation of new conjectures to explain the phenomenon in question. Or, to quote Moretti,

> failures throw a unique light on the whole research process. Failures take us all the way back to our starting points: to those unspoken assumptions that go 'without saying', and thus easily escape critical scrutiny . . . Looking for style at the scale of the paragraph – and, again, not finding it . . . convinced us that a single top-to-bottom theory of the literary text (like that of stylistics) couldn't possibly be right, and opened the way to new hypotheses on textual scale.[4]

In a second phase, close reading turns to what remains of the visible 'data' still awaiting meaning. The software has generated correlations, but without revealing their significance, which is often not immediately apparent. Computational criticism must then sift through the program's

---

3 Sarah Allison, Ryan Heuser, Matthew Jockers, Franco Moretti and Michael Witmore, 'Quantitative Formalism: An Experiment', *n+1* 13 (Winter 2012).

4 Moretti, 'Literature, Measured', p. 4.

diligent contributions – a systematic computation that risks overinterpreting the data – in search of any covert configurations, so to speak, hidden within this 'noise', that might prove meaningful for a future theory. Indeed, *future*, because traditional hypotheses about style, genre or the evolution of forms do not always allow us to reformulate these visible correspondences adequately. And yet, hermeneutic intuition is refined in the process: it recognises a tremor, a surface ripple of reality; these clues, while not decisive, have heuristic value. The next step is to continue the research with other algorithms – ones whose modes of computation might better express the elusive weave of cultural history that, in this moment, remains nearly indiscernible.

The first phase of this close reading of visualisations produced by the digital humanities, then, corresponds – according to Moretti – to Karl Popper's conception of scientific discovery. This is the phase of the '*crucial* test situation', in which a hypothesis or a theory may or may not survive, as they sometimes contain errors so evident as to disqualify them from the race to explain reality.[5] From this also follows the second phase of close reading: the falsification of a hypothesis or theory brings with it the emergence of a new problem, one that a new hypothesis or theory must attempt to explain. The challenge, then, is to articulate this emerging problem in such a way that it becomes testable – something that requires the use of a metalanguage capable of rigorously formulating the problem and evaluating its adequacy in light of empirical reality through a new 'crucial test.'

3.

Popper likens this process of scientific development to the 'critical method':

> It is a method of trial and the elimination of errors, of proposing theories and submitting them to the severest tests we can design. If, because of some limiting assumptions, only a finite number of competing

5 Karl Popper, *Objective Knowledge: An Evolutionary Approach* (Oxford: Clarendon, 1979), p. 10.

> theories are regarded as possible, this method may lead us to single out the true theory by eliminating all its competitors.[6]

Thus, what makes Albert Einstein different from an amoeba, according to Popper, is simply that the physicist seeks to 'kill his theories' in order to come ever closer to the truth, whereas the amoeba operates on the basis of assumptions about the world that are integral to its being, and therefore beyond its ability to examine.[7] In short, Einstein makes use of reason to force himself to be '*consciously critical* of his own theories'.[8]

The Popperian conception defines science through its critical reflexivity: it is about setting rational boundaries against dogmatic explanations of reality. When a theory eliminates any possibility of being refuted by facts – when it 'immunises' itself against any objection, to use Popper's emblematic expression – it ceases to be rational and becomes, for this very reason, dangerous. It may assert itself through persuasion or force, regardless of the reality it purports to explain. This poses both a scientific and a political risk: scientific because, according to Popper, psychoanalysis did not subject its determinism of the unconscious to empirical testing, thus attempting to elevate itself to the status of science by means other than critical rationality; political due to the behaviour of totalitarian regimes, which distort reality and suppress those who challenge their interpretations of it.

Moretti partially inherits this programme: he is concerned with the scientific risk of theories becoming immunised – but he does not share Popper's political anxieties. For him, the digital humanities represent a decisive opportunity to enhance the critical reflexivity of literary studies. Constrained by the computational requirements of programming their hypotheses, literary theory and history are urged to dispel the ambiguities and vagueness of some of their notions. What exactly are the components of style, according to Spitzer? From what data did he conceive them before consolidating them in his essays? And what, precisely,

---

6 Ibid., p. 16.

7 Popper, *Objective Knowledge*, p. 25.

8 Ibid.

must a computer analyse within literary texts in order to test their validity on a large scale?

'Operationalisation' requires the more explicit rendering of a theoretical background that is often left out of the picture, and an enrichment of the metalanguage available for rigorously expressing components of that background. Spitzer's intuition – his ability to 'leap' from a detail to a comprehensive illumination of a work – cannot guide a computer, whose programme must detail every step of its computational process. If Spitzer, in this context, evokes the heraldic image of the lion who brushes away its tracks with its tail to elude pursuers – thus denying the possibility of reconstructing the path of intuition – Moretti, by contrast, insists on laying out the intermediate steps that may have led the scholar of style to 'jump' from linguistic reflections about details to an overarching interpretation of an author or an entire epoch: from Racine's preference for 'flanc' over 'ventre' to that 'muting effect' that characterises the *Weltanschauung* of French classicism.[9]

Intuition must not render hermeneutics unassailable; every tendency towards theoretical immunisation must be resisted.

Between the detail – a word, a verse, a phrase – and the entire body of an author's tragedies or novels, there also lie intermediate levels: the monologue (and the verbal space allotted to various characters) and the paragraph (a segment longer than a sentence but shorter than a chapter). Once identified, these intermediary levels represent the internal steps within the text that a computer must follow in order to reach a more general hermeneutic level – so as to connect individual words to the totality of words and their relationships that constitute any literary work, without the aid of intuition. Inviting stylistics into the realm of digital humanities means first of all rigorously articulating each link in the chain of hermeneutic reasoning that, in particular, leads to the result of a 'muting effect'. The richness of this endeavour lies in its ability to raise new questions that precede any attempt at empirical verification via algorithms: for instance, how do literary theories conceptualise the

9 Leo Spitzer, 'The Muting Effect of Classical Style in Racine (1928)', in Roy Clement Knight, *Racine: Modern Judgements* (London: Palgrave, 1969), pp. 117–31.

paragraph?[10] The precise reformulation of reasoning within the digital humanities can, in turn, enrich the conceptual repertoire of literary studies. On the political front, Moretti takes his distance from Popper. Theories become immunised when they evolve – much like an amoeba – into a restricted register of possible actions, ultimately imposing upon a social group a common sense that no one is able to question anymore. There is no longer any room for criticism. Popper saw in this scenario a threat to the 'open society' – what we would now call liberal democracy.[11] The official detractors of climate change action would undoubtedly, in his eyes, be its enemies today.

Moretti, I believe, is concerned with a different political threat, the matrix for which is not liberalism but Marxism. The immunisation of theories through an undisputed common sense, for him, represents – more radically – a form of symbolic violence intrinsic to social relations of domination. This violence is inflicted not only under dictatorship, but also within the 'open society', albeit in varying degrees. For instance, it explains why workers may vote against their own interests, simply because there is no competing theory capable of revealing the real inequalities they suffer. The critical method, then, does not settle for the consensual model of liberal democracy, but instead adopts the imaginary of dissent – if not of outright revolution: it emphasises the unfair competition between different theories, whether scientific or social. I will return to this point in my conclusion.

4.

Moretti's critical method, then, is not always aligned with Popperian principles, but it certainly is when it subjects literary theory to the calculable tests enabled by the digital humanities. His attention here focuses on the rigorous production of data that can confirm, refine or invalidate

---

10 Algee-Hewitt, Ryan Heuser, Franco Moretti, 'On Paragraphs', *Pamphlet 10* (2015) of the Stanford Literary Lab – at litlab.stanford.edu.

11 Karl Popper, *The Open Society and Its Enemies*, 2 vols (London: Routledge, 1945).

hypotheses proposed by literary studies – but only after those hypotheses have been adapted to the logical and technical constraints of algorithms. 'Operationalisation' is precisely the process through which such adaptation occurs, culminating in a visualisation that renders the results visible – whether the robustness of a theory when confronted with data, or the data themselves as they emerge in puzzling, random or indecipherable configurations.

This conception of scientific discovery is fundamentally dynamic, as it calls for the constant renewal of theories. It is also uncompromising, requiring that theories be formulated unequivocally and tested according to explicit protocols. Finally, it is vibrant, in that the errors discovered enable researchers to take a step forward in understanding reality – and thus, towards truth. However, its application within the digital humanities raises several issues, as it does not fully meet the conditions Popper outlined for the verification of theories.

To begin with, the logical universality required by the falsifiability of theories cannot be obtained by the human and social sciences. What Popper imagines is a world in which the same laws apply in every place and at every moment. It is the world of nature, considered moreover as immutable in its elements, properties and phenomena: 'our laws and our theories must be *universal*, that is to say, must make assertions about the whole world – about all spatial-temporal regions of the world'.[12] This universality is crucial in two respects: it ensures that a counter-example can serve as a falsification *ceteris paribus*, and that an ad hoc modification of a hypothesis does not save a theory by immunising it through exceptions; and it establishes the constancy of reality, allowing science to measure it piece by piece and, above all, to break it down into stable 'states of affairs' (*Sachverhalt*) that are susceptible to precise description.[13] For the 'correspondence' of a statement with reality to be assessable, the empirical perimeter of the fact must indeed be defined exhaustively and unambiguously. Logical universality thus shields us from the temptation to be satisfied with theories that are only loosely coherent or weakly grounded in empirical evidence.

12 Popper, *Objective Knowledge*, p. 197.

13 Ibid., p. 235.

Any form of knowledge that acknowledges a certain historicity in its objects cannot meet this logical clause of *ceteris paribus*. The difficulty here does not arise from the supposed difference between the *Naturwissenschaften* and the *Geisteswissenschaften* – between sciences that analyse physical phenomena and those that study conscious behaviour – but rather from the fact that historical descriptions are tied exclusively to specific and limited contexts. This objection was formulated by Jean-Claude Passeron:

> No definitive description that lists economic, juridical, mental, political, military features, etc., can, in itself, transmit the meaning of a word such as 'feudalism' to a reader who is ignorant of the existence of the medieval West, of the China of the Warring Kingdoms, of Kamakura Japan, etc. No definition of 'feudalism' or of 'capitalism' can be completely generic and constitute an *omni et soli definitio*, nor transmit – and this holds true for Marx as much as Braudel – the meaning of the conceptual denomination to a reader who is not able to relate those generic or trans-historical features which might fall under an enumerative definition to a series of singular configurations considered as historical *idiosyncrasies*, independent of any analysis of such features. The historical concept cannot be reduced either to a simple list of historical 'cases', nor to an analytical summary of the features shared by these historical cases.[14]

In short, when making assertions about the world (to reprise and renew Popper's terms), the human and social sciences always speak about a specific space-time region of the world – never about the world as a whole. Passeron developed this premise – which has such radical consequences – into an alternative epistemology to Popper's falsification model. The subtitle of his major work highlights this contrast: *Un espace non poppérien de l'argumentation* ('A Non-Popperian Space of Argumentation'). Passeron argues that, if we aim to formulate a scientific approach to the historical sciences, Popper's model is insufficient because its presuppositions

14 Jean-Claude Passeron, *Le Raisonnement sociologique. Un espace non poppérien de l'argumentation* (Paris: Albin Michel, 1991), p. 580.

effectively exclude sociology, history, anthropology – as well as literary studies and the digital humanities – from scientific reasoning. And since these disciplines are nonetheless driven by a genuine and rigorous pursuit of rationality, it is Popper's model that must be revised.

5.

The main repercussion of this non-Popperian epistemology concerns the status of formalisation in the digital humanities.[15] If a description of the facts to be tested is never exhaustive, finite or unambiguous – if it is impossible, for instance, to list all the features that define 'the nineteenth-century English novel' – then the translation of problems into the language of variables cannot yield a rigorous falsification of a theory. Algorithmic computation and its visualisations may end up invalidating both the hypothesis under scrutiny (for example, 'the paragraph is an autonomous stylistic entity in the nineteenth-century novel') and the very empirical framing of that hypothesis (if results are inconclusive, perhaps the 'nineteenth-century English novel' corpus was poorly constructed?).

Similarly, the criteria used to describe a literary genre cannot apply to another *ceteris paribus*, if one considers that history affects not only their evolution but also their formation and the degree of formal consistency attributed to them. Perhaps the 'Gothic novel' or the 'social novel' are not 'genres' in the same way that the 'evangelical novel' or the 'anti-Jacobin novel' are.[16] The former shaped writers and readers through their conventions; the latter were coined by critics aiming to assemble texts according to a logic different from that of writing or reading them with the pleasure that stems from adopting an appropriate horizon of expectation.

Following Passeron, we are faced with a kind of 'reasoning constrained by the need to articulate its generalisations predicated on baseline

15 In these terms, Passeron's reflection on the use of statistics in sociology also applies to the use of software and algorithms in the digital humanities. See in particular Passeron, *Le Raisonnement sociologique*, pp. 199–229.

16 Sarah Allison et al., 'Quantitative Formalism', p. 6.

observations that are never fully comparable in every respect', whether we are dealing with the 'Gothic novel' or the 'anti-Jacobin novel', novels set in London or Edinburgh, novels written by men or women, or novels from the 1830s or 1870s – and so on.[17] Passeron continues: 'this is a form of reasoning that, in order to make claims about its object, must incorporate into the interpretation of the stated observations a discourse about the variation of their contexts and about the production of the information it uses'.[18] In other words, to speak meaningfully of the 'nineteenth-century English novel' on the basis of visualisations requires clarification of the methods used to link or compare works that otherwise differ in countless respects not included among the variables (such as the place of publication, the novel's position within the author's publishing history, or the number of references to other writers within the text, to provide just a few examples).

This is what Moretti does. His trademark in the field of digital humanities is, we might say, the step-by-step reconstruction of the whole journey that has led him from an initial intuition to the empirical proof. His scientific contributions are essentially narratives of experiments in which complexities are unravelled through often collective deliberation: Which novels should be chosen to obtain a meaningful sample of the 'Gothic novel'? Where can a digital version of them be found? With which other literary genre – and reference sample – should their components be compared? In which period of the nineteenth century? Which textual elements should be isolated? What is the basis of the relationship between these elements? And what software should be used?

According to Passeron, however, this reflexivity does not stem from the critical method proposed by Popper, but is instead imposed on sciences that historicise their objects, because the world from which they draw their data eludes any strict experimental repeatability of phenomena:

> The conditions of historical observation do not rule out moments of experimental reasoning, but they do require – if one wishes to apply the

17 Passeron, *Le Raisonnement sociologique*, p. 203.
18 Ibid., p. 203.

> results of such reasoning to the world from which the information originates – reflection on the limiting conditions of each experimental reasoning, that is, making observations about the condition of the observations themselves.[19]

Visualisation in the digital humanities can only represent a moment within the reasoning process. An image does not convey through its 'patterns' the conditions of validity that it illustrates.

6.

This problematic status of how evidence is handled through computational visualisations helps explain the strange conclusion of Matthew Jockers's book, *Macroanalysis*.[20] After around a hundred pages devoted to compiling a rich database of nineteenth-century novels – some 3,000 meticulously transcribed works with detailed metadata – the author comments on the visualisation produced by putting the unified corpus of these texts in relation to each other – in other words, the millions of possible connections (statistical deviations between each novel and the others, based on lexical richness, use of verb tenses, pronouns, and so on), reduced to a few hundred thousand considered more relevant than the rest. The final image is stunning: it provides us with a pulse of the cultural past, the life of an epoch extracted from history's most remote archives, like an organism that surfaces from the depths of the ocean, lit up by software as if by the bioluminescence of the archives. The 'data' visualised in Jockers's analysis confirms some of the 'novel's' evolutionary trends previously discussed in the book.

But the nebula of data points surprises Jockers on three occasions. First, the stylistic characteristics of Margaret Oliphant's works lead the computer to distance her texts from those written in the same period by other women writers. Elsewhere, a group of Scottish authors are

---

19 Ibid., p. 204.

20 Matthew Jockers, *Macroanalysis: Digital Methods and Literary History* (Urbana, IL: University of Illinois Press, 2013).

clustered slightly on the margins compared to their English contemporaries. The final visual rupture in the overall coherence is represented by a set of about fifteen titles which, at first glance, share no obvious connection – save for the fact they were written around 1890. 'Here I cannot see anything but noise. Perhaps there are more expert scholars who will manage to see some connection that has escaped me', Jockers concedes in this last instance.[21] This humility does him credit, and above all confirms that the variables and calculations must be interpreted through a metalanguage that is not that of software, but that of literary history – otherwise, they risk becoming meaningless. The computer does not assess either Oliphant's work nor the Scottish productions in light of 'gender' or the 'influence' of Walter Scott. As for the final group of fifteen texts, the image in itself provides no interpretive key. No meaningful inference is possible without a scientifically informed imagination nourished by literary studies.

But perhaps Jockers's discomfort also stems from another factor. How can we determine whether, in the course of the countless interpretive decisions that made possible this 'operationalisation' of literary questions on such a vast corpus, the data encoding or the methods of calculation did not produce relationships between texts whose nature or arbitrariness remains unknown to the researcher? How can we tell whether this 'noise' is the sound of a past awaiting interpretation, or interference created by hidden interactions between the elements subjected to software analysis? Does this noise hide the structure of the world, or the structure of the algorithm? No criterion allows us to decide.

The very idea of a 'crucial experiment' emerges weakened – just like the Popperian framework from which it derives. On the one hand, historical reality is too varied and mutable to aspire to the logical universality of scientific statements demanded by Popper, and therefore to any definitive description of the 'facts' to be tested. On the other hand, the confirmation or refutation of hypotheses made visible by software turns out to be indistinctly empirical or computational, leaving no clear way to distinguish what the past tells us from what the machine tells us.

---

21 Jockers, *Macroanalysis*, p. 167.

7.

The corollary of this non-Popperian stance concerns Popper's expressed need for a scientific meta-language:

> The key to the rehabilitation of the correspondence theory is . . . if I want to speak about correspondence between a statement *S* and a fact *F*, then I have to do so in a language in which I can speak about both: statements such as *S*, and facts such as *F* . . . It means that the language in which we speak in explaining correspondence must possess the means needed to refer to statements, and to describe facts. If I have a language which has both these means at its disposal, so that it can refer to statements and describe facts, then in this language – the metalanguage – I can speak about correspondence between statements and facts without any difficulty, as we shall see.[22]

When formalisations are used in the humanities and social sciences (and thus also in the digital humanities), there is a strong temptation to equate computational programs with metalanguages. Visualisations would then be treated as evidence, because a rigorous description of the facts would incorporate the unambiguous formulation of hypotheses in such a way as to literally *show* the correspondence (or lack thereof) between hypotheses and facts. A coherent arrangement of data would, by its very coherence, demonstrate the plausibility of the hypothesis, while a mess of dots would force one to acknowledge the discrepancy between theory and reality.

However, computational programs are not metalanguages for the digital humanities. They cannot satisfy the criterion of unambiguous description of the facts, as we have already seen, because the variables chosen for computation do not exhaust the empirical content of the hypotheses under examination. Nor do they meet this criterion for another reason: an algorithm does not refer to statements, but to quantifiable amounts. Upstream of the visualisation, a true metalanguage is

22 Popper, *Objective Knowledge*, p. 314.

therefore needed – one that can translate statements into magnitudes suitable for computation; and downstream, the same metalanguage must reintegrate the results of the calculations into a broader description of the phenomenon being studied. And this metalanguage cannot be formalised. It possesses the degree of rigour attainable by conceptualisation in natural language.

Furthermore, this metalanguage has to constantly verify the conditions of validity of its observations. Moretti takes on this responsibility every time the empirical content of his hypotheses concerns the text – its constituent elements, or the relationships between them.

Nothing in literary theory escapes his examination. The formalisation of his reasoning for computational purposes spares none of the presumed certainties of literary studies (style, genre, authorship, and so on), generating a kind of *productive doubt* that leads to conceptual perplexities and sparks theoretical advances. However, when it comes to reintegrating the 'data' provided by the computer into the broader historical context – which algorithms cannot account for – Moretti's hypotheses become more assertive. In a recent article co-authored with Oleg Sobchuk, Moretti rightly criticises the overly simplistic formalisations of history that currently dominate the digital humanities.[23] In most cases, historicity appears merely as a series of effects lined up along a straight, flat line, devoid of oscillation – effects that seem visibly inevitable. The timelines produced by software thus imply, in a surreptitious way, a philosophy of history cleansed of conflict. For Moretti, it seems, the issue derives from the fact that, in his view, historicity has at least two origins: social struggles, whose forces suddenly take form; and forms which, once they have appeared, acquire a dynamic of their own, partly independent of social struggles, and evolve according to branching patterns governed by internal rules.[24] The straight-line approach favoured in many visualisations does not take account of either of these.

---

23 Franco Moretti and Oleg Sobchuk, 'Hidden in Plain Sight', *New Left Review* II/118 (July–August 2019).

24 On this last point, see Franco Moretti, *Distant Reading* (London: Verso, 2013), pp. 121–35.

This political criticism of the digital humanities is timely. It exposes a scientific imaginary marked by such naivety regarding issues that are nonetheless crucial – such as the very forms of time through which we conceive of the past – that it raises the question of whether the academic success of this field might arise from factors that are anything but scientific. And yet, this critique itself stumbles over its own convictions. Popperian or not, it would be good for the digital humanities, through their empirical means, to explore the problem of historicity as such. But this would require the metalanguage used to construct variables and interpret results to break free both from the tacit naivety that currently prevails in the field, and from any form of dogmatism, even if invoked in the name of critical lucidity.

Historical change certainly does not follow a straight line – with all due respect to the Hegelians persuaded by Francis Fukuyama's ideas – and over the past twenty years or so, it has given rise to much more varied models than those highlighted by Moretti.[25] The intense struggle between two opposing camps – a deeply Marxist view – and the autonomous dynamics of symbolic forms, traceable to Popper's Darwinian perspective, have been enriched by partly complementary conceptions within contemporary historiography.[26] Figures such as Walter Benjamin and Ernst Bloch could be rehabilitated through these alternative temporalities, proposing a historicity conceived either as a short-circuit between distant epochs, or as a tangle of asynchronous contingencies whose effects unhinge any present moment ('time is out of joint', to quote Shakespeare) and establish the radical non-contemporaneity of any given era – the *Ungleichzeitigkeit*, to use Bloch's term.[27]

---

25 Francis Fukuyama, *The End of History and the Last Man* (New York: Free Press, 1992).

26 That is, 'the growth of our knowledge is the result of a process closely resembling what Darwin called "natural selection"; that is, the *natural selection of hypotheses*: our knowledge consists, at every moment, of those hypotheses which have shown their (comparative) fitness by surviving so far in their struggle for existence; a competitive struggle which eliminates those hypotheses which are unfit.' Popper, *Objective Knowledge*, p. 261.

27 The short-circuit between different epochs being the starting point of Walter Benjamin, *The Arcades Project*, ed. Rolf Tiedermann (New York: Belknap,

If conceptualisations of our relationship with the past were to be incorporated into the metalanguage of the digital humanities, even as hypotheses – and with the critical depth that characterises them today (namely, an attention to unrealised 'futures of the past' ignored by linear models, and the concern not to reduce an era to a convenient dominant zeitgeist: the statistical average of a cloud of data points) – an entirely new scientific problem would emerge. Can software help us visualise such complex relationships with the past? What kinds of data would we need to produce to enable such modelling? Could an algorithm calculate the cycles, eclipses and diffractions of history? In which programming language – and perhaps more importantly, within what mathematical axiomatisation – could this be done? Core literary concepts like influence, intertextuality, canon and literary field, to name just a few obvious examples, could potentially find promising reformulations in this context.

8.

The digital humanities fall within the epistemological regime of the human and social sciences – the humanities, in the broadest sense of the term – not because of their methods or theories, but because of their objects. The irreducible historicity of the phenomena they seek to model with the help of algorithms prevents them from fully employing Popperian falsification. The non-Popperian framework they thus inhabit is not a fallback for 'inexact sciences', but a specific space of reasoning, whose metalanguage – by resisting any complete logical formalisation – assigns a particular status to computational visualisations.

On this point, Moretti's work has provided a model of the kind of conceptual rigour to which the digital humanities should aspire. Upstream of visualisations, his reasoning makes explicit and integrates certain unexamined dimensions of the human and social sciences – in this case, literary studies; downstream, it interprets results through a

---

2000 [1982]); Ernst Bloch, *Heritage of Our Times*, transl. Neville and Stephen Plaice (Los Angeles: University of California Press, 1991 [1935]).

recontextualising form of close reading. Moretti's critical approach works above all through this labour of 'operationalising' literary theories. But more recently he has also begun to engage with the analysis of the scientific imaginaries at work in the digital humanities. However, in the first case, his critique relies on a philosophy of science whose demands may seem excessive; in the second, it mobilises a conception of historicity that arguably requires deeper discussion.

Can the digital humanities kill their own theories? No. But – returning to the Popper quote used above as an epigraph – this does not make researchers in the field 'believers' condemned to perish with their prejudices. Even if the continual revision of theories does not bring the digital humanities closer to a notion of 'truth' conceived in terms of verisimilitude, it can nevertheless confer a different kind of truth: an epistemological lucidity about their own reasoning, a sign of a rationalism committed to thoughtful consideration of the links between the present and the past.

11

The Roads to Rome: Literary Studies, Hermeneutics, Quantification

Franco Moretti

What relationship, between the quantitative literary history of the past twenty years and the older hermeneutic tradition? Answers have typically been of two kinds: for many in the interpretive camp, the two approaches are incompatible, and the newer one has little or no critical value; for most quantitative researchers, they are instead perfectly compatible, and in fact complementary. Here, I will propose a third possibility that will emerge step by step from a comparison of how the two strategies work. How they *work*, literally; in the conviction that, as Oleg Sobchuk and I have recently written, 'practices – what we learn to do by doing, by professional habit, and often without being fully aware of what we are doing – have frequently larger theoretical implications than theoretical statements themselves.'[1] In that article, 'practice' referred to the different ways of visualising data; here, to the chain of interconnected decisions that shape an explanatory strategy. But the aim is the same: understanding what a research paradigm *does*, rather than what it declares it wants to do.

---

1 Franco Moretti and Oleg Sobchuk, 'Hidden in Plain Sight: Data Visualization in the Humanities', *New Left Review* II/118 (July–August 2019). 'Hidden in Plain Sight' and the current essay are part of a series of reflections on the quantitative study of culture that includes 'Operationalizing: Or, the Function of Measurement in Modern Literary Theory' (2013), 'Literature, Measured' (2016) and 'Patterns and Interpretation' (2017): the last three now collected in Moretti, ed., *Canon/Archive: Studies in Quantitative Formalism from the Stanford Literary Lab* (New York: n+1, 2017), and 'Simulating Dramatic Networks', *Journal of World Literature* (Fall 2020).

With a complication, however: since both the quantitative and – even more so – the hermeneutic approach are actually *many* approaches, often sharply at odds with each other (a Lacanian interpretation having nothing in common with a new historicist or an ecocritical one, and so on), in order to reduce the variables in play I will restrict myself to work I have personally taken part in. This is of course a questionable decision (and the exact opposite of 'Hidden in Plain Sight', which examined sixty-odd articles by over a hundred authors), which I am taking for two distinct reasons: first, because much of what follows will be quite critical, and I find it easier to criticise myself than others; second, because I've been repeatedly taken aback, in the past twenty years, by how different my work ended up being in the two registers. To some extent it *had* to be different, of course (that's the whole point of using more than one method), but there was something slightly uncanny in my drifting away from my own work. Maybe it's just a case of personal inconsistency; maybe the sign of something larger, with an objective significance for the entire field.

1

Hermeneutics first. Nick Adams, the protagonist of Hemingway's short story 'Big Two-Hearted River' (1925), is about to go fishing:

> Nick took it from his hook book, sitting with the rod across his lap. He tested the knot and the spring of the rod by pulling the line taut. It was a good feeling. He was careful not to let the hook bite into his finger.
>
> He started down to the stream, holding his rod; the bottle of grasshoppers hung from his neck by a thong tied in half hitches around the neck of the bottle. His landing net hung by a hook from his belt. Over his shoulder was a long flour sack tied at each corner into an ear. The cord went over his shoulder. The sack flapped against his legs.
>
> Nick felt awkward and professionally happy with all his equipment hanging from him. The grasshopper bottle swung against his chest. In

> his shirt the breast pockets bulged against him with his lunch and his fly book.[2]

First of all – does this passage even need an interpretation? Not really, if interpreting means dispelling the 'obscurity' of a text: here, everything seems perfectly clear. Is it, though? The idea 'that understanding occurs as a matter of course', wrote the founder of modern hermeneutics, is typical of the 'less rigorous practice' of interpretation; for its 'more rigorous' version it is, however, '*mis*understanding [that] occurs as a matter of course, and understanding must therefore be willed and sought at every point'.[3]

Willed at every point . . . Let's start with this, then: that this handful of sentences include *twenty-five* prepositional phrases (those introduced by a preposition: 'from his hook book', 'across his lap' and so on).[4] Twenty-five in 149 words: a lot. But they are there, because they are doing something which is essential to the story: gluing together all sorts of disparate elements. 'The *bottle* of *grasshoppers* hung from his *neck* by a *thong* tied in half *hitches* around the *neck* of the *bottle*.' A Swiss army

---

2 Ernest Hemingway, *The Nick Adams Stories* (New York: Scribner, 1981), p. 190. The analysis that follows condenses the more detailed account I have given in *Far Country: Scenes from American Culture* (New York/London: Verso, 2019), pp. 49–65.

3 The passages come from Friedrich Schleiermacher's programmatic 'Compendium' of 1819: see Heinz Kimmerle, ed., *Hermeneutics: The Handwritten Manuscripts* (Missoula, MT: Scholar, 1977), pp. 109, 110. 'Obscurity', Peter Szondi rightly observed, is for Schleiermacher 'hardly the only occasion for interpretation': *Introduction to Literary Hermeneutics* (Cambridge: Cambridge University Press, 1995 [1975]), p. 27.

4 Here they are, in italics: 'Nick took it *from his hook book*, sitting *with the rod / across his lap*. He tested the knot and the spring *of the rod* by pulling the line taut. It was a good feeling. He was careful not to let the hook bite *into his finger*. He started *down to the stream*, holding his rod, the bottle *of grasshoppers* hung *from his neck / by a thong* tied *in half hitches / around the neck / of the bottle*. His landing net hung *by a hook / from his belt*. / *Over his shoulder* was a long flour sack tied *at each corner / into an ear*. The cord went *over his shoulder*. The sack flapped *against his legs*. Nick felt awkward and professionally happy *with all his equipment* hanging *from him*. The grasshopper bottle swung *against his chest*. *In his shirt* the breast pockets bulged *against him / with his lunch and his fly book*.'

knife: an incredibly compressed and well-organised world. A world *of things*:

> With the *ax* he slit off a bright *slab* of *pine* from one of the *stumps* and split it into *pegs* for the *tent*. He wanted them long and solid to hold in the ground . . . He pegged the sides out taut and drove the pegs deep, hitting them down into the ground with the flat of the ax until the rope loops were buried and the canvas was drum tight.[5]

A world of things, but not only: Nick wants pegs '*for* the tent'; they are 'long and solid *to* hold in the ground', and he hits them '*until* the rope loops were buried'. It's all so *purposeful*: done in order to do something else. 'Know how', Gilbert Ryle called these chains of silent interlinked movements. 'Nick tied the rope *and* pulled the tent up *and* tied it to the other pine.' Always calm, always efficient. But: this is a story. Isn't calm the opposite of what a story needs?

It is. But Hemingway was writing within a very special historical context. We usually turn to stories because our life is not eventful enough; but what if the key experience of an entire generation has been the Great War? Much *too* eventful: and so, the desire for a different kind of narrative arises, where calm has a role to play. War literature, observed Eric Leed, is about 'men who, as a rule, had little or no control over the events which threatened their lives'.[6] No control: that is the key. Hemingway's style is *all about control*: of space, time, gestures, words. 'Nick felt awkward and professionally happy with all his equipment hanging from him': this is the snapshot of a young soldier – before the war. And the same goes for his march through the woods, his reconnaissance, his tent, his camp – he even eats canned food on his trip. While not quite 'playing' at war, Nick is certainly *replaying* it. Rewriting it. Life in the trenches had alternated between tedium and terror; nothing for days, then apocalypse. Hemingway's prose is never boring, and never frightening; clean and cautious, it's the perfect style for *convalescence* (three years later, the central episode – and happiest – of his first great success, *A Farewell to*

5 Hemingway, *Nick Adams Stories*, p. 183.
6 Eric J. Leed, *No Man's Land* (Cambridge: Cambridge University Press, 1981), p. 33.

Arms). This is war literature in the sense that it wants to *recover* from the war: to resolve the dissonance of historical experience, to adapt Lukács's metaphor in *Theory of the Novel*. But on this, more later.

2.

Figure 11.1

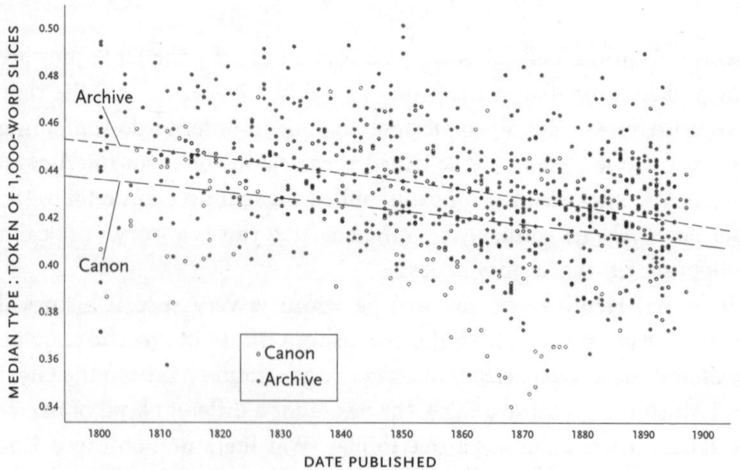

Source: Mark Algee-Hewitt, Sarah Allison, Marissa Gemma, Ryan Heuser, Franco Moretti and Hannah Walser, 'Canon/Archive: Large-Scale Dynamics in the Literary Field', Stanford Literary Lab, Pamphlet 11 (January 2016).[8]

From a few sentences of a single short story, to the most evident novelty of the quantitative approach: the expansion of literary history well beyond a small canon of great works. Time was, a theorist would choose one text – *Don Quixote*, *Robinson Crusoe*, *The Idiot* – and erect upon it a whole theory of the novel. 'Type thinking', Ernst Mayr has called it: '*Tristram Shandy* is *the most typical novel* in all of world literature', as Shklovsky wrote in *Theory of Prose*.[7] In front of the swarm of nineteenth-century

7 Viktor Shklovsky, *Theory of Prose* (Elmwood Park, IL: Dalkey Archive, 1991 [1925–29]), p. 170.

8 The study has now been collected in *Canon/Archive*. Here, too, what follows is only a very abbreviated summary of the original.

British novels in Figure 11.1, though, type thinking is useless: here, one must account for an entire 'population' of novels. Not a very large one, in this case – 1,117, to be exact – but still irreducible to a single text.

The text: this is where the discord between old and new is at its sharpest. It used to be *the* object of literary study; here, it's a dot. It has been *made* to be a dot. Downsized, just like 'events' had been, during the great quantitative turn of seventy years ago. Events used to be as central to historiography as texts to literary study, and for the same reason: because of their uniqueness. 'Historians resembled collectors', wrote Krzysztof Pomian in his retrospective on the *Annales*, 'gather[ing] only rare and curious objects, and ignoring whatever looked banal, everyday, normal . . .' Once events started to be studied 'as elements of a series', however, uniqueness lost its significance, and individual events ended up being 'relegated to the periphery of history, or disregarded altogether'.[9] A history that disregards events: this is the quantitative turn. A history of art without names, Wölfflin once wrote. A history of literature without texts.

Without texts – in the sense that *there are too many of them*, of course, and they can therefore no longer be studied as individual cases: as is indeed the case for the 250 canonical and 850 forgotten novels of Figure 11.1. We wanted to know whether linguistic richness contributed to a novel's survival or oblivion, so all texts were sliced into 1,000-word segments, and their type–token ratio was calculated.[10] And it turned out that the segment with the highest score belonged to Edward Hawker's *Arthur Montague, or an Only Son at Sea* (1850), and that with the lowest one to George Eliot's *Adam Bede* (1859).[11]

---

9 Krzysztof Pomian, 'L'histoire des structures', in Jacques Le Goff, Roger Chartier and Jacques Revel, eds, *La Nouvelle Histoire* (Paris: Retz, 1978), pp. 536, 543–4.

10 Type–token ratio is a standard measure of lexical variety that expresses the relationship between the number of *different* words used (types), and the number of *actual* words used (tokens). 'Good morning, my good friend' has four types and five tokens, hence a type–token ratio of 4/5, or 0.8; 'Good morning, Jim, good morning' has also five tokens, but only three types, hence a type–token ratio of 3/5, or 0.6.

11 Here are two sections of those extreme segments, where the hash sign indicates a word that had already appeared in the segment, and the asterisk a word that did not belong to the initial 'dictionary' of novelistic English (about 230,000 words) created by Ryan Heuser, who wrote the program for this part of the experiment:

That a novel none of us had heard of should have so much more lexical variety than a canonical one like Eliot's was the opposite of what we expected, so we of course read those two segments quite carefully. Hawker's was a description: which makes sense, because descriptions require details, and details increase lexical variety. Eliot's was completely different: a young woman, confessing to having abandoned her child to die, and repeating the same words over and over again (thus uttering the most redundant passage of the entire century), as if she were chained – 'but I couldn't go away' – to that scene of trauma. At this point we read the other segments that clustered around them at the two ends of the spectrum (from *Ennui*, *Tales of a Briefless Barrister*, *Marius the Epicurean*, *Lady Laura*, and dozens of others), and felt we could generalise: high type–token ratio was consistently associated with the prose of the novelistic narrator: written, analytical, impersonal and almost atemporal; low type–token ratio, with the voice of novelistic characters at specific moments of high emotional intensity.

This is what reading texts as elements of a series is like: we no longer wanted to go from the segment of *Adam Bede* to the representation of infanticide and its role in Victorian culture (as I had done with Hemingway); we wanted to go from that segment *to many other segments*, in order to construct a set of conceptual pairs – narrator/character, written/spoken, analytical/emotional, and so on – that would help chart the space of narrative possibilities. Ideally, the *whole* space. Not easy, as we found out – we tried to make sense of the segments lying at the centre

---

Arthur Montague: 'then cut through some acres of refreshing greensward, studded with the oak, walnut, and hawthorn, ascended a knoll, skirted an expansive sheet of# water; afterwards entering an# avenue of# noble elms, always tenanted* by a# countless host of# cawing* rooks, whose clamorous conclaves* interrupted the# stillness that reigned around, and# whose# visits to adjacent corn-fields* of# inviting aspect raised the# ire and# outcry of# the# yelling urchins employed to# guard them from depredation.'

Adam Bede: 'And# I# made haste out# of# the# wood#, but# I# could# hear it# crying# all# the# while#; and# when# I# got# out# into# the# fields#, it# was# as# if# I# was# held fast#-- I# could# n't go# away#, for# all# I# wanted so# to# go#. And# I# sat# against# the# haystack# to# watch if# anybody# 'ud come#: I# was# very# hungry, and# I#'d only a# bit of# bread# left; but# I# could# n't go# away#.'

of the distribution, and failed – but the direction was clear: we were no longer studying texts, but *series* of texts.[12] Different.

3

Twelve sentences; 1,100 novels. The interpretation of a text; the measurement of a corpus. And the question returns: what relationship there is between them?

First of all, they are both perfectly valid forms of knowledge: on this, the broadsides from the interpretive camp are entirely groundless. Both valid – and with a moment of overlap, too. In the midst of measurement, there had been interpretation: we had taken Hawker's 'acres of refreshing greensward, studded with oak, walnut, and hawthorn', and turned it into – which is to say: interpreted it as – 'impersonal analytical prose of the novelistic narrator'. Conversely, the interpretation of 'Big Two-Hearted River' had been triggered by a (very elementary) form of measurement: it was because prepositional phrases were so insanely frequent that I had noticed them, and 'willed my understanding', as Schleiermacher had put it. To some extent, each method had relied on the other, thus evoking the 'oscillation' advocated by various quantitative researchers: a type of work 'moving back and forth between close and distant forms of reading in order to approach an imaginary conceptual centre'.[13]

Moving back and forth. Was that what had happened? I had counted up to twenty-five while working on Hemingway; and yet, this kindergarten

---

12 We failed, because extreme cases like *Arthur Montague* and *Adam Bede* possess an epistemological clarity that average ones lack. For a similar interplay of the extreme and the average, where the latter was analysed a little more successfully, see Mark Algee-Hewitt, Ryan Heuser and Franco Moretti, 'On Paragraphs: Scale, Themes, and Narrative Form', now in *Canon/Archive*.

13 Andrew Piper, 'Novel Devotions: Conversional Reading, Computational Modeling and the Modern Novel', *New Literary History* 46: 1 (Winter 2015), pp. 67–8. Similarly, Hoyt Long and Richard Jean So have urged 'a method of reading that oscillates or pivots between human and machine interpretation, each providing feedback to the other in the critic's effort to extract meaning from texts': 'Literary Pattern Recognition: Modernism between Close Reading and Machine Learning', *Critical Inquiry* 42: 2 (Winter 2016), p. 267.

feat had felt like all the measurement I needed. Same for *Adam Bede*: Hetty's confession was an extraordinary passage for interpretation to work on; we did almost nothing with it, and yet, again, it felt like all the interpretation we needed. And it felt that way because both studies entailed a very clear hierarchy between the two methods: measurement was the means and interpretation the end in Hemingway's case, and vice versa with the 1,100 novels. With 'Big Two-Hearted River', the aim was understanding how a story about trout-fishing could be so significant (its popularity in American universities is legendary) even for readers who presumably couldn't care less about trout; there had to be *something more* than just fishing in it, and when I saw all those prepositional phrases I thought they might help me discover that 'something'. But I was focusing on the *grammar* of the phrases: that there were twenty-five of them, or eighteen, or thirty, made no difference at all.[14] Conversely with *Adam Bede*; we were measuring type–token ratio, and those obnoxious hash tags were the perfect sign of our priorities: they showed repetitions right away, which was what we wanted, and if they also turned reading into a nightmare – well, reading was not the point here. Not for nothing, the next steps we took were a series of correlations of type–token ratio with abstract grammatical categories that got rid of text, reading and interpretation altogether.[15]

I will describe how research actually works, I said at the start, and now you see what I meant: it is in the concrete decisions that at the time seem purely 'tactical' – inserting hash tags, not keeping an exact count of prepositions, turning towards a historical event, measuring another variable of the corpus – it is in these apparently minor choices that 'strategic'

---

14 Better: there had to be enough of them to become visible, as is always the case in stylistic criticism; exactly how many counted as 'enough' could, however, remain vague. See, by contrast, the precision with which Sarah Allison and Marissa Gemma established the link between the register of conversation in the *Longman Grammar of Spoken and Written English* (mean type–token ratio of 30 per cent), and the 500 lowest-ranked segments of our corpus, where type–token ratio oscillated between 27 and 33 per cent: *Canon/Archive*, p. 283. In their reflections, the pathos of research was inextricable from an accuracy that is unimaginable in the hermeneutic tradition.

15 See figures 9.19–21 in *Canon/Archive*, pp. 283–5.

research priorities take form. Priorities, and exclusions: there had been a moment of overlap between the two methods, yes – and then it passed. More precisely, it was dropped. As the work proceeded, interpretation became ever more interpretive, and quantification more quantitative. Once the critical pendulum had started swinging in one direction, it never came back. There was no oscillation here, and no conceptual centre.

But perhaps there could be? Those studies had a one-sided aim from the start, which is why they subordinated one method to the other. Couldn't one design a study in which they had exactly the same weight?

I know of no such study; but in principle it's certainly possible. We can easily interpret Eliot's sentences as thoroughly as Hemingway's, or measure the exact frequency of prepositional phrases in all American short stories of the 1920s. Nothing prevents the two methods from working next to each other. Can they also work *together*? This is the point. Quantification can provide new objects for hermeneutic activity, and interpretations lend themselves to quantitative testing: this we know.[16] What is at stake here, though, is different: it's *the categories* of literary analysis. Can quantitative and hermeneutic categories lock onto each other, so as to *conceptually unify* the two approaches? Aby Warburg's *Pathosformel*, Jakobson's rethinking of poetry and prose in the light of aphasia, Bourdieu's 'field', Schwarz's 'debt' as a key to literary history: plenty of bold conceptual bridges have been launched between distant disciplines in the past. Why is it so difficult this time? None of us is a Warburg or a Jakobson: granted. Is that the only reason?

4

Certain features, writes Georges Canguilhem in his great study of nineteenth-century medical epistemology, 'are termed normal insofar as they designate average characteristics, which are most frequently practically

16 On this, see my 'Patterns and Interpretation', now in *Canon/Archive*, Sarah Allison's *Reductive Reading: A Syntax of Victorian Moralizing* (Baltimore, MD: Johns Hopkins University Press, 2018), esp. pp. 19ff, and Ted Underwood's *Distant Horizons* (Chicago, IL: University of Chicago Press, 2019), *passim*.

observable. But they are also termed normal because they enter ideally into that normative activity called therapeutics . . . the normal state designates both the habitual state of the organs, and their ideal'.[17]

The normal as frequent-habitual-average, and the normal as ideal-normative: one signifier, and two distinct concepts. What relationship, between quantitative and hermeneutic categories? The same: the former focus on the frequent-average aspects of literature, and the latter on its normative side. Normative in the sense Panofsky had in mind when he spoke of art as 'an objectifying conflict, aiming at definitive results, between a forming power and a material to be overcome'.[18] *Bewältigen*: mastering, remoulding, overcoming historical materials by applying the force – *Kraft* – of aesthetic form. This is the normative side of art and literature: one takes what is there, and turns it into something else. And this is also what interpretation works on, or, better, works *against*. Against, because interpretation is always a struggle with the text: it takes those 'definitive results', and tries as hard as possible *to undo the work of form*: to move backwards from the text as it is, through its techniques, to the world around it, and the 'dissonance' that was being addressed. In this sense, interpretation is an understanding of literature that is always tempted to go *beyond literature*: like the essayists described in *Soul and Form*, who pretend to be only discussing books, though they are actually 'always talking about the ultimate questions of life'.

Not that interpretation always goes that far. But it can: whereas the quantitative approach cannot. With the single text that is the typical object of hermeneutics, reverse-engineering may suggest which of the countless aspects of historical reality we should focus on; morphology, acting as the catalyst for historical intuition.[19] With hundreds of

17 Georges Canguilhem, *The Normal and the Pathological* (New York: Zone, 1989), pp. 122–3, 126.

18 Erwin Panofsky, 'Der Begriff des Kunstwollens', *Zeitschrift für Ästhetik und Allgemeine Kunstwissenschaft* 14 (1920), p. 339.

19 The list of major phenomena (let alone minor ones) that could count as 'the world' for any work of literature is virtually infinite. For an American in Europe in the 1920s, it would indeed have included the trenches of the First World War, but also a socialist revolution, cars and aeroplanes, a decade of unprecedented sexual freedom, civil wars, rationalist architecture, the radio, incredible

texts – let alone more – this becomes impossible, and the 'vertical' link between the text and the world is replaced by a 'horizontal' one among texts that are all on the same plane. Hemingway's sentences had led me to the war; Eliot's segment, *to other segments*. It's striking how literature-bound the quantitative approach has turned out to be.

Quantification, imprisoned among books. A flaw? Not at all. If one dimension is lost, in the shift from hermeneutics to quantification, one dimension is gained: we still know almost nothing about how literary systems function, and that's exactly what the logic of measurement shifts our gaze towards. In this sense, the cluster of morphological features emerging from those 1,100 dots had been a small but real step in the right direction: fixing a few stars in the infinite night sky of the literary field. A task, this one, that the hermeneutic tradition, with all its creativity, has never been curious about.

5

What relationship, between hermeneutics and quantification? When I started studying for this essay, I didn't know what the answer would be. Having worked for years now with one method and now with the other – but never together – I had been fantasising about a book to come that might reach a synthesis of sorts: an 'emergent' theory of literature, where the meeting of micro and macro would be more than the sum of its parts. Then I started describing what I had actually done, and the fantasy evaporated: the brief overlap between the two practices, or the lexical proximity of the normative and the frequent, were too weak a foundation for any genuine, long-term synthesis.

Perhaps I should have known it all along. Interpretation *transforms* all it touches: 'this means that'. Quantification takes pride in an utter respect

---

experiments in painting and music, the beginning of hyper-inflation. A single form usually reacts to only a few of these phenomena, which interpretation may succeed in isolating; with a large corpus, however, formal mechanisms multiply in every direction, and the threads that lead from the works to the world become hopelessly tangled.

for its data. The impulses are antithetical. Dionysus, Apollo. Think of how they relate to form. Interpretation moves *between form and the world*, pursuing the broad historical significance of literary works; quantification moves *between form and form*, trying to define the coordinates of an as yet uncharted literary atlas. Here, form is *a force*: an 'overcoming' of historical materials which must be met with suspicion, countered and ultimately unmasked. There, it is *a product*, to be measured with a cool head, and placed within a many-sided system of relations. Interpretation leads towards history, and is animated by the pathos of struggle; quantification towards morphology, animated by the pathos of discovery. Great passions, both of them. But too exclusive to join forces towards a common goal. They can certainly – let me repeat it – work one next to the other, offering new objects of study to their respective fields. But they cannot *intervene in each other's work*. Night and day; one begins, the other vanishes. Always chasing each other, and never becoming one.

For some, this is plenty; for others, maybe even too much; for me, not what I'd been hoping for. But there is a logic to critical work, and we should try to understand it – to understand *what we're actually doing when we're studying literature* – rather than conjuring up a synthesis no one has ever seen. In the end, there is nothing wrong in studying a complicated object like literature in two entirely independent ways. Or at least: this is my view of the matter. Needless to say, I may be wrong, and someone might find a good synthesis – tomorrow. Then, things change. Until then, as Arnold Schönberg once said, the middle road remains the only one that does not lead to Rome.

III

ON THE NOVEL

12

The Serious and the Tragic: Notes on Balzac and Flaubert

Francesco Fiorentino

In the chapter of *Mimesis* on Balzac and Stendhal, Auerbach observed that in the nineteenth-century novel, for the first time on a mass scale, a style was employed that exceeded the boundaries set by classical poetics. 'Low' subjects – those relating to the body, to modest objects, and the social functions of everyday life – which prior to this era and literary season had typically been portrayed comically, could now be presented seriously. Comedy, of course, was not entirely expelled from the narrative; but it ceased to be the inevitable – and even predominant – mode for handling such topics.

The study of the serious style, more identified than explicitly defined by Auerbach, has not, however, received much further scholarly attention. One of the notable exceptions is Franco Moretti, who had the merit of addressing the issue in his own distinctive way – namely, by connecting literary forms to history and ideology. He did so in the essay *Il secolo serio* ('The Serious Century'), included in the first volume of *Il romanzo*, the multi-volume work he edited for Einaudi in 2001: 'Impersonality, precision, the leading of a methodical and regular life, with a certain emotional detachment; in a word . . . seriousness. And, if we want to be quite clear, *bourgeois* seriousness.'[1] For Moretti, the serious style is closely

1 Franco Moretti, ed., *Il romanzo, vol 1: La cultura del romanzo* (Turin: Einaudi, 2001), p. 689. Translated with modifications as 'The Serious Century' in Moretti (ed.), *The Novel: Volume 1* (Princeton/Oxford: Princeton University Press), pp. 364–400 and in Moretti, *The Bourgeois* (London/New York: Verso, 2013), pp. 67–100.

tied to an historical and anthropological notion of class. It is a composite, varied style that can be found in the voices of profoundly different authors, from Daniel Defoe to Jane Austen to Thomas Mann. He describes its multiple stylistic and syntactic components: the free indirect style, the *leitmotiv*, description, narrative fillers . . . But in his view, the literary dimension is only one part of the story.

While this style finds its full realisation in the everyday life of the nineteenth century and in the novels that depict it, Moretti argues that its origins lie elsewhere: we must look not to literature first, but to painting – and not to the Anglo-French axis, but to Protestant Holland. It is in Dutch painting, he claims, that everyday scenes are first depicted seriously: inviting interiors, elegantly laid tables, modest yet functional courtyards: a resolutely anti-metaphysical universe that values material life and its legitimate pleasures. On the other hand, in nineteenth-century novels, a narrative that dwells solely on common sentiments and humdrum actions risks undermining the novelistic quality and failing to evoke strong emotions in the reader. The excesses of passion, the paroxysms of cruelty and suffering, the sublimity of sacrifice, the loftiness of ideals, the exceptional stakes involved – all this tragic *arsenal* can prove useful even to 'realist' novelists, who indeed do not shy away from employing it.

I would therefore like to add a note here to Moretti's essays by exploring the relationship between the serious style and the tragic. If there exists a genealogical kinship between the comic and the serious guaranteeing a certain compatibility, the admixture of novel and tragedy seems far more problematic.[2] As Genette also reminds us, referencing Aristotle, the two genres are not only opposed in terms of narrative versus dramatic modes, but also in terms of low versus noble genres.[3] Thus, the

---

2 There is certainly a comic tone in Balzacian narrative, and above all in that of some 'realist' writers, such as Champfleury.

3 Gérard Genette, 'Introduction to the Paratext', transl. Marie Maclean, *New Literary History* 22: 2 (1991 [1979]), pp. 261–72. The current text reprises some observations already advanced in a previous essay, but from a very different perspective. See my 'Tragico dell'eccesso e umorismo tragico. Balzac e Flaubert', in Piero Toffano, ed., *Il tragico nel romanzo moderno* (Rome: Bulzoni, 2003). pp. 55–70.

tragic in tragedy stands in stark opposition to bourgeois daily life – which, according to Moretti, is the very foundation of the serious in the novel. Furthermore, while the comic provokes and refers to laughter, and the tragic to feelings of pity and terror, the serious seems to lack an exclusive emotional register, or any specific physiological response (like laughter or tears) that it distinctly evokes. It does not possess a clear emotional or bodily dimension as its distinctive feature. So how, then, can it be identified?

In the afterword to the first edition of *La Fille aux yeux d'or*, Balzac offers his diagnosis on the possibility of the tragic and the comic in modernity:

> Modern society, by levelling all conditions and illuminating everything, has eliminated both the comic and the tragic. The historian of manners is thus obliged, as in this case, to take the facts – born of the same passion but occurring in different individuals – wherever they may be found, and to stitch them together in order to create a complete drama.[4]

Social levelling towards the mean brings with it a moral, emotional and stylistic lowering: the tragic represents an excess in the upward direction across all three of these domains, just as the *comic* does towards the bottom. Homogenisation replaces qualitative excess with quantitative multiplication: the same passions, replicated across a plurality of individuals, have replaced the intensity of the passion of a single exceptional individual. Democracy advances in this way, too.[5]

It was therefore necessary to find new modes for creating disruptions – ripples that would stand out against the grey backdrop of the everyday, and against the moral and emotional flatness of the serious. A turn towards something that could replace the tragic and the comic, but

---

4 Honoré de Balzac, *La Fille aux yeux d'or*, in *La Comédie humaine*, 12 vols, ed. Pierre-George Castex et al. (Paris: Gallimard, 1976–81 [1830–56]), vol. V, p. 122.

5 It should be noted that, in the above passage, Balzac underlines how modern society illuminates everything (*en éclairant tout*). The tragic above all presupposes a distance between its protagonists, a veil that covers their lives, which only tragedy has the power to tear aside.

that preserves some of their core characteristics, was essential for renewing the novelistic form in the early nineteenth century.

The tragic, in Aristotle's definition, was meant to evoke fear and pity. But, as early as the eighteenth century, these two emotional registers had already become diluted and separated, giving rise to two narrative subgenres: the *larmoyant* (tearful, sentimental) genre, and that of terror and horror. The new nineteenth-century novel inherited these two registers and willingly recombined them, though no longer within a truly tragic framework. Instead, they fused within what Peter Brooks described as the melodramatic imagination – a mode that pits villains against virtuous characters with pathetic and/or terrifying effects.[6] In this way, drama supplanted tragedy in the aesthetic consciousness of the time.

The practice of drama, however, does not prevent Balzac from continuing to invoke the tragic – not only in a rather banal form divorced from classical tragedy, but also in explicit reference to the genre itself. We can take the example of *Eugénie Grandet*. The most sublime of Balzac's heroines, she has secretly given her cousin the precious coins that her miserly father had entrusted to her, hoping to accumulate even more wealth through her as an intermediary. Her mother realises with horror that the treasure is missing just three days before the terrible Grandet will ask to see it. Here is the narrator's commentary: 'In three days a terrible drama would begin, a drama undignified by poison, dagger, or bloodshed, but fate dealt scarcely more cruelly with the princely house of Atreus than with the actors in this bourgeois tragedy.'[7] Just as classical tragedy was founded on the familial history of Atreus, this tragedy – one of those 'terrible bourgeois tragedies', as they will be called in *Femme de trente ans* – has the family as its locus.

However, unlike the Atreidae, whose royal lineage gave their fate objective significance, the Grandet family's drama carries meaning only in relation to the characters involved (*relativement aux acteurs*). The tragic, then, is transferred into the private sphere, a realm inherently

6 Peter Brooks, *The Melodramatic Imagination: Balzac, Henry James, Melodrama, and the Mode of Excess* (New Haven, CT: Yale University Press, 1995).

7 Balzac, *Eugénie Grandet*, transl. Ellen Marriage (London: Dent, 1973), p. 167; Balzac, *La Comédie humaine*, vol. III, p. 1148.

obscure and overlooked, to which only the modern novel grants the reader access.[8] The terror experienced by the mother and daughter must be shared by the reader, who feels pity for them. Though it involves neither 'poison, dagger, or bloodshed', this private scene is presented as even more cruel. If novelistic tragedy has lost its symbolic power and collective dimension, it nevertheless retains cruelty and emotional intensity, grounded more in feelings than in actions. In the new society, social levelling has diminished the scope of individual stories, but not the intensity of suffering.

Eugénie is a tragic heroine in the manner of Lukács and Goldmann, in that she rebels and refuses compromise. The tragedy involving the daughter's rebellion against her father, following a violent crisis, leads however to an unexpected conclusion: Eugénie receives from her cousin a gold dressing-case worth more than the coins she had given him. Grandet, unable to comprehend the notion of gift-giving, considers his daughter to have done a good deal. Thus, he reconciles with her: 'It was a good stroke of business, little girl. You are your father's own daughter, I see.'[9] With a theatrical touch, the novel defuses the tragic. The tragic tone, which had built up suspense, finds a prosaic resolution. So, what is the value of Balzac's invocation of tragedy, given that it ultimately confirms its incompatibility with the novel? It seems to function as a reading cue, a kind of literary equivalent to a *maestoso* notation in music. It signals intensity and confers distinction on the narrative. Above all, it illustrates how the realist novel introduces a revolution in both style and ideological conception. The comparison between the Atreidae and

---

8 As he writes in *Muse du département* (*La Comédie humaine*, vol. IV, p. 649): 'Il se jouait en effet à La Baudraye une de ces longues et monotones tragédies conjugales qui demeureraient éternellement inconnues, si l'avide scalpel du Dix-Neuvième Siècle n'allait pas, conduit par la nécessité de trouver du nouveau, fouiller les coins les plus obscurs du coeur, ou, si vous voulez, ceux que la pudeur des siècles précédents avait respecté.' ('One of those long and monotonous conjugal tragedies was unfolding at La Baudraye: tragedies that would remain forever unknown if the greedy scalpel of the Nineteenth Century, driven by the need to uncover something new, did not probe into the darkest corners of the heart – or, if you prefer, those corners that the modesty of earlier centuries had left untouched.')

9 *Eugénie Grandet*, pp. 193–4; *La Comédie humaine*, vol. III, p. 1167.

the Grandets, between the high and the low, which was once a topos of burlesque rhetoric and the comic novel, has become serious. The scope of the serious style manages somehow to touch both extremes and to connect them – because these supposed extremes have, in fact, drawn significantly closer. The low is no longer so low, and the high is now within reach.

The reduction of distance becomes clear when the contrast between high and low involves Napoleon, the epitome of exaltation in Balzacian France. The myth surrounding the emperor does not impede a familial diminishment of his figure, which is often stripped of its grandeur to become a kind of bourgeois normality. His sentimental life, notably unexceptional, is frequently and straightforwardly alluded to. In *Maison Nucingen*, 'Bonaparte was as stupid as a bourgeois in his first relations with Josephine'; in *Honorine*, 'Three days before the arrival of Marie Louise, Napoleon lay in his wedding-bed at Compiègne'; in *Contrat de mariage*, 'Like Napoleon, the husband is thenceforth condemned to victories which, in spite of their number, do not prevent the first defeat from crushing him'; in *Une fille d'Eve*, 'Women are sometimes embarrassed for money, and do not wish to tell their husbands, like Joséphine with Napoleon'; in *Cousine Bette*, the Baroness had loved her husband, as Joséphine in the end had loved Napoleon, with an admiring, maternal, and cowardly devotion'.[10] In the bureaucratic environment of *Employés*, he is even cited as an example of a decidedly un-triumphant attitude: 'You, in your sphere, should have done as Napoleon did in his; he bent and twisted and crawled – yes, crawled!'; Z. Marcas, 'another Bonaparte', in the story of the same name, can live on thirty coins a day, like his model. In *Père Goriot*, his austerity is legendary; 'Napoleon didn't dine twice a day, and couldn't take any more mistresses than a medical student

10 *The House of Nucingen*, transl. William Walton (Philadelphia: George Barrie, 1896), p. 11; *La Comédie humaine*, vol. VI, p. 333; *Honorine*, transl. George Bernard Ives (Boston: Little, Brown, 1909), p. 393; *La Comédie humaine*, vol. II, p. 558; *The Marriage Contract*, transl. Katharine Prescott Wormeley (Boston: Roberts, 1895), p. 14; *La Comédie humaine*, vol. III, p. 535; *A Daughter of Eve*, transl. Katharine Prescott Wormeley (Boston: Roberts, 1895), p. 22; *La Comédie humaine*, vol. II, p. 288; *Cousin Bette*, transl. James Waring (New York: Knopf, 1991), p. 25; *La Comédie humaine*, vol. VII, p. 73.

doing his house training at the Capucins.'[11] The emperor is thus remembered for his origins as a self-made man; for his presumed inexperience, his sentimental weaknesses – becoming the figure in whom an entire generation of ambitious young men, such as Eugène de Rastignac and Lucien de Rubempré, could most easily recognise themselves.

In parallel to this domestication of the lofty, one can also see an elevation of the low, which allows bourgeois characters to be likened to him. Thus Nucingen is dubbed the Napoleon of finance, who 'had thus massed his funds, as Napoleon massed his troops'; Gaudissart, who will become the Napoleon of boulevard theatres, boasts, while still a travelling salesman, that unlike the emperor, he would never suffer a Waterloo; Benassis is the Napoleon of his valley; the marchant Birotteau, 'like the Emperor Napoleon at Compiègne', only wants to see the house he is building once it is finished; the old notary Chesnel is as large as Napoleon, 'even bigger'; Véronique, the benefactor of her village, has a will 'stronger than Napoleon's', according to Binchon; Vautrin, 'the Bonaparte of thieves', obtains from his lackeys the same respect that Napoleon received from his soldiers.[12]

Those being compared to Napoleon are invariably bourgeois characters (or, at most, nobles ennobled by him). A great banker like Bucinger, executing daring stock market operations; the consummate salesmen Gaudissart, able to flog anything; an honest and courageous merchant like Birotteau; the capable notary Chasnel; the wealthy landowner Veronique, who invests in and transforms her village; the criminal mastermind Vautrin – all of these figures have become protagonists of the

11 *La Comédie humaine*, vol. VII, p. 1092; *Z. Marcas*, transl. George Burnham Ives (Philadelphia: George Barrie, 1898), p. 25; *La Comédie humaine*, vol. VII, p. 842; *Père Goriot*, transl. A. J. Krailsheimer (Oxford: Oxford University Press, 1991), p. 125; *La Comédie humaine*, vol. III, p. 165.

12 *The House of Nucingen*, p. 87; *La Comédie humaine*, vol. VI, p. 380; *Le Cousin Pons* (*La Comédie humaine*, vol. VII), p. 755; *L'illustre Gaudissart*, (*La Comédie humaine*, vol. IV), pp. 572–3; *Le Medicin de campagne* (*La Comédie humaine*, vol. IX), p. 701; *César Birotteau* (*La Comédie humaine*, vol. VI), p. 165; *Le Cabinet des Antiques* (*La Comédie humaine*, vol. IV), p. 1057; *Le Curé de village* (*La Comédie humaine*, vol. IX), p. 858; *Père Goriot* (*La Comédie humaine*, vol. III), p. 208; *La Dernière incarnation de Vautrin* (*La Comédie humaine*, vol. VI), p. 842.

new bourgeois society. Even the bourgeois courtesan Valérie, capable of amassing great wealth, faces an unexpected challenge but 'preserved her coolness and presence of mind, like General Bonaparte when, at the siege of Mantua, he had to fight two armies'.[13] The social actors have changed, but their qualities – as well as the conflicts and private situations they must navigate – present strong analogies to those of historical figures: 'Our toilers fight against the toilers of the continent by force of misery, as Napoleon fought Europe by force of regiments.'[14] The task of the narrator, as the new historian of manners, is not merely to record this transformation, but to recount it with the same grandeur traditionally reserved for the stories of the old ruling classes:

> Troy and Napoleon are nothing but poems. May this story be the poem of bourgeois vicissitudes, to which no voice has ever given thought, so lacking they seem in grandeur, while being just as immense: for this is not about a single man, but about an entire people of sorrows.[15]

Once again, the whole people stand in contrast to the individual: the serious style tends to be democratic, just as the tragic was aristocratic. But in Balzac's version, the serious style assumes a decidedly elevated register.

Completely different, within the domain of the serious style, is the choice made by Flaubert – as is clearly demonstrated by the relationship his novels entertain with the tragic. In *Madame Bovary*, the adjective 'tragique' appears only once; it is Charles who pronounces it when he wishes to remain at the theatre to see the end of *Lucia di Lammermoor*: 'Ah! Pas encore! Restons! Dit Bovary. Elle a les cheveux dénouées: cela

---

13 *Cousin Bette*, p. 177; *La Comédie humaine*, vol. VII, p. 213. The seriousness of the conclusion of *The Marriage Contract* (p. 179) – in which Paul 'went to bed and slept that heavy sleep which follows immense disasters – the sleep that seized Napoleon after Waterloo' – is quite different from the 'comic' opening of the second chapter of *Promessi Sposi*, in which the agitated slumber of Don Abbondio is compared with that of Condé before the Battle of Rocroi.

14 *Unconscious Comedians*, transl. Katharine Prescott Wormeley (Boston: Little Brown Company, 1896), p. 231; *La Comédie humaine*, vol. VII, p. 1178.

15 *César Birotteau* (*La Comédie humaine*, vol. VI), p. 81.

promet d'être tragique!'[16] In his mouth, the term is ironically deflated into a melodramatic excess on the part of a singer. In *Education sentimentale*, 'tragique' occurs three times, always with an ironic connotation: twice in the phrase *air tragique* and once as a *situation tragique*, referring to a situation that is clearly not so. Similarly ironic is the sole appearance of the word 'tragédie'; it is uttered by Frédéric when he turns to Madame Dambreuse: 'Car, pour plaire aux femmes, il faut étaler une insouciance de bouffon ou des fureurs de tragédie.'[17] Flaubert's aesthetics are deeply averse to theatricality in all its forms, from melodrama to any evocation of the tragic or tragedy itself. And yet, the absence of explicit references to the tragic does not mean that Flaubert's work lacks a tragic dimension. As Brombert aptly put it, Flaubert discovers 'the tragedy of the very absence of Tragedy'.[18]

In his letter to Louise Colet dated 24 April 1852, Flaubert offers an alternative ending for Lamartine's novel *Graziella*, other than the protagonist's death: 'A young man in Naples, by chance, among other distractions, sleeps with a fisherman's daughter and then gets rid of her; she does not die, but consoles herself; this is ordinary and more bitter.'[19] The rejection of the definitive (death) in favour of life continuing, of the irredeemable in favour of the ordinary, the tempering of meaning, produces a lowering of seriousness that manifests as a detached, neutral style suited to the banality being narrated. This tragic quality born of the absence of tragedy nonetheless carries a bitter aftertaste. It is to be found above all in the conclusions of his novels – precisely where, on the contrary, narrative convention would typically expect a concentration of

---

16 'Ah! No more! Let us stay! said Bovary. She has her hair down: this promises to be tragic!' Gustave Flaubert, *Madame Bovary* (Paris: Gallimard, 1972 [1857]), p. 300. In Gisèle Séginger's *Dictionnaire Flaubert* (Paris: Champion, 2017) there is, significantly enough, no entry for 'tragic'/ 'tragedy'.

17 Gustave Flaubert, *L'Éducation sentimentale* (Paris: Le Livre de Poche, 2002 [1869]), p. 541. 'Because, in order to please women, one must demonstrate either the carefreeness of a clown or the rages of tragedy.'

18 Vitor H. Brombert, *Novels of Flaubert: A Study of Themes and Techniques* (Princeton, NJ: Princeton University Press, 1966), p. 90.

19 Gustave Flaubert, *Correspondance*, vol. II (Paris: Gallimard, 1980 [1851–58]), p. 78.

meaning. Thus *Madame Bovary* does not end with the death of Emma or Charles, but with a brisk summary in which the imperfect tense gives way to the aorist, recounting the wretched fate into which Berthe has fallen. The devaluation, the erasure of Emma's existence, the banal squalor: the novel becomes, in Flaubert's words, 'bête comme la vie' (as stupid as life) – and so explains his admiration for the ending of *Candide*.[20]

None of this is told in a tragic or even elegiac tone but through a clinical gaze, 'which is the only means to achieve great emotional effects'.[21] This emotionless account is contrasted with the news of Homais being granted the Légion d'honneur. As he will write in another letter to Louise Colet, 'Irony takes nothing away from the pathetic; on the contrary, it amplifies it.'[22]

This is the very sneer that Crouzet described in *Bouvard et Pécuchet* as 'le grotesque triste': the mingling of conflicting data in a senseless, dysphoric chaos.[23] The epilogues of *Madame Bovary* and *Éducation sentimentale* blend bitter recognition with mocking laughter. Especially in

---

20 Flaubert, *Madame Bovary*, p. 302.

21 Flaubert, *Correspondance*, vol. II, p. 78. In his letter to Louise Colet of 7 October 1852, we find the famous formulation of narrative impersonality: 'When will the facts be written from the point of view of a *superior joke* [*d'une blague supérieure*], that is, as the good Lord sees them from above?' (p. 168). What *Bouvard and Pécuchet* enjoyed in tragedy 'was the emphasis, the discourse on Politics, the maxims of perversity'. Gustave Flaubert, *Bouvard et Pécuchet. Dictionnaire des idées reçues* (Lausanne: Coopérative Éditions Recontre, 1965 [1881]), p. 166.

22 Letter of 9 October 1852 (Flaubert, *Correspondance*, vol. II, p. 172).

23 The expression is from a letter to Louise Colet of 21 October 1846. The *grotesque sadness* differs from the Balzacian grotesque in that, according to Rosen, the latter is 'an inextricable alliance of the comic and the atrocious, or of the familiar and the foreign'. Elisheva Rosen, 'Le grotesque et l'esthétique du roman blazacien', in Claude Duchet and Jacques Needs, eds, *L'invention du roman* (Paris: Pierre Belfond, 1982), p. 140. In relation to the tempering of the *sensanche*, see Jacques-David Ebguy, 'Qul est le sens de tout cela? *L'Éducation sentimentale*, roman du retrait', in Pierre Glaudes and Eléonore Reverzy, eds, *Relire* L'Éducation sentimentale (Paris: Garnier, 2018), pp. 315–36.

places where one might expect an outpouring of pathos, one instead finds a dry style that downplays the story. It's a technique reminiscent of what Freud would later say about humour. Flaubert's seriousness is often tinged with tragic humour.

13

The Novel, History, Politics: Franco Moretti and the Nineteenth-Century European Novel

Françoise Lavocat

The Way of the World was first published by Graziani in 1986, and later republished by Einaudi in 1999 with a new preface.[1] In 2014, *The Bourgeois* was released.[2] Between these two publications, Franco Moretti dedicated many other studies to the novel, especially the European novel.[3]

---

1 The work was translated into English – Franco Moretti, *The Way of the World: The* Bildungsroman *in European Culture*, transl. Albert Sbragia (London: Verso, 2000 [1986]); into French by Camille Bloomfield and Pierre Musitelli – *Le Roman de formation* (Paris: CNRS Editions, 2019); and into Portuguese by Natasha Belfort Palmeira – *O romance de formação* (São Paulo: Todavia, 2020). Other translations are underway, among which we note the Chinese one.

2 Originally written in English – Franco Moretti, *The Bourgeois: Between History and Literature* (London: Verso, 2013); and then translated into German by Frank Jakubzik – *Die Bourgeois: Eine Schlüsselfigur der Moderne* (Berlin: Suhrkamp, 2014); into Spanish by Lilia Mosconi – *El bugruès: entre la historia y la literature* (Buenos Aires: Fondo de Cultura Económica, 2014); into Slovenian by Ana Monika Habjan and Jernej Habjann – *Buržuj: med zgodovino in literature* (Ljubljana: Sophia, 2015); into Italian by Giovanna Scocchera – *Il Borghese* (Turin: Einaudi, 2017); and into Japanese by Yusuke Tanaka – *Burujowa: Rekishi to bungaka no aida*, (Tokyo: Misuzu Shobo, 2018).

3 Compare, in particular, Franco Moretti, *Atlas of the European Novel* (London: Verso, 1998), and the monumental collective work *Il romanzo* (Turin: Einaudi, 2001–2003), translated into English in an abridged version *The Novel*, 2 vols. (Princeton: Princeton University Press, 2006). The celebrated and revolutionary *Graphs, Maps, Trees: Abstract Models for a Literary History* (London: Verso, 2005) also deals with the nineteenth-century novel in a broad manner, but in this current

I intend here, however, to concentrate on these two texts which have much in common, even though they were written almost thirty years apart. The first centres on what Moretti calls the *romanzo di formazione*, encompassing the German *Bildungsroman* (and therefore, beyond *Wilhelm Meister's Apprenticeship* – the genre's founding text – a number of French and English novels up to Flaubert and George Eliot). In this work, Moretti defines the novel, and particularly the *Bildungsroman*, as a compromise – both formally and ideologically. He analyses the variations and vicissitudes of this compromise through the trajectories – decreasingly successful – of a series of heroes (and a few heroines), whose defining trait is youth. Moretti argues that the divergent development of the *romanzo di formazione* in two countries (England and France) coincides with the rise of bourgeois culture and capitalism. His 2013 book *The Bourgeois* addresses the splendours and miseries of the nineteenth-century bourgeoisie through literature and culture more generally (with occasional references to painting and architecture). Moreover, *The Bourgeois* appears to be a continuation of the reflection begun in the 1986 text.

These two volumes allow us to appreciate a different aspect of Franco Moretti's thought – particularly beneficial for those who are more familiar with his theories on world literature and distant reading, and his pioneering work in the field of digital humanities.

How has Moretti's thinking about the novel developed through these two works, and what does it still have to say to us today? The cover of the Italian edition of *Il borghese* (like its English and German editions) features Ingres's portrait of the powerful, imposing and pompous newspaper director Louis-François Bertin, and inspires me to ask a somewhat impertinent question: What kind of love does Moretti nurture for the nineteenth-century novel, which has driven him to dedicate to it a good part of his life as a researcher?

---

contribution I will set aside this more well-known work, which also draws on different approaches.

1. Questions of Method (1986–2014)

1.1. Between history and histories

In his preface to the 1999 edition of *Il romanzo di formazione* Moretti distances himself from the impulse ('perfectly plausible, but happens to be wrong') that had partly animated his earlier work – an impulse, he admits, that dates back to the book's original conception in 1979: namely, 'to establish an *immediate* link between the history of literature and the history of ideology (and especially of political ideology)'.[4] In his introduction to *The Bourgeois*, whose full title ('The Bourgeois Between History and Literature') reaffirms the intent to relate literature to the broader world, Moretti emphasises the absence of any direct connection between these two histories: literary bourgeois characters 'prove exactly nothing about the Manchester or Warsaw bourgeoisie'.[5] Literary history and social history are, rather, two parallel lines, which, in all likelihood, will never intersect. And yet, an indirect relationship exists, metaphorically described as a helical movement, through which literature reconstructs the phases of the development of capitalism over the nineteenth century.[6] Lukács's hypothesis in *Theory of the Novel*, according to which each literary form is the expression and solution of a problem present in the social field or in the life of ideas, remains a cornerstone of both works.[7] In *The Bourgeois*, Moretti claims that, over time, while dissonances may fade, the solutions proposed by the most important literary works – always shaped by compromise – remain mysteriously intelligible. Although literary forms essentially belong to the realm of bricolage (and thus resist being fully theorised), they still allow us to trace a path back to the contradictions that produced them. In this sense, literary form is like a 'fossil' and, ultimately, a tool for knowledge.[8]

---

4 Moretti, *Il romanzo di formazione*, p. 247 n. 10.

5 Moretti, *The Bourgeois*, p. 13.

6 Ibid.

7 Georg Lukács, *The Theory of the Novel*, transl. Anna Bostock (Cambridge, MA: MIT Press, 1974 [1916]).

8 Moretti, *The Bourgeois*, p. 14.

This hermeneutic optimism is underpinned by a very solid theoretical foundation in both works. In the mid-1980s, Moretti returned to the Frankfurt School and structuralism.[9] However, both texts contain only occasional references to Adorno and Benjamin (and always from a critical perspective).[10] The core intellectual and theoretical structure is primarily drawn from Hegel, Marx and Freud; among contemporaries, Lotman; theorists of the novel such as Bakhtin, Auerbach, and Orlando; historians like Marc Bloch; intellectual historians such as Hans Blumenberg and Reinhart Koselleck; linguists such as Weinrich and Benveniste; and the occasional narratologist (Seymour Chatman).[11] So-called French theory does not form part of Moretti's intellectual framework. Barthes is cited several times for his distinction between 'nuclei' and 'catalysts' (which is paired with Chatman's own distinction between 'nuclei' and 'satellites').[12] But Barthes's writings on Balzac are contested.[13] Foucault is cited only once, and again in a critical manner.[14]

---

9 *Il romanzo di formazione* (Turin: Einaudi, 1999), p. xvii.

10 Moretti rightly notes that Adorno concentrated too much on the relation between art and truth to take any interest in the novel (Moretti, *Way of the World*, p. 249), and that he does not represent the most appropriate scholar to do justice to the *Comédie humaine* (p. 144). As for Benjamin, Moretti contests his idea that the hero's death necessarily provides a work with meaning (p. 119).

11 Moretti borrows the distinction between classification and transformation from Jurij Lotman, *The Structure of the Artistic Text* (Ann Arbor: University of Michigan Press, 1970). For the incompatibility between Lotman's thought and a current of French theories from the 1970s and 1980s, see Emanuel Landolt, 'Histoire d'un dialogue impossible: J. Kristeva, J- Lotman et la sémiotique', *Langage et socieété* 4: 142 (2012), pp. 121–40. Aside from the opposition between 'nuclei' and 'satellites', Moretti draws on Seymour Chatman – *Story and Discourse*, (Ithaca, NY: Cornell University Press, 1978) – for the distinction between history and discourse. He also twice evokes Gérard Genette's theses on Balzac, though in order to contest them (Moretti, *The Way of the World*, pp. 96 and 160).

12 In *The Bourgeois*, Moretti replaces this with his own terminology, preferring 'turning points' and 'fillers', translated in Italian as *svolte* and *riemptivi*. Roland Barthes, 'An Introduction to the Structural Analysis of Narrative', transl. Lionel Duisit, *New Literary History* 6: 2 (1975 [1966]).

13 Moretti, *Way of the World*, p. 160.

14 Moretti opposes his own conception of normality – a favourite topic of the *romanzo di formazione* – to that shared by Freud and Foucault, who define it in terms of sickness (Moretti, *Way of the World*, p. 11).

The 'fanfare of deconstructionism' has no place in Moretti's thought or body of work.[15]

This rapid overview would not be complete without the inevitable reference to Darwin, who inspires Moretti's conception of the life and disappearance of literary forms, whose fate depends on their complexity, adaptability and capacity to compete.[16] While this theory operates as a long-term framework in Moretti's thinking about the novel, it remains somewhat peripheral to the argumentation of the two texts under discussion here. Nevertheless, it does inform his keen attention to the decline and death of literary forms.

1.2. European comparatism against universal literature

In the 1999 preface to *The Way of the World*, Moretti explains that the book's approach – originally developed from a course on Goethe, Schiller and Stendhal he taught at the University of Salerno – is explicitly comparatist.[17] However, in a section titled 'Towards World Literature', Moretti strongly advocates for the adoption of a perspective far broader than the one offered by the book itself. The shift from 'comparative literature' (which Moretti narrows to the European realm) to world literature requires the approach of distant reading.[18] And yet, this dual ambition – so programmatic for Moretti's later developments – is not realised in either the 1986 or the 2013 work: both are devoted to the nineteenth-century European novel and rely on close reading. This suggests that Moretti has never stopped pursuing both paths simultaneously.

Moreover, in these works the analysis is limited to a narrow portion of western Europe. *Il romanzo di formazione* is based on the analysis of four

15 Ibid., p. 12.

16 The tendency towards compromise that characterises the coming-of-age novel also allowed it to win out in the struggle against the epistolary novel and the historical novel (ibid.).

17 Moretti, *Il romanzo di formazione*, p. xix.

18 Ibid., pp. xix–xxi. In terms of world literature, the number of works vastly overtakes human reading abilities. In order to overcome this problem, it is necessary to abandon direct reading and instead study the texts through the filter of secondary literature, or by appealing to digital tools. This is the thesis presented in Moretti, *Graphs, Maps, Trees*.

French novels (*The Charterhouse of Parma* and *The Red and the Black*, by Stendhal, *Lost Illusions* by Balzac, and *Sentimental Education* by Flaubert); one German novel and its sequel (Goethe's *Wilhelm Meister's Apprenticeship* and *Wilhelm Meister's Journeyman Years*); and three English ones (Austen's *Pride and Prejudice*, Dickens's *David Copperfield* and Eliot's *Middlemarch*).[19] Russian and American novels are excluded because they are considered too different.[20] In *The Bourgeois*, the corpus is essentially the same, but expanded.[21] In particular, *Robinson Crusoe* is added, along with two novels classified as coming from the (pre-capitalist) European periphery: Giovanni Verga's *Mastro-don Gesualdo* (Sicily) and Bolesła Prus's *The Doll* (Poland). This centre–periphery analysis marks a new development, and draws explicitly on the work of Pascale Casanova.[22]

This corpus, centred on the quintessential French, English and German canon of the early nineteenth century, serves the book's purpose well. The comparison of a very limited number of works allows us to become familiar with the destinies of young protagonists.[23] Comparison of their narratives reveals unexpected affinities (such as that between Wilhelm Meister and Elizabeth Bennet), exceptions (such as Julien Sorel), and contrasts – for instance, between English novels, which affirm faith in justice, and Italian novels (*The Betrothed*), which reaffirm Christian

---

19 I will admit that I find difficulty in understanding why Moretti concentrated on this aristocratic hero in *The Charterhouse of Parma*, without even mentioning Lucien Leuwen, a properly bourgeois hero nostalgic for the revolution and ready – through a union with the noble Madame de Chasteller – to undertake an extraordinary political and social compromise that fails at the last minute due to plots against him. Moretti also cites *Felix Holt* (1866) and *Daniel Deronda* (1876) by George Eliot, as well as Charlotte Brontë's *Jane Eyre* (1847).

20 According to Moretti (*Way of the World*, p. 1), the former provide too much space to religion and the latter to nature. We do see a certain opening in the epilogue, in which the novels of Kafka, Mann and Joyce are evoked in passing.

21 Among other works, Moretti also considers Maria Edgeworth's *Castle Rackrent*, Conrad's *Heart of Darkness*, Gaskell's *North and South*, Dickens's *Hard Times*, Dinak Craik's *John Halifax* and – on the French front – Flaubert's *Madame Bovary*. The book closes with an analysis of a range of pieces by Ibsen.

22 Pascale Casanova, *La République mondiale del lettres* (Paris: Seuil, 1999).

23 Moretti rightly notes: 'What happens with novelistic heroes is what happens with our friends and relatives: we know them perfectly, and we do not know who they are.' *Way of the World*, p. 251.

faith.[24] It also outlines major oppositions: between continental novels, where the plot originates from a disruption between the protagonist and society, and the English novel, which requires the intervention of some 'monster' for the plot to be set in motion.[25] Or between France, which experienced the Revolution, and England and Germany, where revolution is either far off or abhorrent. Indeed, one of the central theses of the book – at the intersection between history and stories – is that the development of the *Bildungsroman* is shaped by how geographically and temporally distant a country is from the French Revolution.[26]

Despite this, one cannot help but dream of a differently comprised corpus. Is it really true that the meagre strand of female *Bildungsroman* is exclusively English?[27] Certainly, Elizabeth Bennet, Jane Eyre and Dorothea Brooke are all English, and, according to Moretti, have no counterparts in France or Europe more generally.[28] However, George Sand, with *Consuelo* and perhaps also *La petite Fadette*, offers interesting examples of feminine education. While Cosette may not possess a strong enough personality to embody a fully developed *Bildungsroman*, *Les Misérables* (1862) – an extraordinary novel in every respect (not least for its sheer number of characters), whose political echoes still resonate today – seems to challenge the historical narrative traced in Moretti's two books.[29] Characters like Marius and Jean Valjean embody the bourgeois figure whose downfall is later dramatised in Frédéric Moreau. Hugo's novels also show that the relationship between fiction and politics is not necessarily one of detachment, and that not all novels are incompatible with revolution.[30]

---

24 Ibid., p. 201.

25 Ibid., p. 207.

26 Ibid., p. 215.

27 *Il romanzo di formazione*, p. xv.

28 I would happily add the heroines of some less well-known novels that were nevertheless bestsellers of their epoch: Maria Edgeworth's *Helen* (1832) and Catherine Gore's *Mothers and Daughters* (1831).

29 I am thinking of Ladj Ly's film (France, 2019) which reprises the title in order to evoke the living conditions of the youth of Montfermeil, a city on the outskirts of Paris.

30 Moretti, *The Way of the World*, p. 64.

1.3. From form/meaning to close reading

The central thesis of Moretti's 1986 work is that the *Bildungsroman* is a 'symbolic form' in the sense understood by Cassirer and Panofsky.[31] Just as the Renaissance discovered perspective, so the nineteenth-century novel invented youth as the embodiment of the spirit of the age: the era of the birth and development of the bourgeoisie and of capitalism. This symbolic form provides a mode of connecting history with histories. *The Way of the World* surveys all the variants of the *Bildungsroman*, through the various ways in which heroes (and, more rarely, heroines) transition (or fail to transition) from youth to adulthood. Thus, the model at work here is relatively abstract: a form-sense that governs comparison at the level of stories, plots and *fabula*. Still, Moretti also shows a keen interest in language, especially in keywords that characterise a specific work – for instance, the key term for Balzac's *Comédie humaine* might be 'over-determination', while for George Eliot's novels it might be 'reform'.

In *The Bourgeois*, the narrative clearly revolves around language and style. Beyond the central term *borghese* itself (and the semantic shift in the Anglophone world from bourgeois to middle class), words like 'utility', 'efficiency', 'comfort' and 'seriousness' (though 'serious' will soon be replaced by the more moralising 'earnest') punctuate and guide the analysis. Moretti also succeeds in conveying to foreign readers the distinctive flavour of the Italian word *roba* (from Verga's novel): a concrete, impassioned, and non-capitalist term for one's possessions. It's a breath of fresh air in the moralistic and sentimental atmosphere of Victorian-era English novels.

The Bourgeois explores the convergence between novels and society, narrative and history, through the lens of language and stylistic inquiry. The grammatical construction of sentences and the use of the gerund in *Robinson Crusoe* reveal a 'style of the useful' based on continuity and accumulation – an aesthetic which aligns with the spirit of early capitalism.[32] The growing prevalence of 'fillers', to the detriment of 'nuclei' or 'turning points', observed across European novels throughout the nineteenth century, is linked to the rise of leisure time and comfort in daily

31 Ibid., p. 5.

32 Moretti, *The Bourgeois*, p. 39.

life. Adjectives lose the concrete value they might still have held in *Robinson Crusoe*, assuming instead an emotional and ethical charge: this transformation mirrors that of bourgeois civilisation, which drifts away from knowledge in favour of a morality steeped in religiosity and emotion. Finally, the use of free indirect style (in *Madame Bovary*) is interpreted as the result of a process of socialisation of both character and narrator, signalling the decline of the *Bildungsroman*.

One may agree or disagree with these hypotheses, but it is undeniable that they form a coherent system. The trajectories of the novel, society, ideas and capitalism intersect continuously and, at the level of the text that Moretti describes as 'molecular', they effectively weave a shared history.[33] It is thus inevitable that the ambivalence of the bourgeoisie – a creature of modernity, whether loveable (above all in its youthful version) or detestable (in the guise of Louise-François Bertin) – should reverberate within the novel itself.

2. An Ambivalence for Novels

2.1. The ambiguities of compromise

Building on Lukács's legacy, Moretti regards every literary form as a form of compromise. Yet it is the nineteenth-century novel – and especially the *Bildungsroman* – that most aptly exemplifies this general law, as it brings together a set of intermediate elements: it belongs to the serious genre, situated midway between the comic and the tragic, and both the characters it portrays and the audience it addresses belong to the bourgeoisie, or 'middle class'. The compromise is ideological and inherent to the novel's form, manifesting itself at the levels of both narrative content and style.

In Stendhal and Balzac, for instance, the compromise lies in the combination of a strong narrator with a weak protagonist. It recurs across numerous formal, narrative and thematic balances: between *fabula* and plot, meaning and productivity, narrative nuclei and fillers, classification and transformation, individual freedom and socialisation, stability and

33 Ibid., pp. 125, 131.

change, bourgeoisie and aristocracy, actions and ideals, conservatism and nostalgia for the Revolution, liberalism and reformism. It is also thematised in the marriages of Wilhelm Meister and Elizabeth Bennet (made possible by the mutual tempering of aristocratic 'pride' and bourgeois 'prejudice'), as well as in the conformism of Lucien de Rubempré and the indolence of Frédéric Moreau.

A 'bourgeois hero' is, in the end, a contradiction in terms; the brilliant invention of the nineteenth-century novel lies precisely in its ability to render compelling destinies that have nothing heroic about them at all. In this way, daily life becomes legitimate material for fiction, and Moretti even suggests that the novel has fostered 'socialization'.[34] In antithesis to 2,000 years of romance, the values and aesthetics embodied by the novel are comfort, labour, honesty, utility, efficiency, clarity, regularity, precision and objectivity. These are the ingredients (in varying and shifting proportions) of realism.

In this regard, Moretti shows that the forms assumed by realism are closely tied to each era's conception of reality; for example, the notion that it contains unpleasant aspects that one must learn to confront (which is precisely what is referred to as the 'reality principle').[35] This is what underlies the bleak endings so often found in novels, particularly for French protagonists, who are, indeed, unable to evaluate reality correctly: Lucien de Rubempré, Emma Bovary, Frédéric Moreau.

2.2. The impasse of the compromise

First and foremost, the miracle of making the uninteresting interesting is a particularly delicate feat, resting on a contradiction that is difficult to overcome. It is telling that Moretti's favourite novel is one in which the compromise is most fragile: *The Red and the Black*, without doubt the novel most ideologically aligned with the French Revolution. The compromise sought through Julien's social ascent falls to pieces due to his own reckless act, and above all, his republican speech before the judges. Moretti, however, criticises Stendhal's novelistic mode, which he equates

34 Moretti, *The Way of the World*, p. 15.

35 Ibid., pp. 94–6.

to *romanzaccio* ('pulp literature').[36] Stendhal's work is redeemed only by the irony of its narrative voice. The Balzacian 'prose of the world' fascinates him, but its characters are hollow, and the frenetic pace of narrative, in Moretti's view, ends up exhausting the reader.[37] His judgement of the English novel is even more severe, as its heroes are, by and large, deemed 'insipid'.[38] The different balance he finds in the English novel, compared to its French counterpart, necessitates the presence of an evil character, reducing Dickens's novels to the level of children's literature. The novels of the Brontë sisters, too, fall into a fairy-tale-like Manichaeism. Indeed, from the entire corpus of English fiction – with the exception of *Pride and Prejudice*, which achieves the joyful maturity typical of the *Bildungsroman* – Moretti spares only *Middlemarch*, the most 'continental' of George Eliot's novels.[39] *Felix Holt* and *Daniel Deronda*, in which the universal is sacrificed for the benefit of the individual, are deemed 'terrible novels'.[40] Moretti's love for novels is extremely selective.

All the more so, given that the representativeness of the chosen corpus is relative. The form/meaning of the coming-of-age novel excludes many other novelistic forms, as well as major works such as those by Walter Scott, Eugène Sue, Victor Hugo and Alexandre Dumas – some of the most popular novelists of the nineteenth century; novels abounding with adventures, in which narrative 'nuclei' undoubtedly outweigh the fillers.[41] Here we find well-tempered heroes (Edmond Dantès, to name but one); and in some of them, such as *Ivanhoe*, the representation of the bourgeoisie is negligible. The conception of normality that forms the subject of *The Way of the World* and *The Bourgeois* is not that of the 'nineteenth-century mass narrative: literature of states of exception, of

36 Ibid., p. 99.

37 Ibid., p. 104.

38 Ibid., p. 11.

39 Moretti considers the *Bildungsroman* to be a category within the coming-of-age novel. Only *Wilhelm Meisters Lehrjahre* and *Pride and Prejudice* are considered to belong to the category of *Bildungsroman*. For him, this form is characterised by a very particular balance that ends with the happy integration of the hero in society's embrace.

40 Moretti, *The Way of the World*, p. 226.

41 On Walter Scott, see Moretti, *The Way of the World*, p. 11.

extreme ills and extreme remedies'.[42] Certainly, Moretti has never claimed that the *Bildungsroman* constitutes the totality of the century's literature; but he certainly considers the most interesting and representative literary form of the new bourgeois hegemonic culture. The crucial question, then, is how literature has been retrospectively canonised. If we take the bestsellers of the period, the picture becomes more complex, dynamic and colourful – and it is not necessarily Ingres's newspaper editor who dominates the scene: there is also the impetuous Prince of Gerolstein (the central figure of *The Mysteries of Paris*), the love-struck hunchback (Quasimodo or Lagardère!), or Gavroche, the child sacrificed on the altar of the Revolution.

Ultimately the greatest limitation of the compromise lies in its very object, in the system, and in the Darwinian perspective underlying the conception of the life of forms. The equilibrium of compromise is both rare and fragile: no sooner is it established than it begins to fracture. In the end, is it not perhaps reserved solely for the turn-of-the-century *Bildungsroman*, of which *Wilhelm Meister's Apprenticeship* and *Pride and Prejudice* are the only true representatives? In *Wilhelm Meister's Years of Wandering*, the balance has already been lost. Fabrice and Julien bear none of the traits of the hero of compromise. After *Pride and Prejudice*, the English novel's forced Manichaeism no longer allows for a satisfactory equilibrium to be sustained. And after *Middlemarch*, 'rien ne va plus'![43] The compromise likewise vanishes after the 'entropic drift' signalled by *Madame Bovary* – in which individuality is sorrowfully absorbed by the social imaginary – and even more so after *Sentimental Education*.[44] But it is only with 1914 and the apocalyptic slaughter of youth that the *Bildungsroman* receives its final death-blow, from which it has only continued to weaken and wither ever since.

What killed it? From Moretti's perspective, the growing crystallisation of capitalism over the course of the nineteenth century, along with the utter discredit into which the bourgeoisie fell due to the many crimes

42 Ibid., p. 12.

43 This is one of Moretti's own subheadings. *Il romanzo di formazione*, p. 250.

44 On 'entropic drift', see Moretti, *The Bourgeois*, p. 100.

it would commit in the following century.[45] The bourgeoisie as promoter of a new culture of freedom and rationality has been overtaken by its deadly double: the capitalist who renders the world unliveable. It is precisely in this sense that Ibsen's lesson remains relevant today. And indeed, these are the final words of *The Bourgeois*: 'Recognizing the impotence of bourgeois realism in the face of capitalist megalomania: here lies Ibsen's enduring lesson for the world of today.'[46]

But is Moretti's own lesson really encapsulated by this dystopian claim?

3. Lessons for the Present

3.1. Art and morality

For the past two decades or so, numerous studies have championed a moral perspective on literature.[47] Amid this chorus, Franco Moretti's voice strikes a refreshingly discordant note.

The Way of the World, and even more so *The Bourgeois*, forcefully articulate a conception of art that is independent of morality. Moretti's benevolence towards the *Comédie humaine* bears witness to this stance. It should be recalled that Balzac – partly due to Barthes's dismissive critique and the fleeting fashion of the *Nouveau Roman* – came close to falling into oblivion.[48] We owe Moretti a debt of gratitude for having

---

45 Ibid., pp. 5, 21, 94.

46 Ibid., p. 187.

47 Martha Nussbaum, *Poetic Justice: The Literary Imagination and Public Life* (Boston, MA: Beacon, 1995); Sandra Laugier, *Ethique, littérature, vie humaine* (Paris: Presses Universitaires de France, 2006); Thomas G. Pavel, *The Lives of the Novel: A History* (Princeton, NJ: Princeton University Press, 2003); Maïté Snauwaert and Anne Carmartin, 'Responsabilités de la littérature: vers une éethique de l'expérience', *Études françaises* 46: 1 (2010), pp. 5–14. In 2016 a seminar in Paris posed the question: 'Le tournant éthique: faut-il le prendre?', *Fabula: La recherche en littérature*, 19 September 2016, at fabula.org. In 2018, an issue of the teaching journal *Repères* took up the theme: 'Le tournant éthique en didactique de la littérature', *Repères,: Recherches en didactique du français*, 15 January 2018, at journals.openedition.org.

48 See Roland Barthes, *S/Z*, transl. Richard Miller (Oxford: Blackwell, 1990 [1970]), which takes issue with 'what is outmoded in Balzac', cruelly defining it as 'a

expressed a markedly different view, as early as 1986. To begin with, he underscores the 'ethical indifference' of the *Comédie humaine* (a point I will not debate here, though it remains contested).[49] This clearly differentiates Balzac's work from the English novels that follow the structure of fairy tales (particularly those of Dickens). As for the clichés, the omnipresent doxa in the *Comédie humaine*, whose heaviness was emphasised by Barthes and Genette, appear entirely secondary in Moretti's eyes, because they serve the narration.[50] This frenzied 'pure narration' that Moretti identifies in the *Comédie humaine* might, as we have seen, stultify and tire the reader.[51] But it is only in relation to Balzac that Moretti speaks of 'literary pleasure'.[52] The origin of this pleasure is the opposite of the 'discomfort' and 'uneasiness' so appreciated by the 'Parisian professors' (who we can imagine, in the 1970s and 1980s, were more concerned with Bataille and Blanchot than with Balzac).[53] The compromise that

---

nauseating mixture of common opinions, a suffocating layer of received ideas' (p. 206). Claude Brémond and Thomas Pavel, in *De Barthes à Balzac. Fictions d'un critiques, critiques d'une fiction* (Paris: Albin Michel, 1998) attempted to rehabilitate him.

49 Moretti, *Way of the World*, p. 131. Moretti's consideration is not baseless. Nevertheless, in the *Comédie humaine*, the distinction between parties for good and for evil is fairly clear. The negative characters often come to a bad end (as in *La cousine Bette*, *Un ménage de garçon*, and *Ursule Mirouët*), while goodness and honesty are often rewarded (as in *Modeste Mignon* and *César Birotteau*, even if the premature death of the protagonist in the latter renders his rehabilitation somewhat bitter). It is fairly improbable that, as Moretti writes (*Way of the World*, pp. 137–8), Gobseck and Vautrin might be Balzac's social references, if by this he means his mouthpieces.

50 And yet it is the narrator's speech that is sometimes heavy in this manner. In *Le Cousin Pons*, for example, there are plenty of antisemitic reflections; it is unclear how these could possibly be to the benefit of the narration.

51 Moretti, *Way of the World*, p. 158.

52 Ibid., p. 160.

53 'Not everyone is an *esprit fort* like contemporary Parisian professors, always ready to launch into the turbulent waters of history, and never having enough of a literature that intensifies discomfort and restlessness. But literary pleasure, for its part, arises from the opposite process – from the perception of a form that reduces and "blinds" the tensions and disequilibrium of everyday experience. What makes literature symbolically necessary is precisely its capacity to mediate and compromise – to teach us how to "live with" disturbing phenomena.' Moretti, *The Way of the World*, pp. 159–60.

generates the pleasure of Balzac's text is that between the exercise of narration and the terrifying complexity of a world abandoned to the whirlwind of capitalism.

Balzac is more or less spared (in a programmatically titled chapter, 'The Worst Defence of Balzac'). But Moretti, as we have seen, is far from gentle with Dickens's novels; nor is he kind to Charlotte Brontë's: the implausibilities in *Jane Eyre* stem solely from the effort to keep the heroine away from any situation that might vaguely resemble adultery.[54] Here, unlike in Balzac, it is the narration that is subordinated to morality.

But it is above all in *The Bourgeois* that Moretti rails against the moralism of the Victorian era (among other eras), in a chapter titled 'Fog', dedicated to the art of concealment in which a certain strain of English prose excels. If the overuse of moralising adjectives almost never allows one to encounter the word 'beautiful' on its own, the same is true for the word 'knowledge'.[55] Its scandalous demotion, in the second half of the nineteenth century, by the very same bourgeois culture that had initially promoted it, still echoes down to our own days.

3.2. Defence of science

'Who loves not knowledge?' asks Moretti, quoting Alfred Tennyson.[56] For Moretti, the fear of knowing – to paraphrase Paul Boghossian – originates in Victorian bigotry and its taste for vagueness, which opposes both the autonomy and independence of human fields of activity, and the clear definition of concepts and objects.[57] The aesthetics of vagueness is the antithesis of the precision that shaped the prose of *Robinson Crusoe*. From Moretti's perspective, the invention of science and objectivity by nineteenth-century bourgeois culture has steadily declined – first into the dilettantism of the gentleman, and then into the anti-intellectualism

---

54 Ibid., p. 209.

55 Moretti, *The Bourgeois*, p. 141.

56 Moretti demonstrates that, contrary to what these words might seem to mean out of context, Tennyson himself considers knowledge to be subordinate to goodness and religion. Moretti, *The Bourgeois*, p. 137.

57 Paul Boghossian, *Fear of Knowledge: Against Relativism and Constructivism* (Oxford: Clarendon, 2006).

of the 'businessman'. The cultured bourgeoisie (*Bildungsbürgertum*) has disappeared, replaced by the bourgeoisie of property (*Besitzbürgertum*).[58] Thomas Mann had already said as much, but according to Moretti, contemporary American culture – centred on sport and entertainment – has only radicalised the trends of the Victorian era.[59] There is obviously much more to be said about the long history of attacks on objectivity and the idea of science, as well as about the contemporary tendency – and not only in America – for 'bullshit'.[60]

Moretti's positive engagement with the sciences permeates the methodological choices of his research. In 1999, he promised a 'truly profane literary history' (these are the final words of the preface to the second edition of *The Way of the World*) – one that would explain without judging.[61] And if in the end he did not abstain from judging (in his eyes, the bad novels are far more numerous than the good ones), he undeniably attempted to privilege rationality. He did so by focusing on the relations between literature and society (inspired by Lukács's Marxism) and on the text itself – on form: plots, narratives, style. He maintained that a phenomenon could only be addressed within the broader context of its own country, and ideally of the world. He also explored the life of words, occasionally making use of databases (as in *The Bourgeois*, which is but one modest example of his work in this field).

4. Conclusions

Franco Moretti's ambivalences about the nineteenth-century novel and the bourgeoisie share the same roots: the observation of a departure from the legacy of the Enlightenment and the French Revolution. If the word *bourgeois*, as Moretti notes, undeniably has French origins, its replacement with the euphemism *middle class* has caused the original meaning

58 Moretti, *Il romanzo di formazione*, p. xiii; Moretti, *The Bourgeois*, p. 3.

59 Moretti, *The Bourgeois*, p. 22.

60 Pascal Engel, *Les vices di savoir. Essai d'éthique intellectuelle* (Marseille: Agone, 2019).

61 Moretti, *Il romanzo di formazione*, p. xxi.

of the word (inhabitant of the *bourg*), and with it the connection between the bourgeoisie and a certain idea of freedom, to be lost.[62] This idea, in the *Bildungsroman*, is embodied by youth. Moretti prefers those young people who feel they were born too late, who secretly harbour ideals at odds with the world (Fabrice, Julien), to those who adapt to it all too well; he prefers novels based on agitation and transformation to those that acquire their meaning only through a concluding marriage; compromises grounded in irony to those based on nostalgia for innocence; the effervescence of adolescence to the purity of childhood; universalism to particularisms; cities to the countryside; French novels to English ones (though not forgetting *Middlemarch*, and a few Italian and Polish examples).

These two works, going against the grain of research focused on reception, emotions and identity, are political works. In an era when the disappearance of the 'middle class' is accelerating, when it becomes difficult to recognise the significant compromises achieved by fiction (often sliding into the realm of the fairy tale and play), and when the humanities, too often privileging morality at the expense of science, have lost much credibility, these works have much to tell us – and perhaps indicate a road ahead.

62 Moretti, *The Bourgeois*, p. 8.

14

Between History and Theory: The Novelistic Form in the Work of Franco Moretti

Enrica Villari

If there is a quality that distinguishes Franco Moretti as a literary theorist, it is his systematically undogmatic method. Throughout his critical sociology of forms, Moretti has adopted a range of models, approaches and perspectives, guided by the conviction that, as Novalis wrote, 'theories are nets; and only he who casts will catch'.[1] For Moretti, heterogeneity is in 'the nature of literature itself' – 'Literature is perhaps the most omnivorous of social institutions, the most ductile in satisfying disparate social demands, the most ambitious in not recognizing limits to its own sphere of representation' – and its examination must reflect this.[2] What unifies such eclecticism is an aptitude for connecting the very small to the very big, the local textual detail to large-scale transformations of culture and history. The result has been a rich and multifaceted account of literary forms and their evolution, foremost among them the novel.

In the following pages I attempt to reconstruct his account of the development of the novel-form across several of his major works, in all their methodological diversity – *Signs Taken for Wonders*, *The Way of the*

1 Franco Moretti, *Graphs, Maps, Trees: Abstract Models for Literary History* (London: Verso, 2005), p. 91.

2 Franco Moretti, *Signs Taken for Wonders: Essays in the Sociology of Literary Forms*, transl. Susan Fisher, David Forgacs and D. A. Miller (London: Verso, 1997 [1983], 2nd edn 1988), pp. 26–7.

World, Modern Epic, Atlas of the European Novel, The Bourgeois – as well as the concomitant evolution of his theory of the novel; for what Moretti has produced is simultaneously theory and history, or rather, a theory that unfolds through a history of the novel's evolution. In reconstructing it, I will single out some central features: the novel's relation to its great rival, tragedy; its problem-solving function; the determinations of geography, whether of the nation-state or the world-system; the interplay between style and character; and finally, some considerations on the theory's political implications.

1. An Unstable Compromise

Given that 'a form becomes more comprehensible and more interesting the more one grasps the conflict, or at least the difference, connecting it to the forms around it', Moretti's starting point is the fundamental opposition between the novel and tragedy.[3] In 'The Great Eclipse', collected in *Signs Taken for Wonders* (1983), he argues that the historical 'task' of Elizabethan and Jacobean tragedy was 'the destruction of the fundamental paradigm of the dominant culture' – absolute monarchy – and that in fulfilling this desecrating function it paved the way for the English Revolution.[4] Moretti portrays this age of absolutism as separated from the age of capitalism by a fundamental historical fracture: 'tragedy belongs to a world that does not yet recognize the inevitability of permanent conflict between opposing and immitigable interests or values, and therefore does not feel any need to confront the problem of reconciling them'.[5] As the offspring of an age marked by the permanent class conflict generated by capital, the novel is instead essentially anti-tragic. Its social function is rather the 'composition of values in conflict', under the sign – always precarious, always unstable – of 'compromise'.

This notion is further elaborated in *The Way of the World* (1987), Moretti's pioneering study of the *Bildungsroman* as a 'symbolic form' of

3 Ibid., p. 26.
4 Ibid., p. 42.
5 Ibid., p. 28.

European modernity. Emerging out of the conflict between the old aristocratic and new bourgeois classes, the *Bildungsroman* inaugurated the great season of the nineteenth-century novel. For Moretti, the genre is structured by a negotiation between the self-determination of the individual and the demands of socialisation – between autonomy and integration. What emerges from his analysis is that, contrary to the Marxist view – from Lukács to the *Dialectic of Enlightenment* – of a heroic bourgeoisie that only relinquished its revolutionary role after 1848, bourgeois values were marked from the start by opposing tendencies, most centrally in the novels under examination, between the embrace of freedom and fear of it. In the classical *Bildungsroman*, 'we find the very opposite of what occurred in the summer of 1789: not a secession, but rather a convergence'. In short, the genre, with its ethos of compromise, narrates 'how the French Revolution could have been avoided'.[6]

Moretti understands that this non-revolutionary image of the bourgeoisie (and of the novel-form) may be unpopular. But he insists that such concerns be left aside:

> Whether, then, it is preferable to weave patiently the veil of compromise, or to slash through it – that is another matter. My purpose here was only to clarify in what way a specific literary genre has encouraged one possible choice to the detriment of the other. Whether this anti-tragic and anti-epic tendency impressed by the novel on Western culture has been a progress or a loss, this is something we must each decide for ourselves.[7]

In his account, it is with the 1815 Restoration that the novel reveals itself to be such a formidable literary form. After the betrayal of the ideals of the Revolution, the harmony between self-determination and socialisation achieved in Austen and Goethe is rendered impossible. Yet the novel's anti-tragic and anti-epic tendencies remain. The notion that the biography of a young individual entering adulthood is 'the most

---

6 Franco Moretti, *The Way of the World: The* Bildungsroman *in European Culture*, transl. Albert Sbragia (London: Verso, 2000 [1986]), p. 64.

7 Ibid., pp. 54–5.

meaningful viewpoint for the understanding and the evaluation of history' was sustained for nearly a century.[8] The youthful protagonists of Stendhal, Pushkin and Lermontov, of Balzac and Flaubert, also come to accept the way of the world; yet, voided of symbolic legitimacy, this now comes at the cost of the integrity of the self.

It is thanks to this formal reconfiguration, Moretti proposes, that modern interiority now makes its novelistic debut – an imaginary life that no longer integrates with reality but pursues its own independent path, free of any constraint, like 'the "strange men" discussed by contemporary Russian culture', who are no longer legible in the manner of Wilhelm Meister or Elizabeth Bennet.[9] With this comes bad faith and all its ambiguities: 'Imaginary life is not – is not only – a storehouse of gratifying lies about oneself; it is also that very same interiority . . . that provides refuge for those values that have been repressed in public behaviour.' So, too, the 'symbolic contradictions' of success, but also the freedom from every constraint that constitutes Onegin's curse, or the confusion between dreaming and mass-cultural consumption that is Bovary's.[10] As their personalities rise above the prose of reality (or aspire to do so), these protagonists inaugurate the modern paradigm of indecision. Yet action is necessary – in life as much as narrative – and so we have the parallel motif of 'arbitrary decisions', gratuitous acts such as Julien Sorel's pistol shot at Madame de Rênal, or Onegin's sudden, belated love for Tatiana.

This phenomenology of modern character enables Moretti to elucidate the epochal meaning of these novels. A new attitude towards life: the 'narrative' attitude which 'has severed all links with comment and judgement as ways of assigning meaning'.[11] The splitting of character also corresponds to an equivalent splitting of the reader: 'the level of discourse treats him as an adaptable, critical and intelligent being – too intelligent perhaps; but the story level speaks to him as a helpless,

8 Ibid., p. 227.
9 Ibid., p. 86.
10 Ibid., p. 90.
11 Ibid., p. 124.

bewildered and irrational creature'.[12] And yet when we shift to British soil, the coming-of-age novel tells a completely different story. There, the identity of its protagonists – Edward Waverley, David Copperfield, before them Tom Jones – is not threatened, because youth is not the laboratory of maturity. Rather, it is a parenthesis that temporarily distances the protagonist from his true self, which is rooted in childhood, and to which the character returns in the novel's denouement. Paraphrasing Virginia Woolf's famous comment, Moretti claims that – with the sole exception of George Eliot – these are not novels written for grown-ups. They are regressive, conservative, beholden to the binary structure of good and evil that one finds in fairy tales.

If we were to stop here, this would certainly represent the most problematic aspect of Moretti's account, and not only for the negative value judgements concerning specific novels that are not always easy to share. But *The Way of the World* offers a further interpretation of the English variant. Having had its revolution in the mid-seventeenth century, mid-nineteenth-century English society was not characterised by the same need for legitimation (or, conversely, criticism) as post-revolutionary France, where the betrayal of the Revolution fractured the novelistic unity of the real and symbolic. It is not that class conflict did not exist in England, but that, just as the Glorious Revolution had effected a compromise between the two factions of the civil war, so too – this is my own elaboration – the plots of the two masterpieces of the English novel which deal directly with industrial conflict (*Hard Times* and *North and South*) show how the class struggle could have been avoided. As Moretti illustrates, the English variant rests on a judicial framework, one that makes the exercise of critical judgement – those distinctions between good and evil – necessary, and which the narrative attitude of the French novel had expunged.

Two great nineteenth-century narrative traditions are thereby distinguished, representative of one of 'the great symbolic contrasts of the modern world': 'On the one hand, the French Revolution . . . On the other, the English Revolution'.[13] Under the sign of politics and the legacy

12 Ibid., p. 125.
13 Ibid., p. 206.

of the Revolution, 'narrative' dominates in the first. In the second, where the culture of the law holds sway, the 'commenting' element survives. Moretti makes no secret of which he regards as the more significant. Yet when, in *Atlas of the European Novel* (1997), he returns to these two branches, he reaches different conclusions. A shift in methodology renders his account of the evolution of the novel at once richer and more problematic.

2. Novel and Nation-State

Moretti's concern in *The Way of the World* is the relationship between the novel and capitalism – or, the novel and the bourgeoisie. *Atlas of the European Novel* represents a notable change of perspective:

> Literary sociology has long insisted, as we know, on the relationship between the novel and capitalism. But Austen's space suggests an equally strong affinity (first pointed out by Benedict Anderson in *Imagined Communities*) between the novel and the geopolitical reality of the nation-state. A modern reality, the nation-state – and a curiously elusive one. Because human beings can directly grasp most of their habitats: they can embrace their village, or valley, with a single glance; the same with the court, or the city (especially early on, when cities are small and have walls); or even their universe – a starry sky, after all, is not a bad image of it. But the nation-state? 'Where' is it? What does it look like? How can one *see* it? And again: village, court, city, valley, university can all be visually represented – in paintings, for instance: but the nation-state? Well, the nation-state . . . found the novel. And vice versa: the novel found the nation-state. And being the only symbolic form that could represent it, it became an essential component of our modern culture.[14]

The novel as symbolic form of the nation-state. And with this reformulation, the English branch suddenly appears the most fertile. While

---

14 Franco Moretti, *Atlas of the European Novel* (London: Verso, 1998), pp. 16–17.

previously the British overwhelmingly represented a conservative rear-guard – suffused with nostalgia for childhood rather than the ardour of youth that characterises the coming-of-age novel in its most achieved form – now it is Scott and Dickens (and Conan Doyle) who dominate the novel's history. How to account for this? The explanation that emerges from Moretti's analysis is as follows: the British nation is a more composite and differentiated space, and therefore more generative for the novelistic form's 'problem-solving' vocation. 'It's a form that (unlike an anthem, or a monument) not only does not conceal the nation's internal divisions, *but manages to turn them into a story*.'[15] Goethe grasped this British specificity when he identified the blossoming of the historical novel with the richness of a nation composed of three kingdoms – England, Scotland and Ireland – each with their own histories and traditions. If this prompted Scott to become a historical novelist, Goethe concluded that it was the comparative poverty of German history that had led him back to private themes after the experiment of *Götz von Berlichingen* (1773).[16]

Moretti's analysis begins anew with Austen, and the way in which two Englands – the 'local gentry' and the 'national aristocratic elite' – give rise to the drama of *Pride and Prejudice*. But it is Scott's *Waverley*, with its protagonist's journey across a landscape of uneven development, from the Hanoverian England in which Austen's novels are set to feudal Scotland and the Jacobite Highlands, which instantiates the centrality of geography, and in particular the dialectic of centre and periphery. In *Waverley* it is the Scottish periphery that generates the plot, but, as Moretti demonstrates, in the tales of two cities – the novels of Balzac and Dickens set in Paris and London – it is provoked by the centre.

Here another divergence arises. While in the *Comédie humaine*, Paris possesses a 'centripetal pull from which no one escapes', in Dickens, London 'has almost no gravitational force: everybody runs away (except scoundrels)'.[17] In Paris the centre prevails – and within it the linear

---

15 Ibid., p. 20.

16 Johann-Peter Eckermann, *Gespräch mit Goethe, in den letzten Jahren seines Lebens, 1823–1832*, vol. 2 (Leipzig: F. A. Brockhaus, 1937), pp. 304–8.

17 Moretti, *Atlas of the European Novel*, p. 120.

movement from the Latin Quarter (youth in search of success) to the Faubourg Saint-Germain – while in London, we witness a retreat: the characters 'withdraw to the counter-world of the suburb, to protect their moral illusions'. Yet, ingeniously, for Moretti it is precisely this lack of gravitational pull that renders Dickens's portrait of the modern metropolis the more radical one. In *Atlas of the European Novel*, the linearity of desire imposed on the complexity of Paris is counterposed – and illustrated with maps of *Our Mutual Friend*, *Little Dorrit* and *Bleak House* – to an enigmatic and quasi-illegible London, a 'mosaic of worlds' without a centre, in which, despite the organising conceit of Dickens's 'notorious family romances', the various narrative threads remain largely unrelated.[18]

The national space that gave rise to the plot of *Waverley* thus finds its equivalent in Dickens's centre-less metropolis. The periphery's capacity to provoke drama – recall Betsey Trotwood's role in *David Copperfield* – shapes the British novel, from Trollope to the Brontë sisters, Eliot and Hardy. And from Scott onwards, the dialectic can be credited with an important 'side-effect' of uneven development: the continuing rethinking of 'modernity' in light of social formations and cultures of the past. The British lineage therefore provides richer examples of how geography shapes the novel's formal properties. But Moretti's argument has implications beyond the borders of Britain – just think of Verga's *The House by the Medlar-Tree* or Lampedusa's *The Leopard*; or the Europe–Russia dialectic in *War and Peace*, or more generally in the Russian novel – and well beyond the nineteenth century.

In *Modern Epic* (1996), Moretti concludes his investigation of a super-canonical lineage of 'sacred texts' – among them *Faust*, the *Ring* cycle and Pound's *Cantos* – with the periphery of the post-war world-system, and the extraordinary global success of Gabriel García Márquez's *One Hundred Years of Solitude*. 'For the first time in modern history, the centre of gravity of formal creation leaves Europe, and a truly worldwide literary system – the *Weltliteratur* dreamed of by the aged Goethe – replaces the narrower European circuit.'[19] Register the homology in

18 Ibid., p. 129.

19 Franco Moretti, *Modern Epic: The World System from Goethe to García Márquez* (London: Verso, 1996), p. 233.

Moretti's analysis, as the possibilities of the novel-form are regenerated not at the centre but the periphery – but this time no longer of the nation-state. And there is more: for the young Waverley, bored by his prosaic youth at Waverley-Honour, Scotland exposes him to an unfamiliar reality that is not the fruit of a poetic invention, but a fact of life:

> Here was a girl scarce seventeen, the gentlest of her sex, both in temper and appearance, who had witnessed with her own eyes such a scene as he had used to conjure up in his imagination, as only occurring in ancient times, and spoke of it coolly, as one very likely to recur. He felt at once the impulse of curiosity, and that slight sense of danger which only serves to heighten its interest . . . It seemed like a dream to Waverley that these deeds of violence should be familiar to men's minds, and currently talked of as falling within the common order of things, and happening daily in the immediate vicinity, without his having crossed the seas, and while he was yet in the otherwise well-ordered island of Great Britain.[20]

The potential for the marvellous that he discovers 'naturalises' the romance of the Gothic novel. As Scott's lapidary postscript observes: 'Indeed, the most romantic parts of this narrative are precisely those which have a foundation in fact' – as if to say, the reality of uneven development produces reserves of the marvellous which no poetics can equal.[21] Likewise, here Moretti illuminates how *lo real maravilloso* puts 'modernism's feet back on the ground'. The term first appeared in Alejo Carpentier's preface to *The Kingdom of This World* (1943), in which he contrasted the European avant-garde characterised by the 'exhausting attempt to invoke the marvellous . . . The marvellous pursued in old prints . . . pathetically evoked in the skills and deformities of fair-ground characters . . . produced by means of conjuring tricks' to the 'marvellous reality' of everyday life he discovered in Haiti.[22] As Moretti explains,

---

20 Walter Scott, *Waverley* (London: Folio Society, 2011 [1814]), pp. 77–8.

21 Ibid., p. 363.

22 Quoted in Moretti, *Modern Epic*, p. 234.

> *Lo real maravilloso.* Not magical *realism*, as it has unfortunately been translated (and as it will inevitably continue to be called), but marvellous *reality.* Not a poetics – a state of affairs. In Haiti, Carpentier writes, surrealism is in the things themselves. It is an everyday, collective fact, which restores reality to modernist techniques: which takes the avant-garde, and sets its feet back on the ground. Does *Ulysses* separate polyphony from any concretely recognizable 'voice' whatsoever? Well, in *Midnight's Children* the opposite happens, and polyphony is re-motivated: there are many languages in the novel, because India is divided into many cultures, and Saleem, with his extraordinary hearing, managed to hear them all. The technical complexity remains, but it is *naturalized* (and also, if the truth be told, somewhat attenuated).[23]

While Joyce's *Ulysses* detached polyphony – the coexistence of different styles and discourses that Bakhtin termed heteroglossia – from any recognisable voice, in García Márquez's Macondo polyphony is produced by the coexistence of five generations. 'And it is not just a question of biological coexistence: through individuals, whole cultures overlap.'[24] Recall the famous trial scene in *Waverley* in which the culture of feudally faithful, chivalric Jacobites clashes with the Hanoverian legality of the nation-state. The story of Macondo, too, is one of accelerated modernity. By placing a character's search for the marvellous in his own time, Scott retained what the Russian formalists termed the 'realistic illusion'. This arrested the tendency, already present in Sterne and Diderot, towards a liberation from anthropocentrism that would triumph in the twentieth-century polyphony of global works. And thereafter, 'magical realism restores the link that Joyce's generation had severed: technique – and anthropocentrism'.[25]

---

23 Ibid., p. 234.
24 Ibid., p. 239.
25 Ibid., p. 235.

3. The Self and the World

While character is fundamental to Moretti's early conceptualisation of the novel and its evolution, this emphasis lessens as his framework shifts to the nation-state and the world-system. *The Bourgeois* (2013) represents an intermediary point. As its introduction explains, the analysis is bifurcated: 'two chapters on bourgeois characters – and two on bourgeois language'.[26] In the central chapter on style, Moretti makes this shift in attention explicit: when 'capitalist structures solidify, narrative and stylistic mechanisms replace individuals as the centre of the text'. According to his analysis, the precise language of *Robinson Crusoe* represented a hallmark of the bourgeois cultural revolution: 'It's a first glimpse of bourgeois "mentality", and of Defoe's great contribution to it: prose, as the style of the useful.'[27] Yet in the Victorian era, this clarity is overcome by 'fog', by a prose charged with adjectives and metaphors. Precision is abandoned for the imposing mobilisation of Victorian values – religious, moral, social – with which the British bourgeoisie cloaked the naked, autonomous dynamics of capitalism. Here, then, is a paradox. Or, to use Moretti's term, a 'dissonance': the greatest capitalist power of the nineteenth century produced the culture most saturated with values. It was in this way, he explains, that it secured its hegemony.

Elsewhere in the introduction, Moretti confesses that he was tempted to make the contemporary implications of this analysis explicit: 'The "American way of life" as the Victorianism of today: tempting as the idea was, I was too aware of my ignorance of contemporary matters, and decided against it.'[28] *The Bourgeois* was published in the same year as Fredric Jameson's *The Antinomies of Realism*, and, as Jonathan Arac has observed, these concurrent works by leading Marxist critics on the realist novel imply opposing political evaluations: 'Jameson writes as if some

26 Franco Moretti, *The Bourgeois: Between History and Literature* (London: Verso, 2013), p. 17.

27 Ibid., p. 39.

28 Ibid., p. 23.

great revolution had been won, Moretti as if it has been lost.'[29] Arac traces this through their contrasting evaluation of Eliot, in particular a celebrated passage in *Middlemarch* where the blackmailer, Raffles, dies at the home of his victim, the local banker, Bulstrode. The ambiguity of Bulstrode is one of the peaks of Eliot's characterisation: 'He was simply a man whose desires had been stronger than his theoretic beliefs, and who had gradually explained the gratification of his desires into satisfactory agreement with those beliefs. If this be hypocrisy, it is a process which shows itself occasionally in us all, to whatever confession we belong.'[30]

Jameson commends the episode as indicative of the overcoming of traditional distinctions between good and evil; for him, Eliot is a leading figure in 'the last stage in the secular struggle against religion and superstition as well as the most fundamental political drive towards democratization'.[31] Moretti, on the other hand, critically counterposes Eliot's approach to Ibsen's radicalism. While Ibsen refuses to resolve the conflict of legality and injustice, Eliot chooses resolution:

> The idea of injustice protected by the cloak of legality – Bulstrode, guilty, wealthy, and unscathed by his early actions – was for Eliot too bleak a view of her society. Mind you, this *is* how capitalism works: expropriation and conquest, rewritten as 'improvement' and 'civilization' ('who would use money and position better . . .') . . . But Victorian culture – even at its best . . . cannot accept the idea of a world dominated by *perfectly lawful injustice*.[32]

Yet, as we have seen, Moretti has elsewhere praised *Middlemarch* in much the same way as Jameson, as the exception to the fairy-tale morality of Victorian novels (and thus 'by far the finest nineteenth-century

29 Jonathan Arac, 'Why Should Marxist Critics Fight over George Eliot?', *Modern Language Quarterly* 77: 4 (December 2016), p. 585.

30 George Eliot, *Middlemarch* (Edinburgh/London: William Blackwood, 1876), p. 459.

31 Quoted in Arac, 'Why Should Marxist Critics Fight over George Eliot?', p. 583.

32 Moretti, *The Bourgeois*, p. 178.

English novel').[33] In *The Bourgeois*, he commends 'the precision so typical of Eliot's prose style', and her expressed desire 'to escape from all vagueness and inaccuracy into the daylight of distinct, vivid ideas'.[34] Moretti was not so much wavering in his judgement as pointing out a specific missed opportunity: to crystallise the episode into a moment of truth – a manifestation of the cohabitation of lawfulness and injustice. The divergence is less between Jameson and Moretti than between Eliot and Ibsen. And it hinges upon characterisation: 'Recognizing the impotence of bourgeois realism in the face of capitalist megalomania: here lies Ibsen's enduring lesson for the world today.'[35]

In this conclusion, we recognise the critical Marxist perspective that Moretti has never abandoned. Is it significant that the final word is given not to a novelist but a dramatist? What the novel's characters signal through their relationship to the world is that, as long as there are individuals, and extended fictional time to tell their stories, there will be room for small oscillations and small choices: to choose to resist the way of the world, or not. A space – limited, isolated – in which the good *Bürger* might indeed resist the destructive force of capitalism. The self and its relation to the world, so fundamental to the novel, is a cipher for a problematic of modernity writ large: the margins for individual agency and the possibilities for changing the world a little (to echo Eliot). In *Middlemarch*, while Bulstrode's aspiration to be a good Puritan is thwarted by capitalist megalomania, Dorothea's dreams of greatness – which are responsible for her unhappy marriage – are instead defeated by the values of bourgeois seriousness. Eliot knew very well that 'there is no creature whose inward being is so strong that it is not greatly determined by what lies outside it', yet at the novel's end, she grants Dorothea's (unheroic, unhistorical) life political meaning:

> But the effect of her being on those around her was incalculably diffusive: for the growing good of the world is partly dependent on unhistoric acts; and that things are not so ill with you and me as they might have

33 Moretti, *The Way of the World*, p. 216.
34 Moretti, *The Bourgeois*, p. 84.
35 Ibid., p. 187.

> been, is half owing to the number who lived faithfully a hidden life, and rest in unvisited tombs.[36]

This is the slow, prosaic, we might even say dull task of reform, in stark contrast to the historic upheaval of revolution. It is *Middlemarch*'s lesson. But it is also the logic of the novel, in contrast to that of tragedy. In one of his finest essays, 'The Moment of Truth', published in 1986, Moretti writes of modern tragedy – of which he identifies Ibsen as the key figure – that in its progress towards what it calls 'truth', this genre has an antagonist unknown to ancient and Renaissance tragedy: 'It is neither blindness, nor passion, nor Fate, nor a conflicting value. It is, quite simply, *life*.' And this antagonism, he explains, 'is none other than the tragic rendering of the generic struggle between tragedy itself and the novel'. Ibsen's lucidity and Eliot's fog are already present in these reflections on the difficulties of modern tragedy, primary among them its 'post-novelistic condition'. In this essay, Moretti expressed hope for 'a culture of the Left that would consider the moment of crisis neither as the only moment of truth, nor as the moment of the only truth'. Underscoring that this need not mean 'unending humiliations and compromises', he concludes with a quotation from Max Weber – 'from whom there is probably still a lot to learn' – which could also stand as a celebration of novelistic character:

> What is deeply striking and moving, on the other hand, is the view of a *mature* man – it doesn't matter whether young or old in years – who, feeling truly and wholly his own responsibility for consequences, and acting according to the ethic of responsibility, still of a sudden does say: 'I cannot do otherwise: I shall not retreat from here.' Here is a truly human and moving behaviour, and such a situation must be possible at any moment for all of us who have not yet lost our inner life.[37]

---

36 Eliot, *Middlemarch*, p. 621.

37 Franco Moretti, 'The Moment of Truth', *New Left Review* I/59 (September–October 1986), pp. 42–4, 47–8.

15

Useless Masterpiece: Notes on Lukács's *Theory of the Novel*

Franco Moretti

When György Lukács is still mentioned nowadays in connection with the study of the novel, it is either for *The Theory of the Novel*, composed between 1914 and 1916, or for *The Historical Novel*, written exactly twenty years later. Either, or: because the two books couldn't be more different. *The Historical Novel* is a very good book – a very *useful* book – written by a serious Marxist professor. The *Theory* is not useful at all. It is an 'attempt' (*ein Versuch*), declares the subtitle; but 'Essay' would be more to the point. The essay: the 'ironic' form, where 'the critic is always talking about the ultimate questions of life', Lukács had already written in *Soul and Forms* (1911), but 'in such a tone, as if it were just a matter of paintings or books'. And in fact, whenever the *Theory* talks about the 'novel', the reader senses that – through the oblique refraction of 'books' – something much more momentous is at stake. But what? What is the 'ultimate question' that the *Theory* is trying to address?

An initial answer could be: it is the transformation of social existence – at some unspecified moment between Dante and Cervantes – into a 'world of convention' whose abnormality Lukács tries to capture through the metaphor of the 'second nature'. Nature, because the 'all-embracing power' of convention subjects the social world to 'laws' whose 'regularity' can only be compared to that of physical nature: 'strict' laws, 'without exception or choice', that are – this is the decisive passage – 'the embodiment of recognized but meaningless necessities'.

Meaning*less* necessities. That is to say: in second nature, 'meaning' is present only in the recollection of its loss. It's the disenchantment of the world first diagnosed by German culture around 1800. When the earth was still 'the abode of the Gods', wrote Novalis in the fifth *Hymn to the Night*,

> Rivers and trees,
> Flowers and beasts
> Had human meaning

But now 'the Gods have vanished' – they live 'in another world', echoes Hölderlin's *Bread and Wine*, written in the same years – and 'human meaning' has vanished with them. 'Lonely and lifeless / Stood nature', continues Novalis:

> Deprived of its soul by the violent number
> And the iron chain
> Laws had come into being
> And in concepts
> As in dust and draught
> Disintegrated the unmeasurable flowering
> Of manysided life.

Meaning, laws, iron chain, life, soul. Novalis's presence in *Theory of the Novel* – whose world, too, 'has been abandoned by God' – is unmistakable: after all, his name appears in the very first paragraph of the book, and remains for many pages the only one mentioned by Lukács. And yet, the present-absent 'meaning' of the *Theory* differs in one crucial respect from that of the *Hymns*: it is not the sign of a (past) divine presence, but of a (past) human activity. Second nature consists 'of man-made structures', writes Lukács; 'structures made by man for man'. True, their 'complex of meanings has become rigid and alien', and may even appear as a ghostly 'charnel-house of long-dead interiorities'. But it was nonetheless *created* by those interiorities – those 'souls' – and in this, it's incompatible with what Novalis had in mind.

In fact, Lukács's 'meaning' comes from a source – Max Weber's sociological theory – that couldn't be more distant from Novalis's lyric. Weber, who had been a crucial presence in the Heidelberg years from which the

Theory emerged, had published in 1913 the first theoretical exposition of his 'comprehending' sociology, as the usual translation has it. 'Comprehending', explains *Economy and Society*, in the sense that the central object of sociology – social 'action' – exists only 'in so far as the acting individual or individuals attach to it a subjective sense'; as a consequence, the comprehension of the 'subjectively *intended* meaning' is the very precondition of sociological knowledge. Somewhat surprisingly, 'meaning' turns out to be as important in Weberian sociology as in romantic aesthetics.

A subjectively intended meaning as the foundation of social interactions. But of course the world of *The Theory of the Novel* is characterised by the opposite state of affairs – by the 'refusal of the immanence of meaning to enter into empirical life'. In placing a Weberian category at the centre of his analysis, only to show its insoluble contradictions, the *Theory* marks Lukács's break with Weber (which was probably precipitated by their bitter disagreement over the First World War). A few years later, the analysis of reification of *History and Class Consciousness* (1919–23) will offer a Marxist way out from those contradictions; but in 1916 this solution was still nowhere in sight, and the problematisation of Weber's thesis had a purely negative quality: a path had been closed, period. In this claustrophobic consequentiality, *Theory of the Novel* belongs to the small circle of masterpieces – Baudelaire's *tableaux*, Flaubert's novels, Manet's paintings, Ibsen's plays, or, indeed, Weber's last lectures – where the rules of bourgeois existence are at once ineluctable and bankrupt. It sounds, often, like the work of an exile.

Such, drastically simplified, is what *The Theory of the Novel* has to say. But just as important as 'what' the book has to say is the way it says it. Here are its opening words: 'Happy are those ages when the starry sky is the map of all possible paths – ages whose paths are illuminated by the light of the stars.' Weber could never have written this. 'The world is wide and yet it is like a home, for the fire that burns in the soul is of the same essential nature as the stars . . . Thus each action of the soul becomes meaningful and rounded . . . complete in meaning – in *sense* – and complete for the senses . . .'

Happy are those ages . . . What kind of a book is this? Certainly, not one that worries solely about knowledge. Make no mistake: there is plenty of knowledge in the pages of the *Theory*, dispensed in countless well-wrought allusions by its prodigiously cultivated young author. Yet that is not what the book is about. The *Theory* is not after knowledge: it is *after meaning*. After meaning, by way of its style.

The style of the essay: reflection, plus emotions: from that 'happy' that opens the book to the 'homesickness', 'weariness', 'despair', 'madness' that we encounter on page after page. It's the heat of emotions that extracts meaning from this world that has become 'rigid and alien'. Or perhaps, better: the heat generated by the collision of emotions and concepts. Of Novalis and Weber. Enigmatically bewitching lyric, and unadorned positive knowledge. 'Every art form', we read in the central section of the *Theory*, 'is defined by the metaphysical dissonance of life . . . every form is the resolution of a fundamental dissonance of existence.' Lukács, too, placed a metaphysical dissonance as the foundation of his book, and then tried to resolve it with the prodigious plasticity of his style. That his style *could* hold Novalis and Weber together – beauty and knowledge – was a miracle that would not be repeated. But perhaps, it should not be repeated. Perhaps, the future of literary theory lies in accepting its fundamental dissonance, without looking for a resolution.

Time Passes

Franco Moretti

1. Almost

'The form mattered almost as much as the content', writes Guido Mazzoni about *Signs Taken for Wonders* and *The Way of the World*. True. Possibly, it was the tradition of Marxist criticism, where form had always mattered a lot. (Almost as much as the content? Almost.) It was the *Jugendstil* prose of the young Lukács, still occasionally visible under the *grisaille* of the Thirties . . . Benjamin's sentences, hovering in the space without gravity of the great Romantics . . . the moments when, having loosened the laces of the System, Sartre and Jameson allow their intuitions to come to life ('the uniquely French tandem of Greed and Literature' of *Mallarmé*, the past that returns to life, 'like Tiresias drinking the blood' of *The Political Unconscious*) . . . Adorno's sentence, nearly exploding for having swallowed the whole arc of the argument . . . the minefield of della Volpe's paragraphs, all asides, italics and concepts . . . Fortini's rhetorical posture, introverted and inflammatory . . . Schwarz's ratiocination, acrobatically straddling irony and complexity . . .

On a minor scale, my way of writing had itself a Marxist origin, rooted in della Volpe's and Colletti's anti-dialectic intransigence. But it was a Marxism placed in the peculiar setting of a long room in the University of Salerno, with two hundred beginners, and a maze of tape recorders piled up on the desk. Perfect, for a Marxist critic who was himself a beginner – perfect, because the 'lecture form' (Mazzoni again) is where criticism meets the world; it's a public event, people have come on purpose, you must make yourself understood, and, much more challenging, *must justify the fact that we are studying literature.* That books are worth reading goes more or less without saying; but studying them doesn't. And there you are, tape recorders turning.

Why study literature? I would begin from this: the pleasure of understanding complex objects in terms of simple elements. Bringing them down to earth. None of us will ever write *The Waste Land*: but we can find out how it's made. How it *has* been made. What changes when Pound crosses out the manuscript's opening page. What is the geometry hidden beneath the turmoil of the *Comédie humaine.* From what series of steps do *The Adventures of Sherlock Holmes* finally emerge. Take a literary product, and bring it back to the *doing* of specific individuals, with their culture and their ignorance, their principles and their hatreds. And the same with criticism. The spoken thought described by Francesco de Cristofaro is a way of laying your cards on the table, presenting your argument as a long chain of things you have learned, and choices you have made: this, and not that (and never, never this *and* that). In the end, writes Jérôme David of the *pamphlets* of the 'Literary Lab', the exposition turns into a genuine narrative, showing how even the most abstract kind of knowledge develops in time, by very concrete trial and error.

Presenting knowledge as a sort of voyage. And then, conveying the delight of arrival. When de Cristofaro makes fun, quite rightly, of the prose which becomes 'martial' and borders on the slogan, I would reply: but of course! You doubt and doubt and doubt . . . but when you reach, I won't say certitude, which is not of this world, but conviction, then why not say it black on white? Having taken apart the grammatical scaffolding of *Leaves of Grass*, close the paragraph with: 'Leaves, of grass'.[1] The comma is ungrammatical, yes, but it allows the reawakening of Whitman's title, unlocking its relationship to a major aspect of American ideology. 'Absentminded – and socialized'.[2] After *The Third Man,* Simmel, the *Bon Marché*, Schinkel, Atget, kleptomania, Gellner, William James, and quite a lot of *Ulysses*, this is how I would summarise Bloom's *stream of consciousness*; see if you're convinced. If that formula succeeds

1 Franco Moretti, *Un paese lontano* (Einaudi: Torino, 2019), p. 35.

2 Franco Moretti, *Opere mondo* (Einaudi: Torino, 1984), p. 131.

in *reinserting literature within social life*: *Ulysses*, with all its eccentricity, within twentieth-century capitalism, with all its normality.

Is it a good reason to study literature? I think so.

2. Historical Materialism

It's 1976, writes Stefano Ercolino, and *Letteratura e ideologie negli anni Trenta inglesi* opens with long quotations from Trotsky and Lenin; ten years later, *The Way of the World* has replaced them with equally long quotes from Mannheim and Panofsky. More explicit than this . . . Yes. But let us take a step backwards. Aside from quoting Lenin and (for the happy few) Trotsky, what did it mean, back then, engaging in Marxist criticism? Concretely, what did one *do*? First of all, one read. Literature, criticism, Marxism – and this is obvious. But above all, *history*. Social, economic, political history; contemporary, and not; Italian, European, world history . . . Western Marxists, wrote Sebastiano Timpanaro once, are those people who think Freud is always right; well, Marxist critics thought *historians* were always right. They pursued 'the effectual truth of the thing'; we, 'the imagination of it'.[3] And an imagination that no longer interested us for the wholesome, realistic 'mirroring' so dear to our predecessors, but for its *distortion*, in which we saw an oblique trace of class conflict.

Studying history not in order to 'contextualise' literature, but to measure its deviation from reality. It was a crude materialism – but materialist, and certainly historical. Then came the interminable deconstructionist winter ('those dark days of the 1980s and 1990s' evoked by McManus), and for a large sector of Marxist criticism materialism became 'little more than an idea', as Brecht put it in the *Kleines Organon*. This version of Marxism, and its increasingly self-righteous intolerance, I have indeed avoided, and in fact opposed; but I have done so, as Ercolino fully understands, *in the name* of materialism and history.

3 'La verità effettuale della cosa' versus 'l'immaginazione di essa': Machiavelli, *The Prince*, transl. Harvey C. Mansfield, 2nd edn (Chicago/London: University of Chicago Press, 2010), p. 61.

Whence my interest in geography, book history and quantification: as many attempts at injecting some concreteness into critical thought. Whence, also, the turn towards evolutionary theory, which provided a fantastic account of the development of forms within history. An account that was just as historical, and more materialist, than Marxism itself.

In some ways, those choices have worked well: to use Ercolino's criteria, in the opening pages of *The Bourgeois*, written a quarter-century after *The Way of the World*, one finds Weber, Wallerstein, Meiksins Wood, Hobsbawm, Anderson, Kocka, Gay, Warburg, Schama, Groethuysen and Koselleck: a lot of history, and quite a lot of Marxism, too. (But not inevitably: because if a conservative thinker like Koselleck explains the role of concepts in history better than the Marxist Williams, then Koselleck's position is the one I will take up.) More generally, *The Bourgeois* tries to follow Roberto Schwarz, the greatest Marxist critic of our times, in viewing forms as 'the abstract of specific social relationships'.[4] Abstract of relationships – and of course of the *conflict* they incessantly generate.[5] And on this point, Ercolino's critique stands. Not that recognising social conflict within the prism of literary form is easy: but my 'extremely selective love' (Francoise Lavocat) for nineteenth-century novels, and for categories such as 'compromise' and 'consent', may indeed have induced me to accept all too willingly 'the ordinary, the tempering of meaning' described by Franco Fiorentino.

'Caramelos y novelas andan juntos en el mundo', wrote Domingo Sarmiento, and I continue to think he was right. But one should succeed in studying candy without becoming addicted, and I probably haven't. Here, Enrica Villari is certainly right in viewing the antithesis of novel and tragedy, and my decision to study the former, as a crucial

4 Roberto Schwarz, 'The Importing of the Novel to Brazil and Its Contradictions in the Work of Alencar' (1977), in *Misplaced Ideas: Essays on Brazilian Culture* (Verso: London, 1992), p. 53.

5 On this point, Schwarz's solution is quite different from the Hegelian zeitgeist rightly criticised by Mazzoni and Miconi, as his formulation indicates the contingent and always unstable nature of such an 'abstraction', rather than an all-pervading spiritual force that supposedly defines entire epochs.

bifurcation. When, in 1990, I moved to the United States, I had in mind a sort of triptych formed by *The Way of the World*, *Modern Epic*, and a book-to-be on modern tragedy; but courses on the novel – not tragedy – were the priority in my new university, and I aligned myself a little too easily with such a request. As the *Atlas of the European Novel*, the five volumes of *Il romanzo*, and the quantitative work of the past twenty years have resulted from that arrangement, it would be stupid to regret it. But . . . But here I am, working on tragedy for the foreseeable future, because the erasure of radical conflict from literary study is a loss – intellectual and political – which should not be accepted.

3. Clarity

The 'lecture form' and the search for simplicity; materialism, forms and history. Although with some difficulties, thus far my research had been reasonably consistent.[6] But in the 1990s something changed. If *The Way of the World* had been fundamentally a historical study of the *Bildungsroman*'s role in nineteenth-century Europe, in *Modern Epic* the pursuit of an evolutionary theory of literature was already as relevant as understanding the historical significance of the epic genre; and in the *Atlas of the European Novel*, more radically, novelistic forms would become merely a means to display the new geographical approach. Without any conscious project on my part, theoretical speculation had supplanted historical research. Its guiding principle was *veder chiaro* ('to see clearly'), mentioned by Federico Bertoni: recognising what was there, first of all, and then, if possible, coming up with a hypothesis on what was *not* visible. If the task of theory, as Popper put it in *Conjectures and Refutations*, consists in moving from what is known to what is unknown, then the 1990s – when I wandered freely from evolution to world-systems theory, from geography to the first attempts at quantification – were my most adventurous years, in which 'the legitimation of scientific

6 One evident problem, indicated by Gisèle Sapiro, concerns the peculiar logic of the literary market. But there are others.

knowledge within the humanities' (Giuseppe Episcopo) was my guiding principle.[7] And it's probably not an accident that it's precisely at the end of that decade that I have come closest to a theoretical formulation in the proper sense, with the 'little system of laws' of 'Conjectures on World Literature' recalled by Mads Thomsen.

And yet, immediately afterwards, the 'research comes to a halt, just when the challenge of constructing a falsifiable scientific method seemed within reach' (Andrea Miconi). Behind this sudden halt, Miconi sees the contradiction 'between divergence and convergence in literary forms' (which is itself the sign of a discord between the Darwinian model and the reality of literary history), and the difficulty in defining 'the ultimate unit of variation over time' (in the absence of which it's impossible to extend 'morphological analysis to the large numbers of ordinary literature'). He is right on both points, and a couple more, of a similar nature, could be added.[8] But the main reason for the decline of that 'falsifiable scientific method' must be sought elsewhere.

Between 2000 and 2010, as digital archives and algorithms entered literary studies, the change of scale and of analytical power had something prodigious about it. We launched into 360-degree explorations on the basis of models – principal component analysis, network theory,

---

7 'It has often been said that scientific explanation is reduction of the unknown to the known', writes Popper in *Conjectures and Refutations*, in a polemical salvo against Nietzsche's 'What Is "Knowledge"? Bringing Back Something Extraneous to What Is Known and Familiar'. 'If pure science is meant', Popper goes on, 'nothing could be further from the truth. It can be said without paradox that scientific explanation is, on the contrary, the reduction of the known to the unknown. In pure science . . . explanation is always the logical reduction . . . of "known" facts and "known" theories to assumptions of which we know very little as yet, and which have still to be tested.' Karl Popper, *Conjectures and Refutations* (London/New York: Routledge, 1963), p. 83. Nietzsche's sentence appears in the posthumous fragments of the years of *Genealogy of Morals*.

8 Very synthetically, I have in mind the difficulty in testing empirically the random nature of cultural mutations, and the impossibility (within the Darwinian model) of conceiving that *political* conflict – neither competition for the same resources, nor a predator–prey relationship, but a struggle supported by powerful principles of legitimation – which is fundamental in human history. Clearly, these issues deserve a separate treatment.

Bayesian statistics, topic modelling: the list kept growing and growing – which only months earlier we hadn't even heard of. At each attempt one found something; something *new*; something *interesting*. And one wrote about it, without worrying too much. Seeing a lot trumped seeing clearly; theory felt like a highbrow, resentful charade compared to the easygoing vitality of practice. And so, a new field emerged, not via a conceptual transformation, but because of *the mere availability of new tools*. A new field, without a new theory, and in fact indifferent to it: it's this unfathomable absurdity that explains the theoretical collapse evoked by Miconi.[9]

And now? Now I look backwards, at the summer of 1990, when I started my twenty-five years of work in the United States, and tell myself three things. First, that I have never managed to become an 'intellectual', as I was hoping to in my youth, and as several friends around me have done. This, I accept: deep down, I've always known I was no more than a professor. But, second, in the United States I have turned into a *laboratory* professor (I even founded one!): the kind that squint when they come out into the sunlight, because they're no longer used to it. This, too, has had its merit; but now it's enough. Because, third, professor for professor, I prefer the one who was teaching in Italy, and cracked the window of the lecture room to let in a little air from the world outside. How to do so now that I am retired, is far from clear; but it's good to have to face a new problem, and even better to find myself in the company of those who have written these pages.

---

9 On this, see the essays collected in Franco Moretti, *Falso movimento. La svolta quantitativa nello studio della letteratura* (Milan: nottetempo, 2021).

The Authors

Federico Bertoni teaches literary theory at the University of Bologna. His books include *La verità sospetta. Gadda e l'invenzione della realtà* (Einaudi, 2001), *Realismo e letteratura. Una storia possibile* (Einaudi, 2007) and *Letteratura. Teorie, metodi, strumenti* (Carocci, 2018). He edited the Italian critical edition of Italo Svevo's *Teatro e saggi* (Mondadori, 2004).

Jérôme David teaches at the University of Geneva. He has published *Balzac, une éthique de la description* (Honoré Champion, 2010), *Spectres de Goethe. Les métamorphoses de la littérature mondiale* (Les Prairies Ordinaires, 2012) and *Martin Bodmer et les promesses de la littérature mondiale* (Ithaque, 2018). He is the co-director of the Bodmer Lab (bodmerlab.unige.ch).

Francesco de Cristofaro teaches comparative literature at the Federico II University of Naples. His essays on literary history and theory have been published in a large range of volumes and journals. He edited *Letterature comparate* for Carocci (new edn, 2020) and, with Giancarlo Alfano, coordinated the four-volume work *Il romanzo in Italia* (2018).

Giuseppe Episcopo is an assistant professor of comparative literature at Roma Tre University. He has published on literature, radio, D'Arrigo, Pynchon and Gadda, and has also edited texts by Franco Moretti and

Fredric Jameson. His last book is *Macchine d'espressione* (Cronopio, 2018).

Stefano Ercolino teaches literary theory and comparative literature at Ca' Foscari University of Venice. He works on the theory and history of the novel, the philosophy of literature and the arts, and critical theory. He is the author of *The Maximalist Novel: From Thomas Pynchon's* Gravity's Rainbow *to Roberto Bolaño's* 2666 (Bloomsbury, 2014), *The Novel-Essay, 1884–1947* (Palgrave Macmillan, 2014) and, with Massimo Fusillo, of *Negative Empathy in Literature and the Arts* (Routledge, 2026).

Francesco Fiorentino taught French literature at the University of Bari. He has written predominantly on seventeenth-century theatre and on the realist novel. He directed the full Italian edition, with translation and commentary, of Molière's *Teatro*. His most recent book is *Il potere spassionato. Corneille, Molière, Racine e altri tre saggi teatrali* (ETS, 2020).

Françoise Lavocat teaches comparative literature at the Sorbonne Nouvelle University. Her books include *Fait et fiction. Pour une frontière* (Seuil, 2016) and *Les personnages rêvent aussi* (Hermann, 2020). Since 2018 she has directed the Société Internationale de Recherche sur la Fiction et la Fictionnalité (fiction.hypotheses.org). She is a member of the Institut Universitaire de France and of the Academia Europaea.

Guido Mazzoni teaches literary theory at the University of Siena. His essays include *Forma e solitudine* (Marcos y Marcos, 2002), *On Modern Poetry* (Harvard University Press, 2022 [2005]), *Theory of the Novel* (Harvard University Press, 2017 [2011]), *I destini generali* (Laterza, 2015) and *Senza riparo. Sei tentativi di leggere il presente* (Laterza, 2025), as well as two books of poetry: *I mondi* (Donzelli, 2010) and *La pura superficie* (Donzelli, 2017).

Patricia McManus teaches literary and cultural history in the Literature Department at Sultan Qaboos University in Oman. Her research interests focus on the history of the novel, especially as a network of genres.

Her most recent book is *Critical Theory and Dystopia* (Manchester University Press, 2022).

Andrea Miconi teaches sociology of media at IULM, where he coordinates a Horizon 2020 project on media systems in Europe. His books include *Surplus digitale. La filiera del valore da Marx al Web* (EGEA, 2019) and *Teorie e pratiche del web* (Il Mulino, 2018).

Mads Rosendahl Thomsen teaches comparative literature at Aarhus University. He has published in the fields of literary historiography, modernist literature, world literature, digital humanities, and post-humanism. He is a member of the Academia Europaea and of the Executive Committee of the International Comparative Literature Association.

Gisèle Sapiro is a director of studies at the EHESS and director of research at the CNRS. Her books include *Los intelectuales: profesionalización, politización, internacionalización* (Eduvim, 2017), *Les écrivains et la politique en France* (Seuil, 2018), *Peut-on dissocier l'oeuvre e l'auteur?* (Seuil, 2020) and *Des mots qui tuent. La responsabilité de l'intellectuel en temps de crise, 1944–1953* (Points, 2020).

Enrica Villari taught English literature at Ca' Foscari University of Venice. Her research focuses on the novel and its culture and aesthetics – from its seventeenth-century origins to the emergence of Walter Scott's historical novel – and on the nineteenth-century realist tradition and its legacy.